An OPUS book

Logic and its Limits

DATE DUE

Patrick Shaw is a senior lecturer in Philosophy at the University of Glasgow.

Logic and its Limits

Patrick Shaw

Second edition

Oxford   New York

OXFORD UNIVERSITY PRESS

1997

Delhi Florence Hong Kong Istanbul Karachi
Kuala Lumpur Madras Madrid Melbourne
Mexico City Nairobi Paris Singapore
Taipei Tokyo Toronto Warsaw

and associated companies in
Berlin Ibadan

Oxford is a trade mark of Oxford University Press
© Patrick Shaw, 1981, 1997

First published 1981 as a Pan paperback
Second edition first published as an Oxford University Press
paperback 1997

British Library Cataloguing in Publication Data
Data available

Library of Congress Cataloging in Publication Data
Data available

ISBN 0–19–289280–0

1 3 5 7 9 10 8 6 4 2

Typeset by Best-set Typesetter Ltd., Hong Kong
Printed in Great Britain by
Biddles Ltd.
Guildford and King's Lynn

to Jane, Rob, and Mike

Preface to First Edition

This book grew out of the conviction, not in itself strange or startling, that the ordinary person can and should think straight rather than crooked.

Most of the time, the ordinary person does think straight. In countless ways social life depends on doing so. Balancing the housekeeping money, locating a fault in a wiring system, planning a day out—all involve, tacitly or otherwise, working out what is compatible with what. I cannot spend this pound and save it; if the bulb works in another socket then the fault does not lie in the bulb; either we catch the five o'clock train or we will not be able to get to the concert. These are the kind of commonplaces that underpin any sort of planned, purposive behaviour. They are largely taken for granted, and any mistakes in reasoning quickly run up against the harsh corrective of experience.

Problems arise when the test of experience is neither so immediate nor overwhelming. People speculate on what the facts might be when the facts are not obvious; and they disagree in their speculations. Also people pronounce upon, and disagree about, what ought to be the case, or whether one thing is better than another. They are not disagreeing about what *is* the case, so they cannot appeal straightforwardly to experience.

When these kinds of disagreement occur, when the competing claims cannot be easily and obviously tested, attention is bound to turn to the route by which a controversial conclusion was reached. We are forced to become self-conscious about the reasoning process. How far reasoning will take us remains to be seen, but so far as it leads we must be sure that it is sound.

In what follows, the aim is to expound some of the rules of good argument and to make the reader more aware of some of the ways in which arguments can fail. Sometimes a conclusion is drawn which straightforwardly does not follow, but sometimes the fault is more subtle: the arguer slips away from the point at issue, or assumes more than an opponent would be willing to grant, or trades too heavily on the emotional overtones of the words he employs.

This book emphasizes the use of logic in helping to settle or clarify disputes. For this reason I have taken examples, wherever possible, from everyday arguments and common controversies. Admittedly there is a danger here that the reader's prejudices will get in the way and the writer's prejudices show too clearly. But the risk seems to me worth taking; logic is relevant, and should be seen to be so. Yet logic cannot determine moral right and wrong; hence the 'limits' of the title. Concentration on the practical uses of logic has determined me to keep formal developments to the minimum necessary for testing arguments. It has also led me to include a number of exercises for the reader to work through on his, or her, own. There is no substitute for practice. Answers are included so that progress can be measured.

The book grew out of my attempts to teach logic to undergraduates and extramural students at Glasgow University. From their questions and difficulties I learned a lot. I hope they learned as much from me. My thanks go to Jane Scollen for reading an early draft, and to the readers of the publishers. All helped to make the final version more polished and more accurate. I would also like to express my thanks to my mother for the typing, to my colleague Michal Scollen for his constant help and encouragement, and to my wife for acting as guinea pig in testing the examples.

Preface to Second Edition

There are some minor changes in the text and the examples from the first edition, including the re-positioning of the chapter on analogy to occur after the discussion of inductive reasoning. There is also a more significant change. The use of truth grids for the testing of arguments has been replaced by truth tables. This should particularly help those going on to do further logic.

The general aims of the book remain the same. They still seem to me worthwhile.

My thanks are due to Dan Lyons for useful criticism and to Ken Brown.

Contents

1 Arguments

I

To the ordinary person logic may be somewhat mysterious, but the adjectives 'logical' and 'illogical' are familiar. A logical argument is one which is sound; a logical person is one who habitually uses sound arguments. Logic, so far as it concerns us here, is an examination of some of the general principles for distinguishing sound from unsound arguments, and an attempt to pick out some of the commonest kinds of error in reasoning.

The study of logic in the above sense—the study of the principles governing good argument—will not necessarily turn the student into a person who argues well, any more than studying a chess manual will turn him or her automatically into a good chess player. The principles have to be applied, and this requires practice and vigilance. People also differ in their natural talent for assessing arguments. Yet anyone who is interested in thinking straight, rather than crooked, is likely to be interested in general principles of sound argument. The first—and in practice the most useful—steps are easily acquired, and they are absorbing in their own right. Much of what is involved is stating the obvious: organizing common sense. Sometimes, however, common sense is not enough.

2

What is an argument? We perhaps think of a couple of people locked in an angry dispute, but from the point of view of the logician an argument does not necessarily involve a dispute or even disagreement. If this strikes the reader as rather eccentric on the part of the logicians, it is perhaps because he gives too much attention to the expression 'argue *with* (someone)'. Logicians tend, instead, to speak of an argument *for* (something). In this sense an argument is a set of statements of which one—the one being argued for—is taken to be established as true on the basis of all the others. The supporting statements are called 'premisses', and the statement they are taken to support is called the 'conclusion'. Only if an argument, so defined, is not accepted will there be disagreement and dispute; an argument in the everyday sense of the word.

Consider the following passage:

Many animals build nests according to a pattern which varies little within the species. In some instances, the offspring have had no opportunity to learn from their progenitors. There must, therefore, be at least some innate tendency controlling the activity. (Boring, Langfeld, and Weld, p. 46)

It is convenient to mark our conclusion, and for this we adopt the sign ∴. Using it we can set the argument out as follows:

- Many animals build nests according to a pattern which varies little within the species.
- In some instances the offspring have not been taught by their parents to build the characteristic nest.
- ∴ There is at least some innate tendency controlling the activity.

The phrase, 'There must, therefore, be . . .' is treated as a signal that a conclusion is being drawn; as an ordinary-language equivalent of ∴.

Contrast the quotation above with this piece of straightforwardly descriptive writing:

The militiamen carried Prince Andrey to the copse, where there were vans and an ambulance station. The ambulance station consisted of three tents, pitched at the edge of a birch copse. In the wood stood the ambulance wagons and horses. The horses in nose-bags were munching oats, and the sparrows flew up to them and picked the grain they dropped. Some crows, scenting blood, flitted to and fro among the birches, cawing impatiently. For more than five acres round the tents there were sitting or lying men stained with blood, and variously attired. (Tolstoy, p. 878)

To label the passage 'straightforwardly descriptive' is not intended to suggest that it is unsubtle. Indeed, it seems a most effective piece of writing. Every sentence is studiously matter-of-fact, yet together they convey a feeling of the pointlessness of war and at the same time mirror the detachment of a person wounded and in a state of shock. But whatever Tolstoy is intending to convey here, it is clear that he is not offering an argument. No conclusion is drawn, and no reasons are offered.

There are cases which can be thought of as akin to, but not quite arguments:

Many fishes carry out long and complex cycles of migration and spawning. The salmon, for example, spawns in fresh water streams, and the young swim downstream to the sea. Later and at the proper time in their maturity, they swim back up the rivers and tributaries from which they came, there to spawn again. (Boring, Langfeld, and Weld, p. 46)

The last two statements provide backing for the first: the statement about many sorts of fish would not be true unless a number of claims such as the one about salmon were true. On the other hand it would seem to be perverse to claim that the statements about salmon (one sort of fish) are offered as a reason for claiming that *many* sorts of fish carry out complex cycles of migration and spawning. Offering examples is akin to offering reasons, but the two are best kept distinct.

3

Our task is the assessment of arguments. However, before we can pronounce arguments sound or unsound we have to be able to identify them. It is good policy to look first for the conclusion, since there are often grammatical clues to guide us—words or phrases that signpost the drawing of a conclusion. In the first example above there occurred the phrase, 'There must, therefore, be . . .'. In the argument below the signpost is different:

All fish are cold-blooded, and no whales are cold-blooded; so whales are not fish.

The word 'so' could be replaced by 'hence', 'thus', 'it follows that', 'one must conclude that' and so on. All these phrases directly high-light the conclusion. They are equivalent to the sign ∴.

Sometimes the conclusion comes first rather than last. Again, there are often grammatical clues to be read:

Whales are not fish; for all fish are cold-blooded and no whales are.

The word 'for' indicates that what follows is offered as a justifica-tion. Again there are alternative modes of expression: 'as', 'since', 'because', and so on.

There are, however, cases where we cannot look to the grammar for help. In these cases we have to recognize the conclusion—and that an argument is being advanced—purely from the sense of what is being said:

The government has no option but to drop the measure. The first clause was defeated in committee stage, and the government has a heavy pro-gramme before the recess.

It seems clear that this is a case where the conclusion comes first. The argument can be reformulated in a more conventional manner as:

- The first clause was defeated in committee stage.
- The government has a heavy programme before the recess.
- ∴ The government has no option but to drop the measure.

Yet one must just look at the passage and see what it says; there are no grammatical clues.

Exercises

In the following passages say whether an argument is given. If so pick out the conclusion. Do not worry at this stage whether the arguments are sound or unsound.

1.1 To make an assessment of modern art is an impossible task. For one can assess a work of art only when there are accepted rules and con-ventions. Modern art has no rules and conventions.

1.2 People lead insecure lives. They don't find reassurance in religion any more; so increasingly they turn to astrology.

1.3 Despite increasingly generous rewards no information was forthcoming about those responsible. Though troops were billeted all over the area they were no match for the rebels.

1.4 Driving too fast in the wrong conditions is the prime factor in road accidents. Stern—and enforced—limits at black-spots would have a far greater effect than an overall curb simply for legislation's sake.

1.5 Who are the real beneficiaries of the technology? . . . Customers are the real winners. If you have ordered before, the operator can call up your name on her computer screen. She can tell you if an item is in stock, or if it isn't how long it will be on back order. (*The American*)

4

Arguments range from the very formal, easily assessed examples on which logicians have traditionally tended to concentrate to the less stylized, less explicit, and less tractable arguments of ordinary discourse. At the extreme there are standard textbook examples such as:

All whales mammals.
All mammals are warm-blooded.
Therefore, all whales are warm-blooded.

(Such arguments are known as 'syllogisms'. They are discussed in Chapters 9 and 10.) The structure is obvious, the conclusion tagged, and the inference in this case clearly sound, or (to use the technical term) 'valid'. However, it is not the kind of argument that would ever be encountered in any ordinary context. Or rather, if it were encountered it might well go unrecognized, for almost certainly it would not be so fully stated. Most likely it would occur as: 'Whales are mammals, so they must be warm-blooded.' The hearer or reader would be expected to provide for himself the unstated premiss, either because it is a commonplace belief that mammals are warm-blooded or because the context in which the argument is advanced makes it plain that this is being assumed. People do not normally spell out what they and their audience take for granted. Life is short, and so is patience.

When the task is to assess an argument as sound or unsound, or when an inference is challenged, background beliefs have to be dragged into the open. It is important to have all the cards on the table, arranged as perspicuously as possible. To find out whether a conclusion follows or not, we must be sure we know from what it is supposed to follow. All of the premisses must be stated, and each of them clearly stated.

There is a place for legitimate worry here: no doubt we should spell out hidden assumptions whenever we are assessing an argument. But can every sound argument in ordinary language be fitted into a form of a sort favoured by logicians? And, come to that, what *are* the approved forms into which ordinary arguments are to be fitted? The answer to both these questions must wait until more has been said about the testing of arguments. But it should be borne in mind that we shall look at only the most basic moves in textbook logic. To that extent there will be everyday arguments that escape our logical net but which would not escape a more comprehensive net.

Exercises

Give the conclusions of the following arguments, and supply any unstated premisses. Try to state the latter as clearly as possible, but do not try to set out the arguments in a formal way.

1.6 William is a churchgoer; so he won't vote for the Communist candidate in the election.

1.7 Oddly enough, a reduction in the present penalty for drunken driving would have a beneficial effect. A mild penalty makes the jury more ready to convict.
   Section 3.

1.8 For many young men in modern industrial society there is no prospect of achieving status through employment. Hence they join gangs and turn to lawlessness.
   Do not worry how good the argument is, but what it is.

5

It must not be supposed that once an argument is laid out in a style pleasing to the logician anyone will be able to see at a glance whether it is sound or not. In our example of the whales it was easy to see that the conclusion followed from the premisses, but sometimes it is much less obvious. Given the premisses

All vitamins are nutritious

and

Some nutritious things are not cheap

does it follow that

Some vitamins are not cheap?

Most people will hesitate over their answer.

It must be stressed that to ask whether a conclusion follows is not the same as asking whether that conclusion is true. From the point of view of logic, truth is not of immediate account. A conclusion follows from the premisses in this sense: if one grants the premisses then one must, to be consistent, also accept the conclusion. If the premisses are true, then the conclusion must be true. Which is not to say that the premisses and conclusion *are* true: whether or not they are is a different problem.

Hence there can be arguments which are absurd from the point of view of truth but which are nevertheless perfectly valid. For example:

All students are teapots.
Our dog is a student.
∴ Our dog is a teapot.

Obviously both premisses are false and so is the conclusion. Yet the argument is logically sound in that the conclusion follows from the premisses. Anyone who maintains those premisses is committed to that conclusion, whether he knows it or not.

This lack of direct concern with truth sometimes disturbs people beginning the study of logic. Their feeling is that truth is the important thing and that assessing arguments independently of truth is not a serious-minded activity. This is to underrate the power of correct reasoning. A valid argument will never take us from true premisses to a false conclusion; so if we begin with premisses which are known to be true and argue from them, then any conclusion we reach, however remarkable or unexpected, will be known to be true also. But before we can have confidence in our conclusions we must be sure we have argued validly, and this means mastering some techniques of logic. Whether we should accept these conclusions depends on whether they really follow. Hence the logician is not indifferent to truth, even though *within logic* questions of truth and falsity are ignored; he merely practises division of labour. He does not lay claim, simply as logician, to knowing facts about the world; rather, his claims are of the form: 'Granted that *these* are facts about the world, then so is this.'

6

We looked at one way in which arguments can be spelled out: by bringing to light assumptions which the arguer thinks too obvious to mention explicitly. There is another sort of 'spelling out' which is sometimes necessary, involving the step from premisses to conclusion.

Suppose we have an argument whose hidden assumptions have all been rendered explicit, and which, expressed in textbook fashion, reads:

All rodents are mammals.
All mammals are inquisitive creatures.
∴ No uninquisitive creatures are rodents.

If the soundness of the reasoning is not at once apparent, we can split the argument into simple argument-steps whose validity is undeniable. First:

All rodents are mammals.
All mammals are inquisitive creatures.
∴ All rodents are inquisitive creatures.

Followed by:

All rodents are inquisitive creatures.
∴ No rodents are uninquisitive creatures.

And finally:

No rodents are uninquisitive creatures.

∴ No uninquisitive creatures are rodents.

At each stage we pick up the conclusion of the previous sub-argument. Each step is trivial and uninteresting, yet the whole process may lead to results which are anything but trivial. It is often supposed that a valid argument cannot have just one premiss. This is not so; the inference above, for example, can be regarded as an argument in its own right.

A great deal of mathematical reasoning can be seen to involve a similar sort of 'spelling out':

Bill is eight years older than John, and in two years time he will be twice as old as John. How old is Bill?

We offer the answer that these premisses imply that Bill is fourteen. However, the inference is not obvious, and we are expected to spell out the argument-steps and operations by which the conclusion was reached. This is done roughly as follows:

Let Bill's age be x and John's age y. We are given that:

(1) $x = y + 8$.

(2) $x + 2 = 2(y + 2)$.

(In two years Bill will be twice as old as John.)

• From (2) it follows that $x + 2 = 2y + 4$.
• Subtracting two from each side we get $x = 2y + 2$.
• Since $y + 8$ and $2y + 2$ both equal x, it follows that they equal each other: $2y + 2 = y + 8$.
• Subtracting $y + 2$ from each side we get $y = 6$.
• John's age is six and Bill is eight years older; therefore Bill is fourteen.

Each of the steps above is of itself fairly trivial, yet there is a considerable distance between problem and answer.

Even in quite ordinary, untechnical prose, arguments are broken down into sub-arguments:

Coal seams have been discovered in Antarctica. Hence the climate there was once warmer than it is now, and hence either the geographical location of the continent has shifted or the whole earth was once warmer than it is now.

The main conclusion is that either the continent has shifted or the earth was once warmer. The premiss offered in support is that coal seams have been discovered in Antarctica. But the passage from premiss to conclusion is made easy by an intermediate step. The sub-arguments can be shown as follows:

Coal seams have been discovered in Antarctica.
∴ The climate there was once warmer than it is now.

And:

The climate there was once warmer than it is now.
∴ Either Antarctica has shifted position or the whole earth was once warmer.

Exercise

Identify the final conclusion and the interim conclusion. Exhibit the two sub-arguments.

1.9 Washing machines often fail to wash really clean. The machine contains a mixture of different fabrics. These different fabrics—particularly synthetic ones—have a liking for different kinds of dirt. As a result the dirt which would once have gone down the drain becomes evenly spread over other garments. (*Guardian*)

7

An argument, it was said, is a set of statements of which one (the conclusion) is put forward on the basis of the others (the premisses). So far it has been assumed that the notion of a statement is self-evident, and for the most part we shall continue to take it for granted. But there are two points here to be briefly made.

First, from a grammatical point of view we can usually pick out statements fairly easily. They are expressed by sentences in the indicative mood, such as, 'It is sunny', 'He will arrive shortly', 'Celtic scored twice.' Such utterances contrast with commands ('Come here!') and questions ('Is it raining?'). But although grammar serves as a guide it is not an infallible guide. Anyone who utters the words, 'Who can doubt that the country is living beyond its means?' is apparently asking a question. However, the question is rhetorical: the speaker is not expecting an answer but is, in effect, making a statement—that the country is living beyond its means—and the question-mark counts for nothing. Similarly commands can look a little like statements: 'I order you to come here at once.'

Secondly, statements are not sentences. If I utter the sentence, 'I have a cold', and Mary utters the sentence, 'I have a cold', both of us have uttered the same sentence but we have not said the same thing; we have made different statements: I a statement about myself and Mary a statement about herself. Again, if I say, 'I have a cold', and Mary says to me at the same time, 'You have a cold', we have uttered different sentences, but despite this we have both made the same statement. There is a sense in which we have both said the same thing; the very same fact which would make what I said true would also make what Mary said true.

Exercise

Identify the conclusion.

1.10 Will capital punishment for terrorists act as a deterrent? I say it will, for two reasons. If it isn't introduced people will take the law into their own hands; and at the moment terrorists serve a few years in gaol and go free—where's the deterrent in that?
See sections 3 and 7.

1.11 Parents can still control some of the schedule [of a child's emotional development], but a large part of it has been wrenched out of their hands by pop culture. Is this a calamity? Not really. Middle class parents are often squeamish and overprotective. (*The New Yorker*)

2 Proofs

I

Arguments are employed mainly to establish truth, thus ending disagreement. Not exclusively so; we may be able to show how one unchallenged belief follows from another unchallenged belief, our motive being simply intellectual curiosity. But, fundamentally, arguments occur where people disagree and one is trying to show the other that something is the case. Arguments are used to prove things, and it is to the question of proof that we now turn.

Not every attempt to persuade a person constitutes an attempt to prove something to him. A person might attempt to persuade by rhetoric rather than by argument. Many disputes, especially in politics and morality, are conducted in highly emotive language which does little to advance the case. To maintain, for example, that capital punishment is wrong because it is a barbarous survival, or that it is right because it is a just and proper penalty, sets a tone (one way or the other) but doesn't say why capital punishment is wrong, or right. It tells us what to think, but not why to think it. This is not to say that rhetoric is always ineffective. Nor, perhaps, is rhetoric always to be condemned. But rhetoric is not our primary concern—simply because, no matter how persuasive, it gives no grounds for supposing the conclusion to be true or correct.

Trying to prove something to somebody places restrictions on the arguer. In the first place, proving something involves arguing validly; the arguer must strive to be consistent, to argue soundly towards the conclusion. Secondly, and a point much more likely to be overlooked, a proof must begin from premisses which are accepted as true by both sides in the dispute. This is a further restriction because, as we saw, a valid argument need not have true premisses. A proof, on the other hand, must start from the truth. The arguer will want to find a starting-point in truth because his aim is to show the truth of the conclusion; only if he goes validly from true premisses can he show the conclusion to be true—otherwise he would simply have shown it to follow from some (perhaps false) premisses. The opponent, too, will want a starting-point in truth. If he does not accept the premisses as true then he will not feel any inclination to accept the conclusion either, even if he sees quite clearly that the conclusion follows from the premisses. It is only if we go validly from an accepted truth that we can hope to arrive at an accepted truth. Indeed, if the premisses are not acceptable to the opponent then they in turn will need to be established by a further argument or by some other means—taking the opponent, perhaps, and showing him that what is being said is true.

A proof, then, is a valid argument starting from premisses which are true and accepted as true by arguer and opponent, and proceeding to a conclusion which previously the opponent was unwilling to accept. It is showing the opponent that, given certain truths (which he accepts), he cannot consistently deny certain others. (Indirect proofs are more complicated, and are considered in Chapter 15.)

2

Proofs are possible only because human beings are fallible, lazy, and intellectually limited. If everyone drew for himself the consequences of every belief he held there would be no call to prove anything and no possibility of doing so either. What happens in a proof is that somebody shows us that we were all along committed to a certain conclusion without realizing the fact. It follows from this that we could never prove anything to a perfectly rational being—one who saw all the consequences of all his beliefs—because we could never surprise him.

We remarked earlier that an argument can sometimes be broken into simpler arguments which are obviously valid and even trivial. For example:

All rodents are inquisitive creatures.
∴ No rodents are uninquisitive creatures.

Trivial arguments are in themselves uninteresting, but they are not unsound. They comply with our definition of validity: if the premiss or premisses are true then the conclusion must be true also.

There is another reason for not excluding trivial arguments. It is that what is a trivial and obvious inference to one person may not be trivial and obvious to another. To a perfectly rational being, as defined above, every move in an argument would be trivial; to the ordinary person, comparatively few. However, almost everyone will find some arguments trivial. Such arguments are valid but cannot function as proofs because nobody would accept the premises without also drawing the conclusion for himself. Considered as proofs these arguments fail because they surprise nobody.

The following piece of reasoning provides us with an example:

God shows Himself to us in the beauties of nature. Therefore God exists.

As an argument this is valid. One cannot without inconsistency accept that God shows himself and yet deny that God exists. The conclusion follows from the premisses. It follows so obviously, however, that as a proof of God's existence it is a non-starter. One cannot imagine anyone accepting the premiss who was not already disposed to accept the conclusion. A proof must surprise us by showing us that we were all along committed to the conclusion without realizing it; but the above would-be proof concerning God is certain is appeal only to the converted. The agnostic or atheist will want to challenge the premiss; the would-be proof begs the question.

In general, an argument is said to 'beg the question' when it blatantly takes for granted precisely what is being disputed. There are degrees here. An extreme case might be the absolutely trivial argument, such as 'It is raining; therefore it is raining.' But in general the notion of begging the question is a somewhat vague one because what the opponent will find blatantly obvious cannot be predicted with certainty in advance.

It has been urged that every valid syllogism begs the question. The philosopher John Stuart Mill wrote in 1843 that

When we say,
All men are mortal,
Socrates is a man, therefore
Socrates is mortal;
it is unanswerably urged by the adversaries of the syllogistic theory, that the proposition, Socrates is mortal, is presupposed by the more general assumption, All men are mortal. (Mill, p. 121)

This is not entirely accurate as it stands. One might well be able to establish that all men are mortal on general biological grounds, without counting and naming every individual man; thus one might know that all men are mortal without knowing that Socrates is (was) a man. It is really the two premisses together—'All men are mortal and Socrates is a man'—which presuppose that Socrates is mortal and which seem to beg the question.

Once the distinction between proofs and arguments is firmly fixed in mind, Mill's problem no longer looks important. If an argument is valid then the premisses taken together must presuppose the conclusion in some sense. They entitle us to draw the conclusion; in the logician's terminology, they 'contain' the conclusion. This in no way affects their soundness as arguments but, depending upon how obviously the conclusion follows from the premisses, it will affect their value as proofs. It is very doubtful if anyone prepared to admit both that all men are mortal and that Socrates is a man would have failed to draw for himself the conclusion that Socrates is mortal. But other formally valid arguments are less obvious, and their value is therefore greater for proving a disputed conclusion.

3

Proof is essentially proof *to* somebody. Hence it is not easy to provide an example, in the abstract, of a proof, in the sense in which I am using the term. A realistic example must first find something that the average reader will hesitate to accept, and then discover acceptable premisses from which to establish it.

A plausible case of a proof in this sense is to be found in the following passage. The author is discussing eclipses:

They take place when the sun, the earth and the moon are in the same straight line, or very nearly so, so that the shadow of the moon falls on the earth, or the shadow of the earth on the moon. When the shadow of the moon falls on the earth there is a solar eclipse. Since the moon must then lie between the sun and the earth, the dark side of the moon must be turned to us: that is, eclipses of the sun always take place at new [crescent] moon.

When an eclipse of the moon takes place the shadow of the earth falls on the moon: the moon must therefore be almost exactly opposite to the sun in the sky, and the fully illuminated face of the moon must be turned to the earth: that is, when an eclipse of the moon takes place the moon must be full. (Evans, p. 119)

We can plausibly regard the passage as an attempt to prove to the general reader (a) that eclipses of the sun take place when the moon is a crescent and (b) that eclipses of the moon take place when the moon is full. The argument is not set out in a formal manner, but offers for acceptance a threefold starting-point: the claim that eclipses occur when sun, moon, and earth are in a straight line; the claim that solar eclipses occur when the shadow of the moon falls on the earth; and the claim that eclipses of the moon occur when the shadow of the earth falls on the moon. Given these facts, the conclusions (a) and (b) follow.

I would hazard a guess that many readers who accept the premises would not themselves have drawn the conclusions from them which Evans draws. We were familiar with the facts from which Evans begins and we were committed to the conclusions he reaches, but we had never made them explicit to ourselves. For some readers the proof may not work. They may be unwilling to accept, for example, that eclipses occur when the moon or the earth casts a shadow. Or they may be unwilling to accept what has so far been tacitly assumed, but not made explicit, that light travels in straight lines. For these readers the quoted passage will not constitute a proof. They will require further steps to establish the starting-point. And other readers will already have seen for themselves the connection which the author spells out. They may accept the passage as a proof, but only in the sense that they think it might serve as a proof to others. The author has not proved anything to them because the conclusion did not need proving to them.

Exercises

Consider the following as proofs. Find what the passages are trying to show, and consider carefully whether the reasons offered in defence of the conclusions are (a) relevant and (b) likely to beg the question.

2.1 Will capital punishment act as a deterrent? I say it will, for two reasons. If it isn't introduced people will take the law into their own hands; and at the moment people serve a few years in gaol and go free—where's the deterrent in that?

2.2 I see that the morality of the methods the government used to bring about the downfall of communism is being criticized. Have those who object paused to consider that they would not be free to criticize had the methods not been successful?

2.3 To allow every man an unbounded freedom of speech must always be, on the whole, advantageous to society. For it is in the interests of the community that every individual should enjoy a liberty, perfectly unlimited, of expressing his sentiments.

2.4 When people decide to leave their village homes for the towns . . . only too often they are unable to find any form of work and do not add to the amount of goods produced in the economy, while they still require food, clothing, and shelter. Houses must be built for them if the growth of slums is to be avoided, and the authorities will sometimes be forced to provide their minimum subsistence needs. Thus, the movement of people causes immediate costs without any necessary increase in total production. (Theobald, p. 40)
One sentence in this is primarily illustrative, expanding a previously made point. Bracket it, then proceed.

4

Proofs, as I have treated them, depend upon what can be taken as granted, which in turn depends on the person with whom one is arguing. This notion of proof is heavily dependent on the notion of 'proving to', and as such it is likely to come under fire from two directions: that it makes proof too subjective, and that it does not fit the notion familiar in mathematics.

As to the first criticism, its force can be somewhat lessened by pointing out that in any society it is possible to take for granted a lot of common ground. There is a shared background of beliefs about the world and its history, a natural starting-point in discussion. Because of this we can anticipate likely sticking-points and offer what would be an acceptable proof to most people in our society. Ultimately we are driven to finding out from the person we are trying to convince where our respective views begin to diverge; proving a thing is proving it to somebody. That degree of subjectivity is unavoidable and, I think, harmless.

Not all would agree. The expression 'prove to' has been condemned by Antony Flew in his book *Thinking About Thinking* on the ground that it confuses proof with persuasion. A good proof may fail to persuade a person too stubborn to listen to reason; while a sloppy argument may persuade somebody willing to be convinced. However, here the fault lies with people rather than in the expression 'prove to'. To prove something to someone is to convince him by rational means. If he is not listening to reason then one will not succeed in proving anything to him, even though the proffered argument would constitute a proof to a more rational person.

There remains the criticism that the above notion of proof does not fit the notion of proof as used in mathematics. This is so, but only because the mathematical notion has become separated from the normal use with the distinction between pure and applied mathematics. A mathematical system contains 'axioms' and 'theorems'. Axioms are laid down as the starting-points of the system. Theorems are shown to follow from the axioms. If the axioms are true, then, since the theorems follow from them, they too will be true. Yet the mathematician regards the axioms as statements whose meaning is not fully specified. In geometry, for example, mathematicians are content to take the notions of 'point', 'line', and 'plane' as undefined terms. They leave it to others to decide what is to count as a line, point, or plane and so to find ways of applying the geometrical system to reality. Truth is the concern of applied mathematics. For the pure mathematician, to say that something is 'proved' is not to say that it has been shown to be true, but only to say that it has been shown to follow from given axioms.

5

Proofs are intended to settle disagreements by moving from an agreed starting-point by sound steps to the correct conclusion. But the question must be asked, How do we establish the starting-point of a proof? There seem to be a number of possibilities.

First, an agreed starting-point may sometimes be the result of a previous proof. The starting-point would previously have been the conclusion of an argument, now used as a premiss in a new argument. This could not be the only way of arriving at agreed starting-points, or every proof would have to rest on a previous proof, and there would be no way of getting started on the process of proving things.

Secondly, an agreed starting-point may be the result of observation. For example:

The castle is built of granite. The nearest source of granite is eighty miles away. So the building-stone must have been transported at least eighty miles.

The first premiss here, that the castle is made of granite, would probably be established by looking at the stone, feeling it and perhaps comparing it with a sample agreed to be granite. Identification need not be easy in a particular case, but practice normally improves performance and makes widespread agreement likely. No area of knowledge would be possible without this kind of agreement.

Thirdly, it seems that there must be a further way of establishing agreed premisses, however. For by its very nature observation is limited and some agreed statements, which could serve to start a proof, could not be established by observation. Consider:

Human beings do not have a functional appendix.

Most human beings are right-handed.

More men than women are colour-blind.

In none of these cases do we seriously doubt the truth of what is asserted. Yet the statements are obviously not established simply by enumerating every case. Not every human appendix has been examined, nor have handedness or the ability to discriminate colours been at all widely tested. Each claim is the result of extrapolating from a small range of cases, regarded as a fair sample. Extrapolation ('induction') is a very widespread method of arriving at general truths. It is considered at greater length in Chapter 12.

6

If the world were a tidier place we might hope that the methods of observation, induction, and proof would offer a rational way of ending all disagreement. This would be to expect too much. Where questions of right and wrong are involved, disagreements are likely to remain, even where the disputants are committed to reason. In these areas it is difficult to find any arguments which cut deep and do not ultimately take for granted what should be shown. The point can be illustrated by considering one case—abortion—in more detail.

Abortion is the murder of an unborn child, therefore plainly wrong.

Whatever one may feel about the rights and wrongs of abortion, as a proof this is hopelessly deficient. To describe an act as murder is automatically to condemn it as wrongful killing; but, since defenders of abortion are hardly likely to accept that it is murder, the argument begs the question. It is less a serious attempt to persuade than a rallying-cry.

Begging the question is not the prerogative of one side only in this dispute. To claim that what a woman does to her own body is her business alone is equally to assume the point at issue, for it is to assume that a foetus is not importantly different from any other piece of bodily tissue.

Yet aside from these weak arguments we find only a great deal of inconclusive discussion about whether and when a foetus is an unborn child. If an unborn child has the same rights as a child which has been born (which seems reasonable), and if from the moment of conception a foetus is an unborn child, then clearly the destruction of a foetus would be tantamount to the destruction of a child—justifiable, if at all, only when the mother's life is in peril.

The problem is that it is not a clear-cut matter of fact that a foetus in its early stages of development is an unborn child. This description would naturally be applied to the foetus in its last month, when it has practically all the qualities of a newly born baby. But a foetus in its early stages lacks practically all of these qualities; eyes, heart, and arteries begin to form in the fifth week, ears in the sixth, and most of the brain has formed by the eighth week. Prior to this time, it would at any rate seem to be stretching the natural meaning of the words 'unborn child' to apply them to the foetus. (Hence a miscarriage is not cause for an inquest, nor is its product normally buried.) Some time between the second and eighth months it becomes natural to describe a foetus as an unborn child.

What is undeniable is that from its earliest development a foetus is *potentially* a child, and that those qualities which it does not possess at first it will come to possess in the course of time. To describe a foetus in its earliest stages as an unborn child is misleading, but to describe it as potentially a child is uncontroversial. But now judgements differ. To the one side it seems wrong to treat potential children as of less moral value than actual children; to the other side it does not. At the one extreme pole are those who feel that its deliberate destruction cannot be justified even by a threat to the life of the mother; at the other are those who think that its destruction is justified simply if the pregnant woman wishes its destruction. Between these extremes are a range of intermediate positions tending towards one pole or the other. Those who take the happiness of the potential mother as the determining factor are likely to regard legislation to limit or prohibit abortion as an intolerable intrusion upon the liberty of the pregnant woman; those who see abortion as tantamount to murder will emphatically *not* regard it as none of their business when a foetus is at risk of destruction—saving a child is a justified intrusion on liberty. This is not like a disagreement about whether Wordsworth was a better poet than Milton, where the contending parties can happily agree to differ. Whatever the law of the land as far as abortion is concerned, one or other of the polar opposite groups will be hoping and probably striving to get it changed.

The problem here is that there is nothing analogous to looking and seeing, no clear test of experience to decide the case. What one side 'sees' as permissible, the other 'sees' as wrong. That being so we are driven back on argument. Can we perhaps find some general principle acceptable to both sides, from which the rightness or wrongness of abortion can be shown to follow? This approach is not easily ruled out, but nor does it seem very promising to follow it. For often people are more convinced in their particular moral beliefs than in any general principles supposed to underpin them. If a general principle leads to the wrongness of abortion, say, then the person who defends abortion may take that as a reason for rejecting the general principle. (This point is developed further in Chapter 18.)

7

The method of proof, as described in this chapter, is likely to encounter recalcitrant cases. But this should not be taken as a reason for despair.

First, it would be a mistake to decide too quickly that a problem, or opponent, is so intractable as to rule out proof from a common starting-point. Perhaps common ground is difficult rather than impossible to find.

Second, it may be that we can tolerate some unresolvable disagreement—even welcome it—as showing just how different people are.

Third, even if there are intractable problems and people, it would be wrong to underestimate the extent of agreement in general and the possibility of reaching agreement by rational means. The very transmission of knowledge of a complex or difficult kind is hard to imagine without the possibility of showing things by argument.

It may be that those cases which resist resolution by proof may be amenable to settlement by some other rational procedure, quite different from anything suggested above. However, there is no widespread agreement about what these radically different methods are, if they exist. At our present stage it is over-optimistic to expect to settle all disagreements by rational argument. But at least rational argument can help to locate and clarify disagreement even in intractable cases. Often that is no small advance.

Exercises

Consider the following passages as proofs. Find out what the passages are trying to show and consider carefully whether the reasons offered in defence of the conclusions are (a) relevant and (b) likely to beg the question.

2.5 Suicide is self-murder, and since all murder is wrong, it must be.

2.6 Two years ago the public sector claimed 51 per cent of Britain's national resources. Last year the figure was 54 per cent. This year it is expected to be higher still. In these circumstances, therefore, any government attempts to extend the public sector must be regarded with disquiet.

2.7 Do you think you have the right to behave so irresponsibly as to advocate the recreational use of a drug capable of changing people's whole attitude to life and work?

   If in doubt about whether this is an argument, reread Chapter 1, section 7.

3 Validity: 'If . . . then'

I

The primary concern of logic is validity rather than truth. It deals with what follows from what, rather than with what happens to be true and what false. A conclusion follows from one or more premisses when it would be inconsistent to accept the premisses and deny the conclusion. In logic inconsistency is the cardinal sin and consistency the first of the virtues. But it should be stressed that the kind of consistency the logician is interested in is consistency at a given time, not consistency *through* time.

Maybe last week Mary believed that the Battle of Hastings took place in 1492 and this week she believes it took place in 1066. We may say that Mary is inconsistent, meaning little more than that she has changed her mind (and perhaps that she is prone to do so). But in a more important sense she is not inconsistent. For she has given up her previous claim. She is only inconsistent in the strict sense if she tries to hold both statements simultaneously. Two statements are inconsistent when they cannot both be held to be true. If the Battle of Hastings took place in 1066 then it cannot have taken place in 1492.

As far as their information content goes, inconsistent statements cancel out; they assert and deny with the same breath. If someone tries to maintain two inconsistent statements and refuses to surrender either, then we have the problem that we cannot make literal sense of his claim. If someone tells us both that his name is John and his name is not John, and will not surrender either claim, then he owes us an explanation of what he is trying to say: perhaps the name on his birth certificate is not John but everybody calls him John, or perhaps his surname is John but not his Christian name. Whatever the explanation, we are owed one, and in default of one we cannot attach sense to his statement.

Sometimes an inconsistency is exploited for effect. If we ask a person whether it is raining we might occasionally receive the answer, 'It is and it isn't.' At face value there is an inconsistency; it cannot both be and not be raining. Of course we know how to interpret this remark: it is raining, but hardly at all. Sometimes the spelling out is more difficult, but we feel roughly we know the lines on which it would be done. There is a well-known aphorism about King James I, that he was the wisest fool in Christendom. Although he was a learned man he lacked good political judgement.

Inconsistencies are frequently unsuspected. Partly this is because people do not connect together their own beliefs on different topics. Beliefs are not always subjected to a close and critical examination. Thus, within a person's overall set of beliefs incompatibilities can survive. But also, an inconsistency can be far from obvious, and statements can long survive unsuspected before being shown to be flawed.

2

Inconsistent beliefs can often be analysed to reveal a self-contradiction. A self-contradictory statement is one which asserts and denies something at one and the same time. Let us represent a statement—any statement—by the letter p. (This is an idea we owe to Aristotle, writing in the fourth century BC.) Then any self-contradictory statement can be represented by

p and not p.

It is any statement which conjoins p with its denial.

There is an inconsistency in believing that John is a bachelor and John is a married man. In this case a self-contradiction can easily be exhibited: if 'bachelor' means 'unmarried man' then the belief can be expressed as:

John is a married man and John is not a married man.

One and the same thing is asserted and denied in the same breath.

Often a self-contradiction is more difficult to unravel. For example, the claim that the square root of two is expressible as a fraction can be shown to involve a contradiction. Yet the inconsistency involves considerable ingenuity to spell out, and few would even begin to suspect that there was any problem here.

One further point about inconsistent beliefs: they cannot always be resolved into a self-contradiction. For example, someone who believes that jet is darker than soot and that soot is darker than jet is manifestly inconsistent in believing both; yet the inconsistency does not take the form of a self-contradiction, *p* and not *p*, as it would be if one held both that jet is darker than soot and jet *is not* darker than soot. Is there perhaps a concealed contradiction, which could be spelled out, given sufficient ingenuity? The problem with this is that anyone perverse enough to maintain that jet is darker than soot and soot is darker than jet would not be compelled to accept things which follow from its denial—things such as: if jet is darker than soot then soot is not darker than jet. So attempts to derive a hidden contradiction cannot get started.

3

We turn now to the question of testing arguments for validity.

The simplest yet the most important step in assessing any argument is to abstract as far as possible from its subject matter. We can get so completely bound up with the truth or falsity of a conclusion that we neglect the route by which it was arrived at. We judge not whether an argument is sound but whether it is sensible. Yet arguments can share the same structure even though some are entirely sensible and others completely absurd. Let us begin with two fairly sensible examples:

If the battery is low then the torch does not shine brightly.
The battery is low. Therefore the torch does not shine brightly.

If Edinburgh is in Scotland then Edinburgh is in Europe.
Edinburgh is in Scotland. Therefore Edinburgh is in Europe.

In both arguments first there is the assertion of an 'if . . . then' statement; secondly, the 'if' part (the antecedent) is asserted alone; and on the basis of those two premisses the 'then' part (the consequent) is asserted alone. We can show the structure of these arguments—both have the same structure—more clearly by using letters.

Suppose we put p for 'the battery is low' and q for 'the torch does not shine brightly'. Then we can set out the argument to show its logical structure or 'form':

If p then q
p
$\therefore q$.

If now we put p for 'Edinburgh is in Scotland' and q for 'Edinburgh is in Europe', we get the same form again:

If p then q
p
$\therefore q$.

Any argument of this form is valid, however absurd its premisses. For example:

If milk is alcoholic then it is illegally sold to children. Milk is alcoholic. Therefore it is illegally sold to children.

By putting p for 'milk is alcoholic' and q for 'it (milk) is illegally sold to children', the reader can confirm that this argument is of the same form as those above. It must again be stressed that the truth of the premisses is not an issue: only whether, granted the truth of the premisses, the conclusion follows. The device of replacing simple statements by letters can help us to see that, in this case, it does. Such reasoning is sometimes known as 'affirming the antecedent', sometimes by its Latin name, *modus ponens*.

4
An argument which looks rather similar to those above, but which is logically very different is this:

If the battery is low then the light is dim. The light is dim. Therefore the battery is low.

As before, we use letters to point up the structure of this inference. Putting p for 'the battery is low' and q for 'the light is dim', we get a form of argument:

If p then q
q
$\therefore$ p.

This argument, and any argument of this form, is invalid. Even if the premisses were true there would be no guarantee of the truth of the conclusion. It may be true that if the battery is low then the light is dim, and true that the light is dim, but false that the battery is low. Perhaps there is some other reason why the light is dim—a bad connection, or a faulty bulb.

This does not mean that the conclusion of an argument of this form is never true; but rather that, if true, it is so by luck rather than by judgement. In the valid form earlier, given that both premisses were true we were led inevitably to a true conclusion. Here the truth of the premisses guarantees nothing, and we are committing the fallacy traditionally known as 'affirming the consequent'. It is a dangerous form of argument, partly because it looks rather similar to the valid form given in the previous section, and partly because many plausible-seeming examples can be found:

If he drank large quantities of alcohol then his speech became slurred. His speech did become slurred. Therefore he did drink large quantities of alcohol.

Putting p for 'he drank large quantities of alcohol' and q for 'his speech became slurred', we get an argument of the form condemned above. Yet is it not valid?

No, it is not. As it stands it is invalid. It becomes a sound argument when we amend the first premiss to read, 'If *and only if* he drank large quantities of alcohol his speech became slurred.' Then the form of the argument becomes:

If and only if *p* then *q*

q

∴ *p*

which is valid. Many fallacious arguments occur from confusing 'if' with 'if and only if'. The latter is a stronger claim, which ideally should always be stated. Unfortunately people often say 'if' when they mean 'if and only if'. When assessing an argument we must try to draw out any such hidden confusions. By tidying up arguments we find it easier to say where (if at all) we disagree.

5

More needs to be said; for the kind of argument I have just condemned appears to be in wide currency. Even scientists sometimes seem to argue by affirming the consequent:

If Einstein's theory is true then light rays passing close to the sun are deflected. Careful experiment reveals that light rays passing close to the sun *are* deflected. Therefore Einstein's theory is true.

The example seems quite typical. Indeed, this style of reasoning seems to be the very thing that Sherlock Holmes, popularly regarded as the model of rational thought, understood by deduction, as in this passage from 'The Boscombe Valley Mystery':

It was about ten minutes before we regained our cab . . . Holmes still carrying with him the stone which he had picked up in the wood.

'This may interest you, Lestrade,' he remarked, holding it out. 'The murder was done with it.'

'I see no marks.'

'There are none.'

'How do you know, then?'

'The grass was growing under it. It had only lain there a few days. There was no sign of a place whence it had been taken. It corresponds with the injuries.' (Doyle, p. 76)

The argument seems to be: if the stone were the murder weapon then it would not have lain there long and it would correspond with the injuries; it hadn't lain there long and was consistent with the injuries; hence it was the murder weapon.

What are we to make of this: that a form of argument which is apparently widely used and even held up as some sort of paradigm of rationality should be an invalid form of argument?

Basically there seem to be three attitudes to the problem. First, it is possible to take a hard line and say that since any argument of this sort is unsound then anyone—scientist or otherwise—who employs this sort of argument is wrong to do so. Any conclusions that are reached by arguing in this fashion can at best be treated as suggestions: a possible way of explaining the bending of light is Einstein's theory, and a possible way of accounting for the stone's being where Holmes found it is that it was thrown there by the murderer. But these are not things which we can unequivocally assert on the basis of the facts given; they await direct confirmation, and until such time as confirmation is forthcoming they remain only suggestions.

This is a drastic step, because it threatens so much of our normal practice and because in some cases (Einstein's Theory of Relativity is one) no simple direct confirmation is possible; all we can hope to do is amass evidence in its favour. We may feel driven to take this Spartan attitude to the kind of argument in question, but it would only be as a last resort.

Second, one could approach the problem in a very tolerant spirit; if it is common practice, especially among scientists, to argue in this way then it must be all right to do so, and too bad for formal logic. This approach is also unattractive, because it is superficial. Not every argument of the form is acceptable, even on very relaxed criteria. The Einstein example may be acceptable, but the example from the Sherlock Holmes story looks distinctly dubious. The stone had not been long in the woods and it had the same shape as the murder weapon; but there are other ways than those given of accounting for these facts. Perhaps the similarity of shape is coincidental, and the stone arrived where it did as the result of a schoolboy testing his throwing arm. However tolerant we are, we must say what it is that makes some of these arguments acceptable and others not; and we must say why, although the conclusion is not guaranteed as in a logically valid form of argument, it is nevertheless acceptable.

There is a third approach, which is to say that our two examples, and other arguments of the same sort, are not fully stated. We saw in Chapter 1 that an argument can rest on assumptions which are not made explicit and which must be properly spelled out if we are to avoid over-hasty condemnation. This seems to me the case here. An argument of the sort we looked at—

If Einstein's theory is correct then light rays passing close to the sun are deflected. They are deflected. Therefore Einstein's theory is correct

—is advanced against a background of competing theories. If it is acceptable it is because only Einstein's of the competing theories would predict (that degree of) bending of light. The Sherlock Holmes example is unsatisfactory because rival theories (a stone-throwing schoolboy, say) would account equally for the facts.

More will be said about this in Chapter 12, where arguments with probable conclusions are discussed.

Exercises

Set out the following arguments, using letters to reveal their logical form, and say whether or not they are valid.

3.1 If there's violence on the football field there is violence amongst the fans. There can be no doubt that society has witnessed a great deal of violence amongst fans this year. It would be right to conclude, then, that there has been violence amongst the players, too.

3.2 If the money supply is held steady, the rate of inflation will fall. It seems clear that the money supply has been held steady, so there will be a fall in the rate of inflation.

3.3 If the rate of inflation is to fall, the money supply has to be held steady. It has been held steady; so the rate of inflation will fall.

6

There are two more argument patterns involving 'if . . . then' which must be considered at this point. They are slightly less obvious than the patterns we have considered so far, but still not difficult.

The first of these is a valid form, 'denying the consequent':

If *p* then *q*
Not *q*
∴ Not *p*.

'Not *p*' and 'not *q*' signify the denials of *p* and *q*, respectively. Let us take the example:

If King Edwards are apples then they are fruit. King Edwards are not fruit. Therefore they are not apples.

This is of the form above, when we put *p* = 'King Edwards are apples' and *q* = 'King Edwards are fruit'.

Here the denial of 'Kind Edwards are fruit' is expressed by putting 'King Edwards are not fruit'. But the denial could be expressed in other ways. More formally, it could be expressed by 'It is not the case that King Edwards are fruit'; less formally by 'King Edwards a fruit? No way.'

As to the validity of the argument above, there is little to be said except consider the example. If King Edwards are not fruit then they cannot be apples; for we are given that if they were apples they would be fruit. In this case the premisses are easy to accept because King Edwards are a variety of potato. But it must be stressed that if we are testing for validity we must take the premisses as given, however much they are open to dispute.

We must learn to recognize a denial even though it does not have the appearance of a negative:

If Golden Delicious are potatoes then they are not fruit. Golden Delicious are fruit. Therefore they are not potatoes.

This is of exactly the same structure as our previous examples. The claim made in the second premiss, that Golden Delicious are fruit, exactly denies the consequent. It does not look like a denial because it contains no negative, but in the context it functions as a denial; it denies the consequent—that Golden Delicious are not fruit. In logic we need to look at how a statement relates to other statements—what job a statement does.

7

If letters are used in the formulation of arguments they must be used intelligently, not to the exclusion of thought but to help thought. Letters are a way of getting us to the heart of the argument. Take our example above:

If Golden Delicious are potatoes then they are not fruit. They are fruit. So Golden Delicious are not potatoes.

How do we set this out using letters?

The first point to grasp is that there is often more than one acceptable way of putting an argument into symbols. The second point to grasp is that to deny 'not p' is the same as to assert p. To deny that it is not raining—'It is not the case that it is not raining'—is the same as asserting that it is raining. To put it in symbols: 'not not p' is equivalent to p.

The most obvious way of proceeding is by reading p as 'Golden Delicious are potatoes' and q as 'Golden Delicious are fruit'. Then the argument becomes:

If p then not q
q
$\therefore$ Not p.

Bearing in mind that any statement is equivalent to the denial of its denial, in this case $q =$ 'not not q', we substitute accordingly:

If p then not q
Not not q
$\therefore$ Not p.

This is a clear example of the valid form, 'denying the consequent'. We have an 'if . . . then' statement; the second part is denied; on the basis of this the first part is denied. We can make it even clearer by bracketing:

If p then (not q)
Not (not q)
$\therefore$ Not p.

8

We have seen that 'denying the consequent' is a valid move. A similar-looking form of argument, but one which is logically a whole world apart, is this:

If p then q
Not p
∴ Not q.

This is known as 'denying the antecedent'. An example which brings out its invalidity is the following:

If Golden Delicious are pears then they are fruit. Golden Delicious are not pears. Therefore they are not fruit.

The second premiss is true because, as we know, Golden Delicious are apples. The first premiss is true because whatever is a pear is fruit. But the conclusion is false. And if we can get from true premisses to a false conclusion then the argument is not valid.

There are more-or-less plausible examples embodying this fallacy. One can be taken in by someone who argues:

If it rained then the ground got wet. It did not rain. Therefore the ground did not get wet.

Any temptation to see this as valid results from reading into the first premiss something which is not stated; that 'if and only if' it rained did the ground get wet. When strengthened in this way, the argument is perfectly sound. As stated, however, it does not rule out the possibility of the ground's becoming wet by some other means: perhaps someone hosed it.

Exercise

Valid?

3.4 History plainly shows that slumps in share prices are bad news for the workforce, for they are always followed by a rise in unemployment. But now the corner has been turned, and share prices are holding steady. Hence we can expect the level of employment to stabilize as well.

> *Try to ignore the variations in ways of expressing the same thought, and concentrate on picking up the basic structure of the argument. Simplify the first sentence and express it as an 'if . . . then' statement.*

9

So far we have considered four rather similar patterns of inference. It may be well to summarize them:

    'Affirming the antecedent':
√ If p then q
    p
    ∴ q. Valid.

    'Affirming the consequent':
× If p then q
    q
    ∴ p. Invalid.

    'Denying the consequent':
√ If p then q
    Not q
    ∴ Not p. Valid.

    'Denying the antecedent':
× If p then q
    Not p
    ∴ Not q. Invalid.

The traditional names of these arguments are unimportant. What matters is that the reader should be able to distinguish them in ordinary speech and writing and know which ones to avoid. It is a mistake simply to try to commit them to memory. If one really understands what is going on in all four cases, and why the invalid moves really are invalid, it is easy to sort out examples of each. All that is really involved is thinking about how we use 'if . . . then'. Some people who know perfectly well how to use 'if . . . then', who normally argue validly when using it, get confused when asked to step back and look at what they are doing. In rather the same way we can run downstairs until we start to think about what our feet are doing; then we lose our rhythm.

Throughout the chapter arguments have been considered valid by virtue of their structure. But there are also arguments and argument-steps which are valid by virtue of the meanings of words involved rather than by virtue of their logical form, for example:

John is a bachelor, so John is unmarried.

This is a valid inference depending on the meaning of 'bachelor'; on the fact that it means 'unmarried man'.

It is tempting to treat the argument above as incomplete as it stands and to add the following 'hidden' premiss:

If John is a bachelor then John is unmarried.

Then (with suitable substitutions) we have turned it into an argument of the form:

If p then q
p
$\therefore q$

—which is a valid form of argument.

However, the additional premiss is not something extra on which the conclusion depends. It is not a new fact, independent of our knowing how to use the word 'bachelor'. The additional premiss is unnecessary. Just as much as the original argument, it depends on the meaning of the word 'bachelor', and the argument was complete as it stood.

Exercises

Express the following arguments, using letters to reveal their logical form and say whether or not they are valid.

3.5 If the President was physically endangered then the alarm expressed was justified. Apparently he was not; so the alarm was exaggerated.

3.6 If advertising of cigarettes is prohibited then the government will lose revenue from smaller tobacco sales. No government will tolerate that, so cigarette advertising will not be banned.

3.7 If each man had a definite set of rules of conduct by which he regulated his life he would be no better than a machine. But there are no such rules; we can conclude that men are not machines.

3* Truth Tables

The casual reader might wish to omit Chapters 3* and 4*. The material in them is self-contained. Those working through 3* and 4* should attempt all the examples.

Our treatment of formal arguments has been unsystematic in the following sense. We have given examples and talked about them, trying to show which were valid and which invalid; but we have not given a way of testing arguments. A fairly simple test procedure is possible, using 'truth tables.'

I

The basic idea is simple. In standard logic, every statement is either true or false; there is no third possibility. Thus a statement, 'It is Sunday', say, can take one of two values: true (T), or false (F). These values are known as *truth values*: to ask for the truth value of a statement is simply to ask whether it is true or false.

If we have two simple, independent statements, 'It is Sunday' and 'It is cold', each of which can be either true or false, there are just four possibilities:

(1) true that it is Sunday, true that it is cold;
(2) true that it is Sunday, false that it is cold;
(3) false that it is Sunday, true that it is cold;
(4) false that it is Sunday, false that it is cold.

The possibilities can be set out in a table, putting *p* for 'It is Sunday' and *q* for 'It is cold':

p,	q
T	T
T	F
F	T
F	F

Now consider the statement, 'It is Sunday *and* it is cold'. Given our assignment of letters above, we can write this as p & q. Under what circumstances is p & q true? It is true only when both parts are true: when it is Sunday and it is also cold. Any statement of the form p & q will be true when both p and q are true; otherwise false.

Similarly, consider any statement of the form *not p* (which we shall write as $\sim p$). Any such statement will be true when p is false, and false when p is true: the sign '$\sim$' reverses the value of p.

We can set out these points quite simply in *truth tables*:

Truth table for &:   truth table for $\sim$:

p	q	p & q
T	T	T
T	F	F
F	T	F
F	F	F

p	$\sim p$
T	F
F	T

The truth table for '&'. As we saw previously, there are four possibilities to consider, which are set out on the left of the vertical line in the table above. On the right of the line is the result of connecting p with q by '&'. Thus, taking the first row of the truth table: two true statements joined by '&' results in a true statement (T & T results in T). Taking, say, the third row of the table: a false statement and a true statement joined by '&' results in a false statement (F & T results in F).

The truth table for '$\sim$'. There are only two possibilities to consider for any statement, p: that it is true and that it is false. These are given on the left hand side of the vertical line, and the result of applying '$\sim$' is given on the right of the vertical line. Thus, the table shows that applying '~' to a true statement results in a false statement, while applying '~' to a false statement gives a true statement.

In Chapter 3, section 6, we asserted that *not not p* is equivalent to *p*. Truth tables show this very simply. We have two applications of '~' to consider, first applying ~ to *p* and then applying ~ to the result of that first operation. We negate *p*, and then negate the negation of *p*. The final outcome is shown in bold type below:

p	~	~p
T	**T**	F
F	**F**	T

The column for ~p is on the right, and is just the same as that given earlier. But there is another operation to be done. We must negate ~p. As before, we negate by reversing the truth value. The column in bold type, ~~p, reverses the values of ~p, and is the same as the column for *p*. Thus *p* and ~~p are equivalent.

Exercise

3.8 *Construct a truth table for the negation of* p & q, *that is, for* ~(p & q)

3.9 *What is the difference between* ~(p & q) *and* ~p & q? *Do the two expressions have the same truth table?* (Brackets matter.)

2

Earlier we looked at statements involving 'if . . . then'. We now introduce the symbol '→' to stand for 'if . . . then', with the following truth table:

p	q	$p \rightarrow q$
T	T	T
T	F	F
F	T	T
F	F	T

The truth table for '→' is less obvious than those for 'and' and 'not', but very useful in testing arguments. Concentrate on the second row. Any 'if . . . then' statement must be false as a whole if the first part is true and the second part false. Consider the claim: 'If Marion called then John was delighted.' Without knowing anything about Marion or John we can say that one thing which is certainly ruled out is Marion's having called and John's *not* being delighted. To assert any statement of the form 'If p then q' is to rule out getting p without q. So the F in the second row of the truth table for '→' is easy to understand. And it is easy to remember that every other row takes T. Thus any statement of the form $p \rightarrow q$ is counted true unless the 'if' part is true and the 'then' part false. (Those who are interested in how '→' relates to the ordinary meaning of 'if . . . then' are referred to Appendix 1).

Given what we have so covered far, testing arguments involving '→' is very easy.

To test for validity: $p \rightarrow q$, $\sim q$, therefore $\sim p$.

First we show all three statements, $p \rightarrow q$, $\sim q$, and $\sim p$, on the same truth table, as follows:

p	q	$p \rightarrow q$,	$\sim q$,	$\therefore$	$\sim p$
T	T	T	F		F
T	F	F	T		F
F	T	T	F		T
F	F	T	T		T
1	2	3	4		5

The numbering of the columns helps the explanation but is not strictly necessary. On the left of the vertical line are the possible combinations of truth values of two statements, p, q. Column 3 is the standard truth table for →. Column 4, representing $\sim q$, reverses the values of column 2, and similarly column 5 reverses the values of column 1.

Now we reason that if the argument is valid then it is not possible to have true premises and a false conclusion. (See Chapter 1, section

5.) So if we can find any row of the truth table above where both premisses have the value T and the conclusion has the value F the argument is invalid: if not, then the argument is valid. In fact, only one row has T for both premisses, and that is in the last row of the truth table, where we also have T for the conclusion. Hence it is not possible for the argument to have true premisses and a false conclusion. Hence it is valid.

Take now an argument of the form: $p \rightarrow \sim q$, $\sim p$, therefore q. We can show that any argument of this form is invalid.

This time the truth table looks as follows:

p	q	$p \rightarrow \sim q$,	$\sim p$,	$\therefore$	q
T	T	T F F	F		T
T	F	T T T	F		F
F	T	F T F	T		T
F	F	F T T	T		F
1	2	3 4 5	6		7

The first premiss is $p \rightarrow \sim q$. Since it is not one of our standard forms we show how it is arrived at. Column 3, p, simply repeats 1, and 5 is, of course, the reverse of 2. Now columns 3 and 5 are connected by $\rightarrow$, resulting in column 4 (written in bold for emphasis). Look carefully at this. The top row alone has the value F because only in this row does the 'if' part have the value T and the 'then' part F.

In testing for validity we must look at both premisses, that is, we look at the truth values in columns 4 and 6. We look for any cases where both premisses are true. This occurs in the third and fourth rows of the truth table. In the fourth row the premisses are true and the conclusion false. Since this *can* happen, any argument of this form is invalid. It is not safe to go from premisses to conclusion. (Row three shows that we might by luck go from true premisses to true conclusion. However, this is not good enough. A valid argument *guarantees* that we go from true premisses to true conclusions.)

Exercise

3.10 Show by means of a truth table that this is a valid argument: 'If Marion didn't call then John was not happy. John was happy. So Marion did call'.

3.11 The truth table for 'p if and only if q', symbolized by '$p \leftrightarrow q$', is given below:

p	q	$p \leftrightarrow q$,
T	T	T
T	F	F
F	T	F
F	F	T

Show that this is equivalent to 'If p then q and if not p then not q'.

4 Validity: Disjunctions and Dilemmas

I

Take an argument such as this:

Either John is clever or he is hard-working. He is clever. So he is not hard-working.

Substituting p for 'John is clever' and q for 'John is hard-working', the form of the argument is shown as:

Either p or q
p
$\therefore$ Not q.

Is this a valid form or not?

I think that this form of argument would be unhesitatingly accepted as valid by many people and unhesitatingly rejected by many others. The reason for this is that the expression 'either . . . or' is to some extent ambiguous. It can be taken to mean 'either . . . or . . . but not both'; it can, on the other hand, be taken to mean 'and/or'. Before we can resolve the question of the validity of the argument above, we must first try to resolve this question of meaning, which affects the first premiss. (When testing for validity we can take the truth of the premisses for granted; but we must where necessary clarify their meanings.)

Let us first put some flesh on the bones of the example above. Suppose a teacher, impressed by a paper he is marking and knowing nothing of the boy who wrote it save his name, says of him 'Either John is clever or John is hard-working.'

If John turns out to be neither—if he had cheated, say—then clearly the teacher was wrong. If he turns out to be one but not the other then the teacher was correct. What if John turns out to be both clever and hard-working? Was the teacher then wrong? There is a division of views on the question.

(a) Some would say straightforwardly, yes. For them, 'either . . . or' excludes both being true. (b) Others would say that though, as it transpired, the teacher could have made a stronger claim, what he said was not false; 'either . . . or' includes the possibility of both being true.

Different people tend to jump different ways on this, and it is not easy to justify a jump in either direction. In favour of (a) it is tempting to point to examples such as 'Either he is alive or he is dead': surely he cannot be both. However, cases like this are indecisive, for it is the meanings of 'dead' and 'alive' which determine that nothing can be both—not the meaning of 'either . . . or'. In favour of (b) we can point to this sort of example: a Rangers supporter bets a Celtic supporter that either Rangers will win the League or they will win the Cup. In the event they win both. Has the Rangers supporter lost his bet?

Which view is the 'common-sense' one, the inclusive or the exclusive use, or whether both uses are widespread, is not an issue which need concern us here. It is much more important to distinguish the two possible meanings than to find out which has the ascendancy in ordinary language. So long as we are clear about the difference between them, and so long as we make it clear when necessary which we are using, no problems need arise.

Returning now to the original example—

Either John is clever or John is hard-working. John is clever. So John is not hard-working

—we can see why there is disagreement. Those who interpret the 'or' as *exclusive* will take it to be of the form—the valid form:

Either p or q (but not both)
p
∴ Not q.

Those who interpret the 'or' as *inclusive* will take it to be of the form:

p and/or q (p or q or both)
p
∴ Not q

—and as invalid because of the possibility of both p and q being true.

2

There is another very basic form of argument involving 'either . . . or', which can be quickly dealt with.

Either John is clever or he is hard-working. He is not clever. Therefore he is hard-working.

Here we have the assertion of an 'either . . . or' statement, followed by the denial of one of the alternatives. It follows that the remaining alternative must be true. The form

Either p or q
Not p
∴ q

is valid. It is so however we interpret 'either . . . or', whether in the inclusive or the exclusive sense. For on both accounts if an 'either . . . or' statement is true, and one of its parts false, the remaining part must be true.

3

It is worth reminding ourselves at this point of the difference between a proof and a valid argument. When testing for validity we are not concerned with the truth of the premises and conclusion, but with the relation between them. We do not worry about who John is and whether he is *really* clever; we take for granted the premises and work from there. When we are looking at a piece of reasoning as a proof rather than testing for validity, we must of course be critical of the premises. A conclusion which follows from false premises has not been shown to be true.

There is a notorious danger in attempted proofs involving

'either . . . or' statements, a trap which often nullifies their conclusions. This is the danger of asserting 'non-exhaustive alternatives':

Either Hitler wanted peace or he wanted war. Hitler certainly didn't want peace. Therefore he wanted war.

This is a valid argument of the sort considered in (2) above. As a proof it is less convincing. It rests upon a premiss which at first glance seems to cover every possibility—exhaust the alternatives—but which does not do so. For it may be that Hitler was completely indifferent between the two; that he neither wanted peace nor wanted war. He may have wanted something else, the aggrandizement of Germany. He may have been confident he would achieve this end, whether by peace (diplomacy) or war, and quite unconcerned which method he used. There is a difference between being willing to resort to war if needs be and wanting war.

Another case of the same sort, but this time a more controversial one, is the argument for the existence of God based upon the existence of order in nature:

Either the order in nature is the result of an intelligent plan or it is the outcome of pure chance. It does not result purely from chance. Therefore it is the result of an intelligent plan.

The argument is formally valid. If the premisses are true then so is the conclusion. Are the premisses true?

The first premiss takes for granted that there is order in nature. Correctly so; indeed, there is a high degree of order. To take examples more or less at random: Aristotle noted that the octopus seeking its prey changes its colour to merge with background stones. Jan Swammerdam, the seventeenth-century biologist, remarked on how well suited are the larvae of mayflies for burrowing in the mud in which they are hatched:

The forelimbs are fitted for digging, as in the Mole . . . Besides their feet, the larvae are also provided with jaws, each with two teeth, like the pincers of Crabs, and these are well suited for working in mud. (*The Bible of Nature*, quoted by Rook, p. 130)

These are just two cases of order and, indeed, of beneficial order. It would be superfluous to multiply examples.

Is the order in nature simply a chance matter? If so, it would be pure coincidence that humans give birth to humans rather than to a whole medley of offspring. It would be pure coincidence that octopuses change colour and merge with their surroundings; one might expect them to change each at random into a whole range of hues. It would be luck that mayflower larvae are all fitted for burrowing, luck that a tree bears all the same species of fruit. This is surely stretching credibility too far. The order in the world cannot be purely a matter of chance.

If it is not chance, then, is the order in nature the outcome of an intelligent plan (and hence of a Planner)? Only if the alternatives— chance or plan—are exhaustive. But there is a third possibility: natural causes. The argument we are examining oversimplifies because it neglects this most obvious way of accounting for the observed order. Indeed, simply to appeal to a divine plan, since it would be compatible with a host of different complex orderings of nature, could not explain the particular order that there is around us. (It would be a lazy explanation.) So I think it is wrong to conclude, as in fact Swammerdam did, that the existence of beings well suited to their environment proves the existence of a divine Planner. The complexity involved can be explained partly by chance—genetic changes thrown up in an unpredictable way—and partly by natural causes, since animals which are well adapted to their environment will be more likely to survive, breed and so transmit to their offspring features which fit them for survival. The complex order in nature can be explained scientifically.

This, it seems to me, shows that the would-be proof, as stated, fails. But it would be unsatisfactory to leave the matter there, because there is a more profound point involved. Even if we can explain the high degree of order in plants and animals by natural causes, these themselves involve an appeal to a kind of order in the universe— simpler patterns by which the more complex patterns are explained. Now these patterns, or perhaps some yet more basic ones if we can discover them, would seem to be the terminus of any possible explanation. But this involves our accepting some sort of order as basic and ultimately inexplicable. Two attitudes to this are possible. There are those who simply accept that explanation has to stop somewhere, and maintain that any attempt to go further is pointless and unverifiable speculation. The other approach is to regard this ultimate order as the manifestation of the will of a Planner, who is himself beyond explanation (self-caused). Whether this last move is justified, and if so how, is a crucial question in philosophy, but one which lies beyond our scope.

Exercises

Show the structure of the following, using letters, and say whether or not they are valid. If validity depends on which meaning of 'or' is used then say how.

4.1 The choice is clear. Either the witness really saw the accused enter the bank or he is an unmitigated liar. That the witness is lying is not to be countenanced. It follows that he really saw the accused enter the bank.

4.2 Either the statesmen of the period were gullible fools or they were lining their pockets at the expense of the ordinary citizen. It is quite clear, unfortunately, that they were gullible fools. But at least it follows that they can be pronounced innocent of the second charge.

4

So far we have considered argument-forms involving two statements which can be symbolized using the letters p and q. It is necessary now to look at arguments involving three or more statements variously connected. We symbolize the different simple statements by p, q, r . . . —as many as are needed. Fortunately the argument-forms which have to be examined are not difficult to grasp, and there are no fallacious but resembling forms to confuse us. In fact there are only two types of argument to consider, one of which will not long detain us.

The hypothetical syllogism is a valid argument. Its form is:

If p then q
If q then r
∴ If p then r.

If the sun shines then the family will go to the beach. If the family goes to the beach then Janet will go swimming. Therefore if the sun shines Janet will go swimming.

One might wish to dispute the premisses, but if they are accepted then the conclusion must also be accepted. The form of argument is valid and obvious, and there seems no need to say more about it. It is used in chains of reasoning, and the chain can be extended in the same fashion indefinitely:

If p then q
If q then r
If r then s
∴ If p then s.

And so on.

5

Finally, there is the dilemma, which contains 'either . . . or' statements as well as 'if . . . then' statements within its structure. An example of the dilemma in its basic form is this:

Either he walks or he catches the bus. If he walks then he will get wet. If he catches the bus then he will arrive too early. Therefore, either he will get wet or he will arrive too early.

The argument is formally valid. Putting p = 'He walks', q = 'He catches the bus', r = 'He will get wet', and s = 'He will arrive too early', we can set the argument out in the usual way:

Either p or q
If p then r
If q then s
∴ Either r or s.

What is going on can be stated less concisely in words. Given that one or other of two statements (the horns of the dilemma) is true, and given that each has a consequence, then one or other of the consequences must be true. (It does not matter whether 'either . . . or' is interpreted as inclusive or exclusive.)

To repeat, the dilemma is a valid form of argument. Traditionally, though, there was much discussion of how to refute dilemmas. The discussion was aimed at dealing with them as proofs rather than as arguments, and there were three widely recognized ways of proceeding.

One way was to escape between the horns of the dilemma. Where the alternatives in the first premiss are non-exhaustive, it is possible and sometimes correct to accept neither alternative, to find a third possibility which the 'either . . . or' premiss ignored:

Either I work all the time or I play all the time. If I work all the time then I shall be poor company. If I play all the time then I shall be a poor scholar. Therefore, either I shall be poor company or I shall be a poor scholar.

There are manifestly more sensible ways of organizing one's time than either of the possibilities raised in the first premiss.

A second strategy was to tackle one of the horns of the dilemma, showing that it did not carry the consequences alleged. Consider this argument against compulsory medication:

Either medication is beneficial or it achieves nothing. If it is beneficial there will be no need to force it on people; and if it achieves nothing it is wrong to force it on people. So either there will be no need to force medication on people or it is wrong to do so.

Here it is the first horn of the dilemma which is open to challenge. It is by no means obvious that if medication is beneficial people will spontaneously adopt it. Whether compulsory medication is justified or not, the case against it given above is simplistic.

We have seen, then, that the 'either . . . or' premiss may be challenged as non-exhaustive, and that one of the 'if . . . then' premisses may be challenged as untrue. The third method of challenge is less straightforward and more interesting. It is traditionally known as a rebuttal. There is a widely quoted example of an Athenian mother whose son decided to enter politics. She was unhappy and tried to deter him by reasoning as follows:

Either you speak justly or you speak unjustly. If you speak justly then men will hate you. If you speak unjustly then the gods will hate you. So either men will hate you or the gods will hate you.

To this the son replied:

Either I speak justly or I speak unjustly. If I speak justly then the gods will love me. If I speak unjustly then men will love me. So either the gods will love me or men will love me.

In fact this does not raise a challenge to the mother's argument, but simply shows that other, more desirable consequences follow, as well as the ones previously shown. Instead of the simple denial of a premiss, we have something more subtle, rather like the riding of a punch. For the two arguments, of the mother and of the son, are entirely compatible. Both agree that either the son acts justly or he acts unjustly. If he acts justly, says the mother, men will hate him. If he acts justly, says the son, the gods will love him. Both may be true. It may be that if he acts justly then gods will love him *and* men hate him, while if he acts unjustly men will love him and the gods hate him. A rebuttal leaves the original dilemma intact. It accepts the conclusion but tries to show that there are other consequences which must be taken into account: the consequences are less black than they seemed.

6

Two variations on the basic theme.

Frequently a trivial first premiss is omitted altogether, for example:

If he speaks then he will be regarded as foolish. If he says nothing then he will be regarded as cowardly. Therefore he will be regarded either as foolish or as cowardly.

(Either p or not p)
If p then q
If not p then r
∴ Either q or r.

This is a truncated version of the standard form of dilemma.

Another form which deviates from the standard pattern is the so-called 'simple dilemma':

Either p or q
If p then r
If q then r
∴ r.

Either we retreat or we make a stand. If we retreat we will be cut down. If we make a stand we will be cut down. Therefore we will be cut down.

The same grim consequence follows from each of the alternatives.

Those missing out 4* should proceed to the examples on page 55, and tackle part (i) of the exercise.

4* More on Truth Tables

When using truth tables it is usual to work with the inclusive rather than the exclusive 'or' (discussed in Chapter 4, section 1). The symbol for 'or' is normally 'V'. The truth table is as follows:

p	q	$p \lor q$
T	T	T
T	F	T
F	T	T
F	F	F

The only case which is false is the fourth row, where both parts of the disjunction are false. So if I say 'Either Mary speaks French or she speaks German', and it later turns out that Mary speaks both, then what I said was correct. If I wish to use the exclusive 'or' then I must do so explicitly: for example, 'Either Mary speaks French or she speaks German, *but not both*'. The truth table then looks as follows:

p	q	$(p \lor q)$	&	$\sim(p \ \& \ q)$
T	T	T	**F**	F
T	F	T	**T**	T
F	T	T	**T**	T
F	F	F	**F**	T

The final outcome is given in bold type. The right-hand column comes from negating the standard truth table for $p \ \& \ q$.

Now consider the argument:

Either John is clever or he is hard-working. He is clever. So he is not hard-working.

Putting p = John is clever, q = John is hard-working, we can test by truth table as follows:

p	q	$(p \lor q)$,	p	$\therefore$	$\sim q$
T	T	T	T		F
T	F	T	T		T
F	T	T	F		F
F	F	F	F		T

The argument is invalid, since in the first row both premisses are true and the conclusion is false.

A similar pattern of argument is:

Either p or q
Not p
$\therefore q$

Using truth tables it is easy to show that any argument of this form is valid.

Exercises

4.3 *Show by means of a truth table that with the* exclusive *sense of 'or' the argument: 'Either John is clever or he is hard-working. He is clever. So he is not hard-working', is valid.*

4.4 *Show by means of truth tables that on both senses of 'or' the argument: 'Either John is clever or he is hard-working. He is not clever. So he is hard-working', is valid.*

Truth tables can be extended to deal with arguments involving three or more statements. If there are three statements then there are eight possibilities (and eight rows of a truth table) to consider. No new principles are involved. Earlier we considered the simple dilemma:

Either we retreat or we make a stand. If we retreat we will be cut down. If we make a stand we will be cut down. Therefore we will be cut down.

Putting p = we retreat, q = we make a stand, r = we will be cut down, the validity of the argument is shown by the following truth table:

p,	q,	r	$p \vee q$,	$p \to r$,	$q \to r$ $\therefore$	r
T	T	T	T	T	T	T
T	T	F	T	F	F	F
T	F	T	T	T	T	T
T	F	F	T	F	T	F
F	T	T	T	T	T	T
F	T	F	T	T	F	F
F	F	T	F	T	T	T
F	F	F	F	T	T	F

Here, for example, $p \vee q$ is false where both p and q are false, that is, in the last two rows of the truth table.

The argument is valid since there is no row in which all three premisses have the value 'T' and the conclusion, r, has the value 'F'.

Exercises

4.5 *Show that arguments of the form* p $\to$ ~q, q $\to$ ~r $\therefore$ p $\to$ ~r *are invalid.*

4.6 *Show that arguments of the form* (p & q) $\to$ r $\therefore$ p $\to$ (q $\to$ r) *are valid.*

In the same way truth tables can be extended to deal with four or more component propositions. There is a drawback, and this is length. With four propositions the truth table takes up sixteen lines, and with five component propositions it takes thirty-two lines. There are shorter ways of dealing with arguments of such complexity, but they are beyond the scope of this book.

Exercises on Chapter 3 and 4

(i) *Show, using letters, the structure of the following arguments and say whether they are valid. Relevant chapter and section numbers are appended for guidance. (ii) Test the arguments marked with an asterisk by means of truth tables.*

4.7*   If and only if the fuse blew did the light go out. Clearly the light did go out, so it must be concluded the fuse blew.
       Chapter 3, section 4.

4.8   Either air traffic will grow in future, or air traffic will decline. If it grows jobs will increase. If it declines then noise nuisance will abate. Either way there are advantages.
       The conclusion is informally stated here; it will need spelling out more prosaically. Chapter 4, section 5.

4.9   Consider 4.4 as a proof rather than an argument. Construct a rebuttal of the dilemma.
       Chapter 4, section 5.

4.10* If there is no resurrection of the dead then the Christian faith is empty. For if the dead rise not then is not Christ raised. And if Christ be not raised your faith is in vain.
       Chapter 4, section 4.

4.11* Unless the book contains pornographic passages it will not be widely read. But it does contain pornographic passages. So it will be widely read.
       'Unless p *(then)* q' = *'If not* p *then* q'. *Chapter 3, section 7.*

4.12   Public ownership of an industry is either unjustified or unnecessary. If an industry is making a loss it should not be propped up with taxpayers' money, and if it is making a profit there is no point in taking it over.
       After setting out the argument formally, consider the example as a proof. Could either horn be tackled? Both? Is it possible to escape between the horns? Chapter 4, section 5.

4.13   Unless the government reduces disparities in income there is no real hope of reducing inflation. But if the government does reduce these disparities, investment will slump and employment will fall off. So either we learn to live with inflation or we resign ourselves to accepting a low level of economic activity.
       Chapter 4, section 5.

4.14* You always hurt the one you love. So if you hurt someone that shows you love them.
Express the first statement in terms of 'if' . . . then', and say which of the argument-forms in Chapter 3 it most resembles.

4.15* Without slavery of some kind there can be no civilization. For there can be no civilization without leisure, and unless there is slavery leisure does not exist.
Identify the conclusion. Set out the statements in terms of 'if . . . then', and say whether or not the argument is valid. Chapter 4, section 4.

   NB Any 'if . . . then' statement has an equivalent formed by switching the parts and negating: 'if p then q' = 'if not q then not p'.

4.16 *For this and the following examples bear in mind that 'only if p (then) q' = 'if not p then not q' = 'if q then p'.*
There is no obvious way that Jones can run his business profitably. Only if he carries more stock will he attract enough customers to pay his way; but if he carries more stock he'll run up crippling debts.
The first sentence states the conclusion in a loose fashion. Draw a conclusion independently, using the premises given. Chapter 4, section 6.

4.17* Only if motive, means, and opportunity were present is the accused guilty as charged. It is clear that they were present, and that therefore the accused is guilty.
Chapter 3, section 4.

4.18* No negotiator is acceptable unless he takes a responsible view of labour relations. But if he takes a responsible view he is committed to maintaining a capitalist society. So only if he is a committed capitalist is a negotiator acceptable.
Chapter 4, section 4.

5 Getting the Premisses Right

It is time to recapitulate.

- Arguments consist of premisses and conclusions advanced on the basis of the premisses.
- An argument is valid if the conclusion follows from the premisses.
- A proof is not the same thing as a valid argument. A proof, starting from premisses which are true and accepted by both sides, goes validly and non-trivially to its conclusion. A valid argument need not start from true premisses and can be trivial.

The last two chapters were concerned with validity. There were exceptions, dictated mainly by tradition: we looked at different ways of dealing with the dilemma, treating it thereby as a strategy of proof rather than simply as a (valid) form of argument. But our main concern was with validity and invalidity.

Assessing for validity is a precise business, but ordinary language is not always tidy. So in constructing examples like those at the end of the previous chapter there are twin dangers: on the one hand, of making them artificially simple, such as never occur outside the logic books; and on the other hand, of expecting the unfortunate reader to trace a faint logical path through a jungle of luxuriant verbiage. The difficulty is not simply that there are many ways in ordinary language of saying the same thing—'If it rains I shall get wet', 'My keeping dry depends on the rain's holding off', 'Unless the rain holds off I shall get wet', 'It can't rain without my getting wet', and so on. What is ultimately more troubling is the fact—raised briefly before—that in ordinary everyday speech we omit obviously intended premisses from arguments. Attempting to supply the missing premisses, and to turn a casual inference into the sort of argument that can be properly tested, can be very frustrating indeed.

Let us look more closely at two of the exercises set in Chapter 1 and see how far they are amenable to formal treatment. The first is relatively straightforward:

Oddly enough, a reduction in the present penalty for drunken driving would have a beneficial effect. A mild penalty makes a jury more ready to convict.

The first step is to pick out the conclusion, which is that a reduction in the penalty for drunken driving would have a beneficial effect. Put more familiarly, the conclusion is that if there is a mild penalty for drunken driving then it will be of benefit. One premiss, given, can be restated: if there is a mild penalty for drunken driving then juries will be more ready to convict. There are perhaps two more unstated premisses: if juries are more ready to convict then drivers will drive more cautiously; if drivers drive more cautiously then it will be of benefit. Thus, with some conjecture and minor amendments, the argument turns out to be a valid chain of reasoning of the sort discussed in Chapter 4, section 4.

Turning this argument into a valid chain of reasoning does not make it any more convincing as a proof. Here is a conclusion, at first glance surprising, based on a stated premiss plus some hidden premisses. Spelling out the argument will not, in all probability, render the conclusion more secure, because the first, the stated, premiss is somewhat controversial and so is one of the unstated ones: if penalties are mild drivers might not be motivated to avoid them. In Chapter 2, by contrast, we came across a conclusion—that eclipses of the moon occur when the moon is full—which was rendered more secure by the argument that led to it. The spelling out of premisses and argument-steps may often pass by the doubts of the sceptic without engaging them. In such cases there is little point in altering an argument so as to bring out its formal structure.

Sometimes it is not just unnecessary but very difficult or impossible to set out an argument in an appropriate, tidy form. The next example, like the one above, also concerns motoring:

Driving too fast in the wrong conditions is the prime factor in road accidents. Stern—and enforced—limits at black-spots would have a far greater
effect than an overall curb simply for legislation's sake.

It seems that the first statement is offered as a reason for the
second:

Driving too fast in the wrong conditions is the prime factor in road
accidents.

∴ Stern and enforced limits at black-spots would be better than an
overall curb on speed *simply for legislation's sake*.

The link is less easy to construct. Perhaps the first thing that should
be pointed out is that the conclusion is controversial, but the stated
reason for it somewhat vacuous. Partly this is because 'too fast in the
wrong conditions' contains a redundancy: 'too fast for the conditions' would say as much. But partly it is because 'conditions' would
be widely taken to include the weather, traffic volume, and road sur-
faces—as well as things such as sharp bends and bad junctions which
can reasonably be termed accident black-spots. To concentrate on
accident black-spots would be to assume that the other conditions
in which people drive too fast are either unimportant as a source of
accidents or unable to be easily affected by legislation on speed. Until
we know which assumption is made we cannot be sure what the
argument is. The phrase 'simply for legislation's sake', italicized
above, perhaps suggests that an overall limit cannot be (or will not
be) enforced. Again, it is unclear just what we are being asked to
assess, and we cannot reasonably guess. The argument is unclear and
its underlying structure cannot be discerned.

Often our approach must be a tentative one. We should begin by
asking what a purported proof is trying to show: what is its conclusion? Then we ask how the conclusion is supposed to be established.
A clear formal structure may then emerge, which can be tested.
Sometimes we will find that on examination the premises seem
ambiguous or unclear, as in the case above. Only if they are clear can
we ask whether they provide a relevant and mutually acceptable
starting-point for a proof.

This chapter will be looking at arguments as proofs.

2

Most of those who say they believe in capital punishment do not really believe in it. For if they were called upon to carry out an execution themselves they would not be able to bring themselves to do it.

There is an unstated assumption underlying the argument above, namely that anyone who sincerely believed capital punishment was right would be prepared to carry out the punishment himself. This assumption carries the burden of the proof, and once exposed it looks very suspect. A person might surely fail to carry out an execution because he regarded executions as unpleasant rather than wrong. It is only too possible to shirk unpleasant tasks which one thinks ought to be done, leaving it to others to perform them.

On the other side of the capital punishment debate one sometimes hears this argument:

The vast majority of those who criticize capital punishment are insincere because if a close friend or relative of theirs had been murdered they would want the death of the murderer.

This seems to me no better than the other. It is quite possible for a convinced abolitionist to feel like that in the conditions envisaged—and the assumption being made is that his feelings then would be a true reflection of his beliefs about capital punishment. But the assumption is suspect. People's judgements are notoriously bad when they are distraught with grief, and there is no reason why moral judgements should alone be exempt from error. There is no doubt that a person *might* regard his vengeful feelings as indicative of his true beliefs; but equally he might later come to regard them as a shameful aberration.

These two examples make clear the necessity of exposing and examining the beliefs on which an argument rests. But there is a danger here. One must be fair to the arguer and not foist upon him or her extreme or far-fetched beliefs. At one point the philosopher Antony Flew violates this precept. He is discussing an argument by the Abbé Sieyès, against a second chamber in government:

that if the second chamber agrees with the first it is superfluous while if it disagrees with it, it is obnoxious.

(A dilemma; the reader should try to set it out formally—see Chapter 4, section 5.) Commenting on this argument, Flew writes:

there is no intellectual or other merit in simply asserting these drastic propositions. By doing so you make, without supporting, the totalitarian assumption that all dissent on any point must be immediately and automatically overridden. (Flew, p. 22)

One may well accept that the original argument is dogmatic and unfair to the case for a second chamber; but to suggest, as Flew does, that anyone advancing it is tacitly committed to totalitarianism is wild in the extreme. In any legislative system there comes a point when dissent is overruled—but in general not immediately and automatically. When there is a single chamber, presumably a single vote can decide what will become law, although there may be a custom of voting at committee stage, and so on. When there is a second chamber with blocking or delaying powers, more votes and presumably more debates will be needed before a bill becomes law. If there is a hidden assumption in the argument used by the Abbé Sieyès, it need be no stronger than this: that since the legislative process must terminate at some stage, it might as well be the province of one chamber as of two, or three, or four. Now whether it 'might as well' or not is a complicated matter, involving the composition and powers of the second chamber. But there need be no presumption that in a single-chamber system of government all debate will be stifled or ignored.

It is obviously tempting to see in an opponent's argument hidden assumptions which are implausible or objectionable. His argument is then so much the more vulnerable. Yet we should ask ourselves if the opponent would really accede in the belief we are ready to foist on him—or where possible ask the opponent himself. Another good rule of thumb when there are hidden beliefs underpinning an argument is to ask what is the minimum belief or set of beliefs needed to carry the argument through. One cannot safely attribute more than this. By the same coin one should not accept too lightly the beliefs which an opponent claims to detect underpinning one's own arguments. An opponent is subject to the same temptations to over-simplify or overstate *your* case.

3

We looked earlier at would-be proofs which beg the question, which take for granted what is in dispute. Sometimes it is very obvious what question is begged and how, and there is unlikely to be any puzzlement. That was the case in our earlier example which moved from the premiss that God shows himself in the beauties of nature to the conclusion that God exists. No atheist or agnostic would for a moment accept such a premiss, for he would see all too clearly what it committed him to. Sometimes, however, begging the question occurs in a slightly more technical or complicated context, and the reader may be bamboozled, getting the feeling that something is wrong but unable to say precisely what.

Here is a somewhat technical example:

[That] there are round squares, for example, is not something that could possibly be believed, and the impossibility in question is not just *psychological*. That somebody should believe both (and at the same time) p and not-p is itself a self-contradictory supposition. The frequent claim that people, alas, are capable of holding self-contradictory beliefs notwithstanding, the statement 'X believes . . . that p and not-p' is itself self-contradictory. It entails 'X believes . . . that p and X believes . . . that not-p', and hence 'X believes . . . that not-p'. But if someone reports that he believes that not-p we all deduce . . . that he does not believe that p; no psychological assumption about the workings of his mind is needed to justify the inference. In other words, part of what is meant by 'X believes that not-p' is 'X does not believe that p'. (Pap, p. 173)

In this passage the author is arguing against the received opinion, which is that people sometimes believe self-contradictory things— things of the form '*p* and not *p*'. He claims that this belief leads to a contradiction. In essence he argues as follows:

Assume X believes *p* and not *p*.

- We infer X believes not p. (If he believes both he believes each.)
- Whence it is not the case that X believes p. (Part of the meaning of 'X believes that not p' is 'X does not believe that p'.)

But this contradicts the original assumption that X believes p as well as not p. So the assumption leads us into self-contradiction.

We shall examine this kind of proof more closely in Chapter 15. For the moment let us concentrate on the second step. This step is the dubious one. It is hard to see why anyone who held the orthodox opinion should be inclined for a moment to accept it. For why would they reckon it safe to infer from the fact that X believes not p that he does not believe p? After all, their claim is precisely that someone might believe both. Despite its apparent rigour, the argument begs the question by appealing to a step whose validity is immediately tied to the proposition in dispute.

An example of a less technical but perhaps more complicated kind is this:

We must assume that human beings are programmed by superior powers, if only because to refuse to accept the idea would only show how well we are programmed.

To repeat, the first step in examining any argument, whether for validity or in order to see how well it measures up as a proof, is to ask, What is this piece of reasoning designed to show? What is the conclusion? Here is one case where simply identifying the conclusion can help to turn vague feelings into a clear approach.

In this example the conclusion is that we must assume that human beings are programmed by superior powers.

Having found the conclusion, we can go on to ask what we are offered in support of it. From what premiss or premisses is it claimed to follow? All that we are offered here is that if we assert that we are not programmed then that only shows how well we are programmed. But there is really no reason whatever to assume that this is what it shows: perhaps the assumption that we are not programmed is correct. It is true enough that if we were programmed then our denials of the fact could not be taken at face value, for the pro-

grammers might have programmed us to deny that we were programmed. But the argument was supposed to be proving, not assuming, that we are programmed. It begs the question.

The reader who is not already persuaded that we are programmed
is, I imagine, unlikely to be convinced by the 'proof', but some confusion is understandable. For it is a commonly urged objection to
the claim that we are programmed that we don't feel we are. The
objection is not conclusive: we might have been programmed to feel
that we are not programmed. But now this perfectly sound defen-
sive point is promoted into evidence *for* the thesis that we are all
programmed. There is no warrant at all for this, but in the heat of
discussion it is easy to suppose there is, and that it flows from a
subtlety one has missed.

Exercises

What hidden assumptions are made in the following passages?

5.1 We may safely reject materialism on the ground that, if it were true,
man's cherished hopes, his ideals, and his yearnings for a future life,
would be as dust.

5.2 . . . .our sexual instinct, as it now is, has gone wrong.

You can get a large audience together . . . to watch a girl undress
on the stage. Now suppose you came to a country where you could
fill a theatre by simply bringing a covered plate on to the stage and
then slowly lifting the cover so as to let everyone see, just before the
lights went out, that it contained a mutton chop or a bit of bacon,
would you not think that in that country something had gone wrong
with the appetite for food? (Lewis (1), p. 86)

4

Sometimes a proof will fail because it moves from mutually inconsistent premises. Usually, but not always, this occurs when there is
anxiety to justify some practice. Several reasons are offered in its
favour, each aimed at mollifying a different set of critics, and inconsistencies creep in. One example (invented, but not all that far from
reality) is this:

There are two good reasons why so much university housing is occupied by professors. One is that it is an inducement to distinguished academics who might otherwise hesitate to accept a chair. And secondly the property is old and rambling so that few people want it anyway.

Comment is superfluous.

A more interesting example, not aimed at defending a policy, is the 'first cause' argument for the existence of God:

Everything has a cause. There cannot be an infinite regress of causes, however. So there must be a First Cause, namely God.

It is not clear how far one is justified in identifying a first cause with God, but that is a question which we need not discuss. More interesting is the question of how we are to treat the premisses, and in particular the second premiss. What is an infinite regress of causes?

Suppose we consider some event or object, A, and ask the question, What caused A? Some other thing, B. Now suppose we ask in turn, What caused B? Some other thing, C. And what caused C? . . . It is clear that our schematic answers to these questions lead us to suppose that we have a series, somewhat as follows:

$$\ldots \Rightarrow C \Rightarrow B \Rightarrow A$$

The series has a last member, A, but does it have a first member? There would seem at first glance to be two possibilities. Either one can work backwards for ever asking, and in principle able to answer, the question, What caused . . .? Or there is a point beyond which we cannot work back; our series then has a beginning as well as an end.

If, as the second premiss claims, there cannot be an infinite regress of causes then we cannot work back for ever, and there must be a first member of the series—a first, uncaused cause beyond which, working backwards, we cannot go. But now we have admitted an uncaused thing—the first member of our causal series. And yet the first premiss was that everything has a cause, that is to say that there are no uncaused causes. Our first premiss says, in effect, that the causal series cannot have a beginning, and the second premiss says that it must have a beginning. The premisses contradict one another, and the argument as it stands proves nothing.

There are various ways in which we might try to modify the argument, but what is perhaps more interesting is why it has seemed so powerful. My conjecture is that the inconsistency between the first and second premises often escapes detection because both premises seem self-evidently true. It goes against the grain to admit that anything is uncaused, and it also goes against the grain to admit an infinite regress. Yet one or other of these must be admitted. In fact neither is impossible.

Until the eighteenth century practically every philosopher accepted as a necessary truth the proposition that every event must have a cause. They regarded an 'uncaused event' as impossible, like a round square. In the eighteenth century David Hume mounted a successful challenge. Hume did not deny that in fact every event has a cause; what he doubted was that every event must, logically, have a cause. He maintained that the notion of an uncaused event is not a contradiction in terms: an uncaused *effect* is a self-contradictory notion because an effect is defined as an event having a cause; but all events are distinct and separately conceivable. The belief in universal causality, Hume argued, arises from experience; it is a matter of fact, not of words.

More recently many physicists have come to doubt even this fact of causality, claiming that certain changes involving subatomic particles of matter are uncaused. Whether or not this is the case—perhaps the physicists have given up the search for causes too quickly—the idea of an uncaused event cannot be ruled out as impossible.

Regarding an 'infinite regress', what causes the problem here is that some infinite regresses *are* unacceptable. For example, the philosopher Gilbert Ryle criticized the theory that every intelligent activity has to be planned. He pointed out that planning something is itself an activity which can be done intelligently or otherwise so that an intelligent act of planning would itself have to be preceded by an act of planning to plan, and this act by an act of planning to plan to plan and so on. Thus any intelligent activity of a person would have to be preceded by an infinite number of intelligent activities, and intelligent activity could never get going. (A similar argument was used in Chapter 2 to show that not every premiss can be proved.)

That a theory leads to an infinite regress is here used to destroy the theory. For people cannot perform an infinite number of successive acts in a finite time. But an infinite regress of causes is possible in an infinite time—that is, if the universe has always existed. Then there would be causes, dependent on causes, these in turn dependent on other causes and so on without end. There would then be no problem about how the series got going because it would never have got going; the universe would always have existed.

As I have stated, I think that both an infinite regress of causes and an uncaused cause are logically possible. It is the difficulty of coming to terms with either which gives the argument from causes its power. Logically it is—at least in the version discussed above—a bad argument. But it confronts us with fundamental questions.

5

By way of summary of this chapter, four rules of thumb.

- First, when trying to establish a conclusion, try to discover why the opponent dissents from it. Otherwise you might end up at cross purposes by taking a starting-point which he considers irrelevant. For example, some people defend capital punishment on the ground that it deters would-be murderers, others on the retributive principle of a life for a life. Anyone arguing against capital punishment should try to find out which ground his opponent subscribes to.
- Second, do not assume premisses which your opponent will obviously have nothing to do with. You have to convince him, not yourself.
- Third, sometimes an argument involves unstated assumptions. Do not burden an opponent with stronger hidden beliefs than are needed for him to carry through the argument. For instance, if all he needs to assume is that most Scots are dour, do not foist on him the belief that *all* Scots are dour.

- Fourth, consider warily any hidden beliefs which an opponent professes to find lurking behind your argument. He is subject to the temptation to misrepresent your position, as you are to misrepresent his.

Exercises

Assess the following as proofs. Ascertain the conclusion, and see how well they are supported by the reasons given. Do not ask yourself about the truth or falsity of the premises or conclusion; just whether the premises support the conclusion adequately.

5.3 Everything must have a cause. For otherwise it would have to cause itself; that is, exist before it existed, which is impossible.
How does this beg the question?

5.4 I can't see why people get so steamed up about the use of corporal punishment. It's the most effective deterrent there is, and the vast majority of people prefer a short sharp penalty to a long drawn out punishment such as imprisonment.
See section 4.

5.5 The atheist says that the pain and waste of the evolutionary process prove to him that there is no God. But, I ask him, who is he to pass judgement on the Divine plan?
Is the reply satisfactory?

5.6 Our ban isn't the result of some objection in principle to the recreational use of soft drugs. It's just that if everybody spent most of their time spaced out on drugs there would be no significant work done. That's the reason for enforcing a ban.
How good is this defence? What other activities would the justification above rule out?

5.7 We can't reform schools outside the state system simply by supporting some of their pupils out of state funds. For, first, the presence of such pupils would not make a bad school better: and few such schools have standards higher than those of a good comprehensive. Secondly, we would still be isolating these children in an élitist way. And finally, they would continue to divert more good teachers from state schools than the country can support.
See section 4.

5.8 But the article fails to note that these—[kabuki, calligraphy, flower arranging, and prints]—were pastimes for the wealthy few in a society where the vast majority had one preoccupation—to get enough to eat. Similarly, few Japanese today, most of whom are preoccupied with trying to afford a house, have the time or money to devote to such activities. It thus is unfair to criticize the Japanese as failing to appreciate their traditions. (Letter, *Washington Post*)

6 Sticking to the Point

1

Proofs go from mutually accepted true premises by a valid argument to a conclusion which the opponent previously denied or doubted.

This offers an approach to the assessment of arguments, but ordinary arguments are not always tidy. Often one has to detect the basic pattern through a screen of obtrusive detail; like finding hidden objects in a puzzle picture. Diversionary phrases and irrelevant thoughts overlie the logical structure. There is no substitute for practice in sifting out the irrelevancies: what a book can do is signpost the commoner pitfalls.

One surprisingly frequent error is slipping away from the point. It is to consideration of this mistake and near relatives of it that we turn now.

2

Every reader must at some time have done this: begun by arguing for a certain conclusion and found himself at the end of the discussion defending a view which was not his own and which he would normally disown. In terms of our pattern, what has happened is that an attempt to prove some statement, p, does not establish p at all, but some other statement. A simple example is the following:

I have been accused of speaking irresponsibly. Let me deal with that one. It is not I, but those who accuse me who are speaking irresponsibly. For they are attacking freedom of speech, and what can be more irresponsible than that?

The speaker is attempting to defend himself against the charge of speaking irresponsibly. He does not really answer that charge but rather asserts his right to be allowed to speak, irresponsibly or otherwise. It may be that the speaker's critics are attempting to silence him and that this is irresponsible. It may be that they are simply subjecting his remarks to criticism, in which case they can hardly be said to be attacking freedom of speech. We do not know how far the speaker's complaints are justified and it does not matter. What we can say is that he fails to address himself to the charge of irresponsibility which he says he is going to answer; he slips away from the point at issue.

Another misdirected argument is this:

The belief in an afterlife has inspired some people to acts of great courage in resisting social tyranny, and deterred many from living a life of narrow selfishness. So it cannot be dismissed out of hand.

To claim that a belief cannot be dismissed out of hand is to claim that there is reason to believe it may be true. Yet what is offered by way of support is not a case for the truth of the belief in life after death. Instead we are given reasons for holding the belief to be socially valuable. If the point at issue is the truth of the belief then the argument would seem to be irrelevant. It may not be irrelevant. Perhaps the arguer is taking it for granted that a socially valuable belief is likely to be true: if so, further questioning would elicit the fact. But it is more likely that there is no such assumption, and that the arguer is simply missing the point.

Shifts of this sort most frequently occur in dialogue rather than in writing. In general we can see why this should be so. A person writing to convince has all the steps of his argument laid out in front of him. He can amend, elaborate, anticipate objections, and above all take time to think. In conversation, time is short and there is pressure to say something. This can often lead to wild changes of tack. In a broadcast discussion some years ago the following exchange occurred; the topic was some alleged 'wonder food'— wheatgerm, honey, or something—for which large claims were being made:

'And do you really think that this elixir will help women to retain their beauty even into old age?'

'I do indeed. The trouble is that our society concentrates on young girls of twenty and fails to realize that maturity and experience bring character and beauty to a face.'

Whatever the truth of the claim about our society, that observation does nothing to show that the elixir has any effects at all, let alone the ones claimed for it.

A more weighty version of the same mistake occurs in this passage. The topic is affluence, and whether it is a good thing:

However . . . rising consumption . . . might still be attacked as likely to foster the self-regarding motive of personal material gain, as opposed to more altruistic motives. But I doubt whether the acceptance or rejection of the goal of higher consumption by politicians or intellectuals will make much difference to the average person's motives, which surely go too deep to be so easily changed. Of course the action of politicians can (within limits) thwart the motive of material gain, as by imposing heavy marginal rates of taxation. But this will not alter the motive itself, which will continue to exist whether consumption rises rapidly or slowly. To achieve a basic change in motivation would require a much more elaborate change in our society. (Crosland, pp. 218–19)

The author shapes as if to refute the charge that rising consumption fosters the motive of personal gain. But he certainly does not answer the charge and, indeed, he comes very close to conceding it. The nub of his reply is that politicians and intellectuals cannot profoundly alter people's motives—cannot create or destroy motives. But the objection was not that rising consumption creates the motive of personal gain, but that it *fosters* the motive of personal gain. The author does not explicitly concede this, but he does concede that the actions of politicians can thwart motives, and consequently it becomes difficult to resist the conclusion that they can foster them too.

3

The above argument illustrates a particular form of slipping away from the point; this is the emasculation of the point at issue. A strong claim seems to be advanced, yet as the argument proceeds it becomes clear that a very much weaker claim is being defended. In the case above a strong claim—that rising consumption does not foster the motive of personal gain—was turned into a weaker claim—that it does not bring the motive into existence.

Another example occurs in Robert Ardrey's *The Territorial Imperative*. Ardrey maintains that the urge to defend territory is innate, and that this fact can explain many aspects of human history and society:

I submit, of course, that the continuity of human evolution from the world of the animal to the world of man ensures that a human group in possession of a social territory will behave according to the territorial principle. What we call patriotism, in other words, is a calculable force which, released by a predictable situation, will animate man in a manner no different from other territorial species. (Ardrey, p. 232)

Ardrey instances the response of Americans (including himself) to the Japanese attack on Pearl Harbor, which he believes was too rapid and widespread to have been the result of social conditioning. Patriotism, he believes, is not something that we are taught, and the territorial principle will lead a nation to resist when its territory is attacked.

Yet there are certain obvious exceptions to this rule. In Europe in the Second World War, for example, a large number of people accommodated themselves to German occupation. Ardrey deals with these apparent exceptions to his thesis by weakening the thesis:

Shock and immediately applied overwhelming power might crush the defences of a nation: it was the essence of the blitzkrieg. Poland, Norway, and the Netherlands fell, for the multiplication of territorial resources cannot be extended indefinitely. (Ardrey, pp. 237–8)

This is Ardrey's explanation of some territorial conquests. His explanation of the conquest of France weakens his thesis more drastically:

The fall of France shocked the world far more, I suspect, because of the collapse of the French will to resist than because of the failure of French arms . . . the French collapse seemed a kind of cry against nature, an evolutionary sin for which the French have been demonstrating guilt and neurosis ever since. And yet, one must suggest, the fall of France was an event less dramatic in territorial terms than the evidence would warrant. France in the years between the wars had slipped, like Italy, to the status of a noyau, the society of inward antagonism which it yet, in all probability, remains. (Ardrey, p. 238)

(A 'noyau' is a group of people or animals held together by mutual animosity.)

What seemed like a strong claim—that patriotism is an instinctive calculable force released by a predictable situation—now begins to look distinctly watery: patriotism is in some cases an instinctive force; sometimes it is non-existent.

But, crucially, it is barely open to Ardrey to introduce the quali-fication at all. If patriotism is innate and unlearned (p. 235) it is hard to see how only some people can have it, how French people lost it some time between 1914 and 1939, how the Italians failed to possess it. And this is just a special case of a more general difficulty. For it is apparent that there is a great deal of learning involved in patri-otism, which makes an attack on a piece of land perhaps thousands of miles away—and which perhaps one has never seen—an attack on one's country, an attack on one's fellows. At times Ardrey seems to concede this, retreating to the claim that patriotism requires some unlearned element, a territorial instinct which may take different forms:

When we discuss behaviour patterns, such as the territorial, we deal with these open patterns of instinct. The disposition to possess territory is innate. The command to defend it is likewise innate. But its position and borders will be learned. And if one shares it with a mate or a group, one learns likewise whom to tolerate, whom to expel. (Ardrey, p. 24)

In fact he repeatedly shifts between two claims. The first is that there is an instinct to defend (some) territory, but that it is not resolved which, nor what happens when loyalties conflict. The second is that patriotism is natural, and one's country is one's territory. The first claim is more easily defended; the second more likely to attract attention.

Exercises

In each of the following passages the arguer shifts his ground. Find what is initially claimed and what is offered in support. Say how the supporting reasons shift the ground of the discussion.

6.1 One might argue that the search for truth is something that emerges naturally in all intelligent people; just as they express themselves in art and music, so in philosophical thinking. If a person sees no value in philosophy then he is not intelligent enough, or is maybe unfitted by inclination, to undertake a serious course of study; either that or he has not been properly taught to think.

6.2 I don't consider that advertising has anything to do with alcohol abuse. Home influences are more important—from the extremes of parents who drink too much to parents who won't let a drop into the house . . . There is a case for taking steps to persuade people to be more careful with alcohol. Some of the money the government makes from the industry should be spent educating the less strong minded not to drink so much. (*Glasgow Herald*)

6.3 There is every justification for spending millions of pounds on space exploration. It is part of man's nature to seek truth and adventure—and no doubt if the money were not spent in that way it would not be spent in any better way.

4

The final example illustrates the need for clarity in defining a problem, as well as the dangers of slipping away from the point (all the greater if the point is unclear to begin with). It is an extract from a radio discussion from the 1950s between Malcolm Muggeridge and Bertrand Russell on whether progress is possible. The extract is a lengthy one, but it well repays study. It is a perfect example of how two very intelligent and controversial debaters can get virtually nowhere towards agreement, even on where to disagree. It has the authentic and familiar ring of discussion of a big topic.

   One note of caution. The protagonists perhaps suffer a bit from having their conversation preserved, blemishes and all. That is the price of fame. I imagine that few of us would do so well.

The debate begins by Muggeridge defining the problem as he sees it:

MUGGERIDGE: My position is this—I consider that one of the major factors in reducing the world to its present rather melancholy condition has been the circumstance that human beings have been conditioned, for a variety of reasons, to believing that in some extraordinary way human life must, or can, get better and better. Now I regard this as a complete fallacy. I don't think it gets better, nor, indeed, do I think it gets worse. And I think that the only way human beings can live sanely in this world is by recognizing that, and therefore I contend that the idea of progress has been a disintegrating idea, a fundamental error, and that there's very little hope for us until it's ultimately exploded. (Muggeridge, pp. 23–5)

Notice that Muggeridge is not very precise in expounding what he sees as the problem. He regards the belief in progress as mistaken and harmful, but he runs together two quite separate beliefs about progress:

- that human life must go on getting better and better;
- that human life can go on getting better and better.

In opposition, Muggeridge claims:

- that human life does not get better or worse at all;

and he implies:

- that human life has been made worse by the belief in progress and that if that belief were dropped it might perhaps be made better.

It may seem pedantic to fix on these different interpretations. Isn't it enough, one is tempted to say, that Muggeridge is against progress? Not so. As we shall see, the failure to specify more precisely what is to count as 'progress' leads to a great deal of talking at cross purposes.

Rather than destroy the continuity of the conversation I shall use letters in the margin to refer to my further comments which follow. The reader will best approach the passage by reading it straight through to begin with, then working through it making reference to the comments as he does so.

RUSSELL: Well, if one accepted the view that nothing that anyone can do will make the world either better or worse, one might just as (a) well take to drink and sink into the gutter. And it seems to me that it's not the view that you really take, and you don't really believe it.

MUGGERIDGE: I must utterly disagree with that, because I don't think that not believing in progress—believing as, for instance, Christians have always believed, that human life is inherently imperfect, and that it cannot be other than imperfect, because they are imperfect—I don't believe that that has produced a sort of ennerva-(b) tion. There's absolutely no reason why people shouldn't become richer, why they shouldn't invent things, why they shouldn't make their lives more comfortable. All that's got no bearing on the par-(c) ticular question that we're discussing. What we're discussing is whether human life itself is progressing, is getting finer, richer, better. In my opinion, not.

RUSSELL: There are, you admit, changes in our circumstances. What you do not admit is that these changes are either for the better or for the worse. You've maintained that they're ethically neutral, and if you hold that, honestly and sincerely, it does follow that it doesn't (d) matter what you do at all, and that all ethical standards—all ethical and moral standards—are at an end.

MUGGERIDGE: Not in the least. I'm not saying that changes in human life don't matter. I'm saying that they don't alter its essential character, and that if people attribute to them qualities that in fact they don't have they are pursuing a fallacy, and ultimately wreck their lives. In other words, it may or may not be desirable that you should have things like radio, this strange invention that is enabling us tonight to be heard by other people. It may or may not be an advan-(e) tage that that exists, but it has no bearing on this idea of progress. On whether you or I are better people, more likely to understand the circumstances of our existence.

RUSSELL: I don't think one ought to confine oneself to scientific discoveries. Now, there have been savage societies in which, when a man got old, his children sold him to neighbouring cannibals, to be eaten, and I think you and I would agree that that was a bad system, (f) and we prefer the system in which old men are allowed to go on.

MUGGERIDGE: I should have said, myself, that if you added in the appalling cruelty of the time we've lived through, both collective and (g) individual, it would create a world record, and I believe there's some connection between that and this extraordinary illusion that human beings are progressing. Because I think that what really makes human beings humane and kind is humility, and the idea of progress is an

(h) arrogant idea. And that is probably its greatest moral disadvantage.

RUSSELL: I think that we've got to get down to a certain point. Are we thinking of better or worse only in moral terms, or also in other terms. Now, if you're thinking only in moral terms, then I think there's a great deal to be said for your attitude, but I should say that a community is better, for example, in which people are healthy than

(i) one in which they are ill, although that's nothing to do with virtue.

MUGGERIDGE: Then you would look for the best human beings— for the highest achievement—in those communities which had successfully mastered the problem of their material existence, and if you

(j) did that, you would be bitterly disappointed.

Now the comments:

(a) Russell selects one of the problems thrown up. He addresses himself to Muggeridge's claim that there is no progress at all. He makes the point that it would be difficult to live by that belief.

(b) Muggeridge tries to meet the point by claiming that not all who deny the possibility of progress become morally apathetic. For example, Christians believe that a perfect world is impossible, but they are not morally apathetic. However, the counter-example does not squarely meet the case. For though Christians believe that life can never be other than imperfect, it does not follow that they believe life can never be improved at all. They do not believe that things can ever become perfect, but they may believe some progress is possible.

(c) Muggeridge qualifies (and thereby weakens) his claim by ruling out changes in wealth and comfort as irrelevant.

(d) Russell ignores or does not notice the argument in (b) and the concession in (c). He reiterates his earlier argument that if there is no possibility of improving things at all then there ceases to be any point in trying to do good. It is clear by this time that an exact definition of the thesis under discussion would be a very great help. Russell is attacking the very strong view that it is not possible for human life to get better at all; it may be that Muggeridge only wants to say that in fact it hasn't got better, and that it can't go on and on getting better indefinitely. If a discussion starts off unclear, the confusion is often compounded by the fact that each of the disputants cannot see what the other is driving at; each sees the other's remarks as missing the point.

(e) Muggeridge repeats his previous point in response to the preceding criticism. Russell has accused him of holding the belief that no desirable change (no real progress) is possible. Muggeridge replies that he does think desirable change is possible, but not change of the sort which he would call progress. Muggeridge wants to restrict the word 'progress' to advances in moral sensibility.

(f) At last we come to the beginnings of a discussion on whether there has actually been change of an essential sort for the better. Russell's example would be a case of progress.

(g) Muggeridge claims, in effect, that to focus on this example is to focus too narrowly. Overall, our society is no better than those in which the old were put to death. Contact, at last!

(h) The claim is that belief in progress prevents progress, because it prevents humility, which is a necessary part of true progress. Russell began by claiming that the belief in progress is necessary in order to prevent apathy. Are they both talking about the same belief? Russell, it is fairly clear, thinks that to avoid apathy it is necessary to believe that one can leave things better than one found them (some progress is possible). I think that Muggeridge is attacking the belief that things will go on getting better and better (continual progress). This is, perhaps, an arrogant and dangerous belief. Failure to clarify the question in the first place is largely to blame for the confusion here.

(i) Russell doesn't respond explicitly to Muggeridge's argument in (g), though perhaps he tacitly concedes it. He draws a distinction between moral progress and progress in other respects—he instances health, and might perhaps add things such as knowledge and security. Moreover he seems prepared to concede that there is no moral progress, although he maintains that there is progress in these other areas.

(j) Muggeridge is not listening. Russell has conceded that material progress does not necessarily go along with moral progress. Muggeridge accuses him of holding the view that the best people are to be found in the wealthiest societies. Far from holding this view, Russell has tended to side with Muggeridge in denying it.

As the debate continued, the question on which the dispute centred was the relative importance of moral and non-moral progress, with Russell holding to the position that the elimination of extreme poverty is the most important task, overshadowing spiritual values, and Muggeridge claiming in response that only by the pursuit of spiritual values is extreme poverty likely to be eliminated. In the lengthy extract we have looked at above that issue has hardly even begun to surface.

It is interesting to reflect how confusion has resulted from the vagueness of the proposition up for discussion. The result is a quite bewildering thread of argument which, even frozen on the page, is difficult to follow. Yet this debate is typical of spoken controversy on a complex subject which evokes different value-judgements in the participants; a mixture of half-grasped criticisms, shifting ground, emotional responses, and thought-provoking ideas. Written controversy has a better chance of being well structured. There is time to grasp an objection and assess it properly. Even so it is difficult enough. In conversation, under pressure of time, it is next to impossible to grasp all that is going on. One could not change this even if one would.

5

We have considered in some detail in this chapter the importance of clearly defining the issue and sticking to it. Sometimes in a very short passage the author will stray from the point, sometimes weakening the point, so that what looks at first a very controversial view turns into something much more commonplace.

Speech and writing bring different problems when one is trying to assess an argument. In conversation it is often very difficult to avoid being swept along. Time is at a premium. Therefore, even when one suspects that something is going wrong, some fallacious step being made, it is often difficult to say just what. Very often, unless one can say quickly what is wrong, the moment is past.

In printed argument, where the reader can go at his or her own pace, there is not the same problem. The crucial passage, the dubious move, can be examined again. But there are other problems, of which the chief one is length. What the author says on page 50 may square ill with what is said on page 10, but the mass of material in between may conceal the conflict from author and reader alike. Both have been led by gentle steps, and both have been led astray. When one suspects an author is shifting the ground one can painstakingly check out one's suspicion. Even here, print has some advantage over conversation, where the same sort of shift can occur but where one's suspicions are less easily put to the test.

Exercises

As before, find how the supporting reasons shift the ground of the discussion.

6.4 Some medical scientists have argued that there can be no cure for schizophrenia. What reason is there for believing otherwise? Quite simply that to adopt a negative belief at this stage would mean the end of hope for thousands of people, whereas if research goes on there is still hope. It shows complete irresponsibility to condemn people to despair in that way.

6.5 Only someone with an excessively contemptuous view of British stout drinkers and British margarine buyers would believe that they are being manipulated by the not very hidden persuasion of Guinness or Summer County posters into buying products which, but for all those irrelevant cartoons and irrelevant pictures of unspoilt countryside, they would not prefer to the available competition. For the advertiser the aim is, presumably, to generate goodwill and to keep the name of the product in the public mind. And if, all other things being equal, I choose Pirelli tyres because I have enjoyed their calendars, is that a bad or a silly reason? (Flew, p. 111)
   Compare the first and last sentence.

6.6 There is no doubt that the loss of religious faith has made the world a worse place. Nor is it any objection to point to religious wars or the intolerance religion sometimes engenders. Any movement, not just religion, will lend itself to exploitation by the unscrupulous. And excesses of zeal, which characterize great movements, are no worse than the apathy of today's prevailing faithlessness.

6.7 *Assess the following piece of dialogue.*

LORD JAMES OF RUSHOLME: I want to know what's wrong with the methods we use to select our political leaders.

MUGGERIDGE: What's wrong with the methods is that you are basing your test primarily on intelligence . . . I would use the simple method that the man who wants power gets power.

LORD JAMES: But that gives us Hitler.

MUGGERIDGE: Yes. It gives us Napoleon, it gives us Lenin, it gives us Roosevelt, it gives us all the people who've exercised power in our time. But I hate them all because I hate power. (Muggeridge, p. 153)

6.8 There was reasonable-to-good evidence that low-level radiation was beneficial. Studies on rats in Japan had shown that animals which received periodic doses of low-level radiation and were then exposed to a high dose were less susceptible to cancers than those who had not received low-level doses. (*Guardian*)

7 Meaning and Definition

Insensitivity to word-meanings can lead to pointless or confusing debate. Indeed, it has often seemed to philosophers that much controversy is simply the result of failure to attend to the meanings of the key words in any discussion. The theme runs through the writings of British philosophers from Locke onwards; to the extent that many philosophers in the 1950s thought that all philosophical problems arose from misunderstandings of the language we use. Be this as it may—and most philosophers today would see it as a gross overstatement—there is no doubt that ambiguity and shifts in meaning can be treacherous. This chapter explores some of these shifts, showing how they can lead to misunderstanding and error.

In the passage below, W. S. Beck argues against dualism. This is the philosophical belief in, as Beck puts it, 'the absolute separateness of mind and body':

When an experience leaves a memory there must be some material imprint in the brain (according to current evidence), since it is clear that brain function at all levels involves . . . patterns of neuronal discharge. It is not necessary to visualize these material imprints as little scenic bas-reliefs scattered throughout the cranium: the phenomenon bears a closer resemblance perhaps to what happens in the course of magnetic tape recording. Thus memory—and consciousness too—has a physiological basis. (Beck, p. 44)

However, most philosophers who have subscribed to dualism would not dispute the kind of evidence that Beck sets out. Their belief in the separateness of mind and body is a belief that consciousness and brain are not identical. They are fully prepared to concede that changes in the brain go together with changes in consciousness, and will often concede that changes in the one can bring about changes in the other. In that sense the two are not absolutely separate, any more than a dog and its shadow are absolutely separate. Nevertheless, a dog is not the same as its shadow—neither, dualists would say, is a brain the same thing as a mind; and in that sense the two are absolutely separate. Beck thinks he has found objections to philosophical dualism, but they turn on misconstruing what is meant by 'absolute separateness'. Whatever the shortcomings of the theory, it is not so easily refuted as that.

Our second case of a shift in meaning comes from Thomas Carlyle's *Lectures on Heroes*:

I am well aware that in these days Hero-worship, the thing I call Hero-worship, professes to have gone out, and finally ceased. This . . . is an age that as it were denies the existence of great men; denies the desirableness of great men. Show our critics a great man, a Luther for example, they begin to what they call 'account' for him; not to worship him, but to take the dimensions of him—and bring him out to be a little kind of man! He was the 'creature of the Time', they say; the Time called him forth, the Time did everything, he nothing—but what our little critic could have done too! This seems to me but melancholy work. The Time call forth? Alas, we have known Times *call* loudly enough for their great man; but not find him when they called. He was not there; Providence had not sent him. (Carlyle, pp. 193–4)

The view under attack here is an interesting one: that great men are simply talented individuals, the products of their age, well able to exploit the situations in which they find themselves. Carlyle will have none of this, believing that great men are heaven-sent. However, in Carlyle's argument there is little of real substance. Carlyle exploits the confusion of 'called forth' with 'called for'. His opponents claim that the great man is called forth (produced) by his time. Carlyle claims that great men have been called for (sought) frequently enough, without being sent. The reply does not directly meet the case; to believe that every great man is a product of his time is not to believe that every time of crisis produces its great man.

A common shift in meaning concerns the word 'God':

Everyone has some god. Everyone worships something. If it is not the God of Christianity or some other religion then it is ones country, or family, or the dog, or even the car.

If people were not so keen to accept the conclusion they would be much more critical of the route to it. To worship is, in its original use, to adore as divine; in another common use it can simply mean to adore—to regard with deep respect or admiration. A person may well worship family or car in this second, more colloquial sense, but there is no reason for taking seriously the suggestion that anyone lavishing tender loving care on either family or car really regards them as divine.

When the ambiguity in the meaning of the word 'worship' is pointed out, what looked like a religious claim has become a psychological one: that everyone lavishes great care and attention on *something*. (This claim, too, is fairly dubious; for most people spread their affections and enthusiasm more thinly over many objects.)

H. G. Wells argued in the same manner, for effect:

I have a practical mind, and I judge a man's religion by the line of conduct he pursues. If, for example, he persists in getting drunk, and if he goes to great trouble and abandons most of the other good things in life to get drunk and keep drunk, then I do not care what battered religious labels may be sticking to him, Baptist, Greek Orthodox, Sunnite, Hindu, Christian Scientist, Atheist, his real God is Drunkenness. And if he estimates the values of life in terms of dollars; if he thinks that losing Dollars is failure and calls accumulating and spending Dollars in a showy and successful way 'making good', then his creed does not matter in the least to me; his real working God is the dollar. (Wells, p. 105)

There are links between the idea of a being with power over us and the idea of the outstanding concern in life. Wells exploits the connection deliberately in order to shock and provoke.

2

As we saw in the previous chapter, what starts as a bold claim is often unwittingly weakened and qualified in the course of discussion. Such meanderings are sometimes made easier by shifts in the meaning of certain key words.

In this example of stretched definition the author argues that words or expressions have meaning in so far as they refer (or bear a 'referential relation') to states of affairs:

There is little trouble defining the class of objects or events to which a word like *telephone* refers, but it may be difficult to identify the referents of words like *jealousy, teach, concept*. Some signs, like *Hi* and *Thanks*, bear referential relationship only to certain kinds of social situations. Other signs refer to relations between referents; words like *in, of,* and *and* have this function. The particular sequential arrangement of signs may have a referential function; this is evident in the comparison of the string *man bites dog* and *dog bites man*. The word *to* in an infinitive phrase like *to be* may be said to refer to something in the grammatical structure of the sentence in which it appears. (Carroll, p. 6)

The main criticism to be levelled against the passage is that it so widens the use of the word 'refer' that what is said is not informative. To refer to something normally involves picking it out or directing attention to it. So a proper name—Mary, Tom, or whatever—can direct attention to the person who bears that name among the speaker's acquaintances. And perhaps it is reasonable to say that 'telephone' refers to (because it directs attention to) a class of objects, and that words like 'in' and 'of' refer to relations. But what of words, or rather one-word sentences, like 'Hi' and 'Thanks'? Even if they are uttered only in certain kinds of social situation they hardly pick out or direct attention to those kinds of situation. (Otherwise, instead of saying 'Thanks', I might say 'Someone just did me a service'—which applies to the right sort of situation but does not actually thank anyone.) The suggestions that word order and the infinitive use of 'to' refer to something in the grammatical structure of the sentence are simply too vague to assess without further information.

At best the notion of referring is rather vague. By widening its meaning Carroll renders it still more vague. He does this in the interest of laying down a general theory of how words work. Yet the quest for a theory of 'how words work' may be misguided, if it tends to suggest that all words work in the same way. It is more realistic to suppose that different sorts of words all work in different ways to build up the meanings of sentences.

Another example of stretched meaning:

Academics are in no position to complain about the fact that nowadays University degree courses tend to aim at satisfying the job market rather than indulging an urge for abstract understanding. Academics are in the education business, and, like any business, those working in education should aim at meeting their customers' demands.

Notice here the extended use of 'business'. According to the ordinary dictionary meaning, a business is 'a commercial or industrial concern'. Here, however, it is treated as equivalent to 'an establishment having income and expenditure'. On this wider definition many things become businesses which are not businesses in the ordinary sense—not just education but art, the family, and religion, for example. Now whereas commercial and industrial concerns might well be dedicated to meeting the wishes of their customers, the same is not necessarily true of businesses in this wider sense; so, whether true or not, the conclusion is too hasty. (Of course, any establishment will continue in existence only so long as enough people want what it offers, so there may be problems if people's wants change. This is not, however, the same as saying that the aim of the establishment should be to follow the changed wants. For example, a religion will persist only so long as people want what it offers; but the aim of a religion is not to court popularity, but to communicate the truth about God.)

Exercises

7.1 In this period of austerity every one of you will be asked to make sacrifices. We in government felt that we, too, should make sacrifices. So we are making drastic cuts in government expenditure.
What does the phrase 'government expenditure' mean?

7.2 The Prime Minister is to be congratulated. His motive in allowing a free vote on his side of the House may have been largely tactical, but he has nevertheless restored to Parliament an air of honesty and responsibility.
What is the PM being praised for?

7.3 Human nature being what it is, we are justified in speaking of the interest earned on savings as the reward for the sacrifice involved in waiting to spend one's wealth, accumulating it rather than spending it all at once.
Section 2.

7.4 The scientific worker, whatever his upbringing may have been, and whatever sectarian labels he may still be wearing, does in fact believe in Truth—which is his God—in a God who is first and foremost Truth and mental courage.

3

In both cases above we have seen a change in meaning brought about by widening the normal meaning of a word. More things under the new meaning count as businesses, and more things count as cases of referring. Redefinition can also narrow the normal meaning of a word, so that fewer things than usual count as cases of whatever it may be.

This covert narrowing of the normal meaning may be accompanied by the word 'true' or 'genuine'. If so, then we have what Anthony Flew has happily dubbed the No True Scotsman Fallacy. It runs somewhat as follows:

No Scotsman, it is claimed, would wear a kilt along with a tee-shirt, eat haggis deep fried in batter, or put lemonade in whisky.
— But lots of Scotsmen do these things!
— No true Scotsman would.

The original claim is thus protected by screwing up the definition of Scotsman to exclude many of those who on all normal criteria fit the bill.

A manœuvre as transparent as this might seem too obvious to deceive anyone, even the perpetrator. But it is not always so obvious what is going on. Consider this challenge to political action aimed at relieving hardship in America:

Everyone is supposed to comfort the suffering, uplift the disadvantaged and 'feel your pain.' The trouble is that compassion so casually dispensed is debased. (*Washington Post*)

There follows an account of a number of proposed government initiatives. The author claims, variously, that the problems they address are exaggerated, or that the initiatives are directed at the wrong groups or will be ineffective or will have bad effects. (These claims may well be right; for our purposes it does not matter.) Then comes this passage:

To feel for the plight of others is usually a worthy instinct, and although genuine compassion is often private and quiet, there's obviously a place for it in public life. But the passion for its public expression has gotten out of hand. This sort of compassion is a mushy concept that confuses many ordinary setbacks and choices with 'suffering' and supposes (often wrongly) that many can be erased by collective intervention. Genuine compassion has been cheapened, and the quest to be seen as caring has had a corrupting effect on public life.

Now compassion in its normal meaning is 'sorrow for the suffering of another'. Feeling compassion in the normal sense of the word may well be 'mushy', in so far as it does not imply that one has correct beliefs about how best to relieve suffering, or that it only arises when the other person's suffering is severe or unusual. But in the author's use of the word, compassion—genuine compassion, that is to say— is discriminating. It is not felt for those suffering the ordinary misfortunes which life brings, and with it comes knowledge of how and when it is appropriate to act. Very few people will qualify as compassionate in this new, stricter sense.

So what motivates this stipulation? Why doesn't the author simply make the point that compassion doesn't guarantee good results? The most likely answer is that he cannot bring himself to admit that the political initiatives in question are even sincere. Thus he concludes the passage above by speaking of the quest to be *seen as* caring. He unwittingly slides from saying that the politicians are not genuinely compassionate in his new, strict sense, to saying that they are not genuinely compassionate in the old sense either.

A further example of 'high redefinition' concerns happiness:

> We cannot be happy without being good; for amongst the many instincts which crave for fulfilment are those essentially altruistic in their aims, such as the maternal instinct and the social instincts. In this respect happiness differs from pleasure, which can be utterly selfish, for it is the expression of individual instincts which may be entirely egocentric. We cannot be happy unless we have right relations to others, and such right relations imply goodness in conduct. The psychological ideal must exclude . . . any conception of happiness which is antagonistic to the good. (Hadfield, p. 92)

Again, we have what looks like a bold statement of fact—that one cannot be happy without being good—turning upon examination into what looks remarkably like a verbal stipulation. All those people whom we thought to be bad but happy were not feeling happiness at all. Pleasure, yes; but not happiness. The claim comes to look less significant than we thought, because the distinction is a fine one. If we ask people which they are feeling—pleasure or happiness?—they will probably be unsure what the difference is; and if we simply refuse to call bad people happy, regardless of what they themselves would claim, then we are simply redefining the word 'happy' to exclude bad people.

It is not surprising that the author should want to tamper with the meaning of the word 'happy' in this way. In context it is clear that he is trying to link the concept of psychological health to the concept of goodness. If this can be done then any accusation that psychiatry is morally subversive will be shown to be without foundation. Redefinitions of this sort are rarely undertaken gratuitously; they occur under pressure or for a purpose.

4

Shifts in meaning are often connected with worries about 'real' definitions. Where there are disputes about, say, what happiness involves, people are tempted to ask what is the real meaning of the word. Normally those who ask are not simply seeking a dictionary definition, for the question often seems to them more serious and profound when the dictionary lists more than one meaning. They feel that somehow, lying behind the way that people use words, lying behind the dictionary definitions, they will find some facts which will constitute an answer to their question. The search for the 'real' meaning, the 'right' definition, is surely a misguided one. However, there lies behind it something important, albeit ill-expressed.

The quest for the 'real' meaning is misguided because it suggests that meanings are not conventionally fixed. It suggests that the everyday meanings of words, recorded in dictionaries, are only approximations to some meaning to be teased out by pure thought. But words are ultimately conventional. Where a word can be defined in different ways—'worship' meaning 'adore as divine' or simply 'adore, regard with deep respect and affection'—there seems no sense in asking which is the right definition or which is the real meaning. One definition might be, in context, more useful or less misleading than another—but not, out of context, right or wrong, true or false. Indeed, it is perfectly possible to stipulate the meaning of a word for a given context. If I stipulate (to borrow an example from Lewis Carroll) that I shall use the word 'glory' to mean 'a nice knock-down argument', and then go on to claim that a Beethoven symphony contains nothing of glory, my claim will be an obviously correct one, although expressed in a completely perverse manner. A Beethoven symphony does not contain bits of nice knock-down arguments, but it is stupid and confusing to redefine the word 'glory' as a preliminary to saying so. Not all stipulations will be as silly as this, of course. We saw the need to distinguish between the inclusive 'or' and the exclusive 'or' in an earlier chapter. The labels 'inclusive' and 'exclusive' were stipulated to apply to the two senses of 'or' and have since become accepted labels for the two senses; this is logical jargon, which saves time and will be understood immediately by logicians.

Behind the search for 'real' definitions there is often a serious purpose. Once we begin to think of definitions in terms of useful or confusing, convenient or misguided, rather than right or wrong, real or mistaken, we are tempted to see disputes about what is the true meaning of Christianity or the real definition of socialism as rather trivial. Yet they are often far from trivial, and our view that meaning is ultimately conventional should not lead us into supposing that it does not matter what we call things. Take, for example, a word like 'socialism'. It has acquired a whole group of connected meanings, so that for different people it means different things. For at various times and in various countries a large number of only partly related ideas have been put forward as socialist, or have been expounded by the spokesmen of workers' movements. The ideas have fared differently at different times. Some which have come to seem practicable were once held to be utopian. In other cases the opposite shift has occurred. Sometimes what seemed a single idea has on analysis resolved itself into a number of different strands. Hence, by different people at various times, the most important characteristics of socialism have been thought to be workers' co-operatives, the public ownership of the means of production, production for use rather than profit, a planned rather than an unplanned economy, an equal society. These are a number of the main ideological strands woven into the history of socialism. Disputes about what is 'true' or 'real' socialism, or about the true or real meaning of socialism, can often be seen as covert bids to shape the direction of socialist thought by claiming to keep the pure wine of its doctrines intact. It is wrong to think that there is a pure wine. To think so is to forget that words and movements have their histories. But it is legitimate to emphasize some elements in the tradition and play down others. Those who worry about what socialism really is are trying to ascertain how it will or should develop.

Exercises

Look out for ambiguities and shifts in meaning:

7.5 If patriotism is an unreflective acceptance of the doctrine that it is noble to fight and if needs be die for one's country, then it is outmoded, costly, and dangerous. Reinforced by a nostalgic dwelling on past glories and routine flag-waving, uncritical patriotism resists economic change and prevents the working out of a sensible system of world trade.

7.6 Our Church has been accused of taking a casual attitude to divorce. It just is not the case. No one can, and nor do we, divorce those who are truly joined together in the eyes of God, because those couples who are really made one will never seek divorce.

5

Obviously what holds of our example of socialism holds of many others. A word often lacks a single, clear meaning not because it has two quite distinct meanings (as 'bank' means either the side of a river or an establishment for the custody of money) but because it contains a whole cluster of more or less related ideas. Another source of imprecision is that some words lack a clear descriptive meaning but embody a clear commitment in attitude, either of approval or of disapproval. We have already encountered one such example: the word 'progress'. It may not be clear what sort of changes progress involves, but it is fairly certain that to describe them as progress is to signify approval of them.

Sometimes an argument can turn on the in-built emotional attitudes which a word conveys. We do not spell out its descriptive meaning, but fall in with the attitude evoked uncritically, as here:

A capitalist society essentially involves freedom, and freedom is the very antithesis of dictatorship. So capitalist society is by its nature democratic.

A little reflection promotes scepticism: Franco's Spain and Pinochet's Chile were capitalist dictatorships. So where has the argument gone wrong? It turns on the notion of freedom. But a society can be free in some respects and not others. It is failure to specify exactly what freedoms are involved that have led to unsound argument. Different senses of the word 'freedom' have been conflated.

Capitalism essentially involves a number of freedoms: freedom to buy from a range of competing goods, freedom to choose whether to spend or save, freedom to compete for the jobs on offer and, for those who can afford it, freedom to own the means of production—machines, factories, raw materials—and to hire and fire workers. The antithesis of dictatorship is political freedom, which involves the ability of ordinary citizens to vote on national policies or to choose between competing political parties. The two sorts of freedom do not necessarily coincide or even overlap.

The word 'freedom' needs to be used with care, partly because it is non-specific (we need always to ask what sort of freedoms are under discussion) and partly because it is something towards which we have a favourable attitude. If any measure can be represented as promoting freedom it is so much more likely to find favour, while if it is seen as involving a threat to freedom it is likely to be unpopular. But one person's freedom can limit the freedoms of others, and some freedoms are more important than others; so the appeal to freedom should not be accepted uncritically.

6

Many of the words we use have built-in overtones of approval or disapproval. To describe someone as mean, or cowardly, is to give some indication of the sort of the sort of behaviour they go in for, but it is also to criticize. Again, to describe someone as honest, or considerate, is not simply to describe, but also to give praise. And earlier we commented that the word 'freedom' has a wide meaning but implies a favourable attitude on the part of the user.

Much of our political vocabulary is emotionally loaded in this way. For example, we use the word 'terrorism' in such a way that terrorism is a bad thing. The common dictionary definition of terrorism is 'an organized system of intimidation', that is to say, the attempt to exert influence by violence or the threat of violence. However, the dictionary definition does not account for the fact that terrorism is universally regarded as a bad thing. Most people think that organized intimidation is, however regrettably, sometimes justified, but nobody thinks that terrorism is justified. The government of the United States of America might well admit to having orchestrated the intimidation of Saddam Hussein through taking the lead in the United Nations Security Council, but it believed its intimidation of Saddam Hussain was justified. 'Terrorism' is always used of intimidation which is felt to be unjustified. Violence which is felt to be justified will be described in other ways. So, for example, where one nation intimidates another it will talk of the legitimate use of force; where a government intimidates insurgents within its own territory it will talk of counter-terrorism; where a government supports insurgents in another country it will describe them as freedom fighters. Also, no group will describe itself as a terrorist organization, however violent or coercive its attempts to win influence. Other people sometimes support terrorists, but *we* support only those whose threat or use of violence is justified.

'Terrorism' has an aura of disapproval attached to it in nearly all its uses. Hence, even when people agree about the straightforward facts of the case they might disagree about whether to apply the term 'terrorism'. In such a situation their disagreement would turn on whether the actions in question were justified or not. In describing actions as terrorism we show that we regard them as unjustified. Many other words have emotional overtones in some contexts, but 'terrorism' is a particularly clear example because the overtones are universal and one-way. Contrast it with a word such as 'socialist', which often has emotional overtones but which are not one-way. In some parts of society to call somebody a socialist is abusive, but in others it is regarded as a compliment. One can imagine circumstances in which socialists might be reluctant to declare their beliefs. They may be afraid that the after-dinner conversation will get too heated, or think that their careers will suffer. Amongst like-minded people, though, they will be perfectly content to accept the label 'socialist'. Socialists consider themselves to be socialists in a way in which terrorists do not consider themselves to be terrorists.

We can use self-ascription as a rough test of when a term has connotations of disapproval: would those who are labelled with it accept the label as fair? If so, then the label is either neutral or complimentary. The test is only a rough one, because a term of abuse can sometimes be adopted as a badge of honour. It is in this spirit that some homosexuals refer to themselves as 'queer', in preference to using the more positive label, 'gay'.

In the context of moral and political dispute we should treat non-neutral words, whether favourable or unfavourable, with some caution. The danger is that a non-neutral label indicates the speaker's attitude to the facts but does not of itself justify that attitude. In effect, the use of non-neutral labels assumes that the justificatory case need not be made out. If the audience shares the attitude of the speaker then the strength or weakness of the justificatory case is not tested, while if the audience does not share the attitude of the speaker then the dispute can easily get locked into name-calling.

Exercises

In the next three examples look for key emotion-setting words.

7.7 I'm not advocating censorship. I believe that we should seek to ensure greater responsibility on the part of those in charge of broadcasting, not greater control.

7.8 Freedom does not mean prosperity or security, desirable though these may be. The worker today is better off than his forefathers were; he is less dependent on the sayso of his employer. That is security, not freedom. Freedom in politics means freedom from the bureaucratic controls of government, and in that sense it is not clear that we are freer today than we were last century.

7.9 Extremism in the pursuit of liberty is no vice and moderation in the defence of freedom is no virtue. (Barry Goldwater)
Section 6. Are both parts of the claim equally acceptable?

7.10 Once more it will be said that sport is above politics. But as always those who maintain that sport is unconnected with politics are inconsistent. For they are indulging in politics themselves in trying to keep politics out of sport.
A difficult example. Are they inconsistent?

8 Divisions and Distinctions

1

We have looked at problems arising from failure to fix the meaning of words precisely and from failure to stick to a single meaning in a given context. This chapter considers some errors arising from the attempt to make language precise. Now it might seem absurd to suppose that precision in the use of language can lead to error, and by and large I think this is true. The mistakes which we shall be examining are not the result of using language precisely, but arise from worries about how language can apply to a changing reality in which there are few sharp divisions. They are the sort of mistake which does not arise at the level of the naïve use of language, but only after reflection on its use.

It is, then, necessary to precede consideration of these arguments by some remarks on language, in order to explain how we may be tempted into error.

2

Language divides: animals from plants, trees from shrubs, strings from percussion, fiction from non-fiction, puddles from ponds. Yet although we say that language divides these things, this seems a careless way of putting the point. Surely all these things are what they are independently of language? They would still be different even if nobody had learned to call them by different names. However, words seem precise where often the reality is less so. We divide the spectrum into red, orange, yellow, and so on. The words are sharply distinct but the colours are not—red shades into orange,

orange into yellow. Language, to put the case metaphorically, has sharp edges where reality is smooth.

This connects with what was said in Chapter 3, that in logic either something is so or it is not so, and there is no third possibility. Either a given shade of colour is red or it is not red; one or the other. But then what about the shades midway between red and orange, those which one would not happily place in either category? And it is not only colour-words that seem out of step with the underlying reality. Consider the words 'clothed' and 'unclothed'. We say that everybody is either clothed or unclothed, and we feel confident that we can decide by simple inspection which people are in which of these states. But even here one can dream up various exotic possibilities which would cause us to hesitate. Is someone wearing only carpet-slippers clothed or unclothed? Is someone, otherwise naked, over whom a large sheet has been dropped? With an effort of imagination any number of borderline cases, where neither the term nor its opposite clearly applies, can be constructed; not just for 'clothed' and 'unclothed', but for practically any pair of mutually exclusive terms.

3

Why do borderline cases arise and how do we deal with them when they do?

They arise partly from the nature of the reality which we are trying to describe. The spectrum between red and orange is continuous, with no natural divisions for our language to follow. But the other source of borderline cases is the way we learn words. As many have remarked, some words are learned largely by having examples pointed out to us. Colour words fall into this category. Parents select standard objects to point out to a child when they are teaching him or her the word 'red'. They point to pillar boxes, ripe tomatoes, favourite toys which are central shades of red. And when they teach a child the word 'orange' they will select a very different set of sample objects. The child learns to label objects closely resembling the first group 'red' and those closely resembling the second group 'orange'. There are objects intermediate in colour between the first group (the standard red things) and the second group (the standard orange things). The child has been taught what to count as central cases of red and orange (and other colours too) but he has not been taught how to deal with intermediate shades. What happens when the child tentatively labels one of these intermediate shades 'red'? His parents are likely to say something like 'Well, yes, a sort of orangey red', or 'It's halfway between red and orange'; or 'I think it's more orange; reddish-orange, though'. The parents reflect something of the hesitation that the child feels. Presumably it would be possible to tighten up our use of colour words; to fix on a shade and decide that it is the last shade of red and its neighbour the first shade of orange. But normal people differ in their ability to discriminate and remember fine differences in shades of colour, and for practical purposes the rather unsystematic way of treating the boundaries between colours works perfectly well.

To illustrate the point by analogy: suppose there are two kingdoms, separated by a sparsely populated stretch of jungle. The two kings may agree to draw a line on a map which will divide the jungle and mark the common boundary of their kingdoms. Or they may not bother. If there are no taxes worth collecting they may simply agree that somewhere in the stretch of jungle the one kingdom gives way to the other, but since neither bothers where, they can leave the boundary unmarked and undecided. I suggest that we should think of the distinctions we make in language as being like this. We could, with some pains, make very precise distinctions, but we find it convenient to have boundary areas rather than boundary lines. Just as the two kings claim all the land between them—though in the stretch of jungle they aren't sure who claims which bit—so our colour words 'red' and 'orange' exhaustively divide that stretch of the spectrum between them, even though we cannot decide of some shades whether to count them as red or not.

The same goes for our earlier example, clothed/unclothed. We learn what to count as clothing by learning what are the central cases. We do not make clear-cut decisions on every strange possibility that we can dream up. As and when they arise we will find some way of describing them. 'Clothed' and 'unclothed' are opposites and exhaust the possibilities between them; but again this leaves room for boundary indecision in certain cases.

4

Unless there is an overwhelming need for precision we will probably be content to tolerate borderline cases. This does not mean that any system of classification is as good as any other. In some cases a twofold classification will seem perfectly natural. In the case of 'clothed' and 'unclothed' the possibility of borderline cases is not very noticeable because in practice the borderline cases are somewhat contrived. However, there are cases when a twofold division would seem intolerably clumsy because the boundary areas between the two words would be much more intrusive. Suppose we had to divide men by height. If we allowed ourselves just two groups to put them into, 'tall' and 'short', I suspect that the classification would quickly come to chaos. Since most heights cluster fairly closely around the average and few men are either particularly short or particularly tall, most of the people to be classified would be borderline cases. If we gave ourselves three classifications, tall, short, and medium height, although we would not exclude borderline cases—people falling between medium height and tall or medium height and short—we would have a more workable system. This is purely because of the way men's heights cluster around an average; but I repeat that even a threefold classification would not rid us of difficult decisions. (Our normal use of 'short' and 'tall' presupposes, I think, a threefold classification; but sometimes both terms get extended.)

Suppose, on the other hand, we had to classify by height a group of men half of whom were jockeys and half basketball players. Here a twofold, short and tall, classification would work excellently. There would not be one average height in the group around which the heights clustered. Instead there would be two points of cluster. In this case, unlike the former, the facts would not force us to rethink our twofold classification.

What this suggests is that there is some choice in what system of classification we use, but that some classifications are a better 'fit' than others.

5

Borderline cases cannot always be tolerated.

Suppose it seems to a doctor as he treats his patients that tall men are more susceptible to a certain disease than other people. So far it is just an impression that he has, but he sets out to get evidence for this proposition. One of the first things he will have to do in testing the proposition is to decide what is to count as a tall man. As it stands his conjecture is vague because what some people will count as a tall man others will not. Our ordinary talk, containing expressions like 'tallish', 'middling tall' and so on, becomes a liability. The doctor will have to draw a boundary line, specifying a height (six feet, perhaps) below which a man will not count as tall. Scientific knowledge demands precision where everyday know-how often does not.

Another area where boundary lines often need to be drawn is law. Periodically disputes arise because something emerges as a borderline case. When hovercraft first came into operation it was necessary to decide in law whether they were ships or aircraft. It had to be determined what sort of licence was needed to pilot a hovercraft. Some years ago a court was asked to decide whether a toffee apple is a sweet or a fruit. Such a case sounds frivolous, but money was at stake, for how toffee apples were classified determined how much tax was paid. As well as seeming frivolous, at times, such questions can also seem rather sterile. It sounds like a recondite fact which the judge is expected to determine, but the previous sections suggest that what is required is a more or less arbitrary decision. Well, in such cases, I think, the judges do not scrutinize the facts and look for deeper facts behind them. Rather, they look for previous judgements which may be relevant to a decision and make their decision with some eye to the consequences of coming down on one side or the other. It is not some mysterious insight into the essence of the toffee apple that is sought, but rather a decision about what is the fairest or the best way of classifying toffee apples.

6

We now come to a crucial point and a source of error in argument. The existence of borderline cases does not show that a distinction is unreal. This is clear enough in the cases we have considered. No matter that we have colours which we describe as halfway between red and orange. No matter that we are reluctant to classify some colours as unambiguously red or orange. So long as there are clear central cases of red and clear central cases of orange, that is all that is necessary to make a real distinction. We can normally tolerate an area of indecision. To revert to the analogy of the two kingdoms, even if there is a hazy boundary area between them, there is no doubt that there are two kingdoms and not one.

This consideration is sometimes missed. It is argued that where there are no clear dividing lines there can be no distinction. Or it is asked, But where do you draw the line?—again with the clear implication that if a line, sharp and clear, cannot be drawn then the distinction is spurious. To repeat, the existence of borderline cases does not show that a distinction is unreal.

An instance of the fallacious move—there's no clear line so there's no real distinction—comes from the writings of one of the greatest American philosophers and logicians, W. V. O. Quine. There is a venerable distinction in philosophy which Quine attacks, the distinction between analytic and synthetic truths. Analytic truths are held to be true by virtue of meaning alone; synthetic truths are held to be true by virtue of the facts. The most frequently cited example of an analytic truth is 'All bachelors are unmarried', a claim whose truth follows from the meanings of the words 'bachelor' and 'unmarried'. An example of a synthetic truth, one true by virtue of the facts and not by definition, would be 'Ripe strawberries are red'. Quine mounts a vigorous and justly praised attack on the distinction, but among his arguments is an unconvincing one:

I do not know whether the statement 'Everything green is extended' is analytic. Now does my indecision over this example really betray an incomplete understanding, an incomplete grasp of the 'meanings', of 'green' and 'extended'? I think not. The trouble is not with 'green' or 'extended', but with 'analytic'. (Quine, p. 32)

What this comes to is that Quine has found a borderline case, a statement—'Everything green is extended' (i.e. takes up space)—which he finds it difficult to classify either as analytic or synthetic. On the strength of this he seems prepared to regard the distinction as unreal. In this case, as in others, it may be impossible to draw a sharp boundary. That does not show that there are not clear cases on either side. It may be worrying to philosophers that one of their key concepts is so imprecise; but it does not follow, from the existence of borderline cases, that there is no distinction to be drawn.

For a less technical example we can revert to the abortion controversy. I said earlier that at some time between the second and the eighth month it becomes natural to describe the foetus as an unborn child. That is much too vague, and was left deliberately so. But in law something much more precise is necessary. A foetus which miscarries in the twenty-eighth week of pregnancy is legally regarded as a prematurely born child, but a foetus which miscarries earlier is not. It is sometimes said that it is absurd to draw a sharp line in this way and the distinction is unreal. Well, drawing a sharp line does look thoroughly arbitary even though it may be legally necessary to have the distinction, but the boundary area that the sharp line is drawn through does represent an important stage in the development of the foetus. At around this time the foetus becomes capable of existing outside the womb; of taking oxygen and nourishment other than through the umbilical chord and ridding itself of waste matter. This is a plausible way, at least, of establishing the distinction between a foetus which is an unborn child and one which is not: whether it is capable of independent life. (To repeat what was said on page 21, an answer to the question of when a foetus can appropriately be called an unborn child does not settle the question of whether a foetus at an earlier stage is entitled to be aborted. Opponents of abortion often deny the difference between a foetus at the moment of conception and a child, when what they really (!) wish to deny is that there is an important difference.)

Exercises

8.1 It might seem at first sight that the contradictory of 'William is wise' is 'William is not wise' (or unwise). But this would be to assume that there is no other alternative, that William, and by implication everyone else, can be placed in one of two clear-cut categories, the wise and the unwise. (Emmet, p. 59)
'Wise or unwise', 'wise or not'; are they equivalent? Are they clear-cut?

8.2 Nobody can really say that some commodities are necessities and others luxuries. Things which our grandfathers would have counted as luxury we regard as indispensable; and besides, there are people prepared to go short on food for things like alcohol and tobacco.
Assess.

8.3 There's no such thing as objective right and wrong, despite what we want to tell ourselves. People disagree on all sorts of moral issues—capital punishment, sexual behaviour, genetic engineering, and so on.

7

A similar and sometimes associated mistake is the 'genetic fallacy':

X comes from Y, so X is really Y.

Our example is from C. S. Lewis, or rather from some critics whom Lewis quotes as arguing against him as follows:

Isn't what you call the Moral Law simply our herd instinct, and hasn't it been developed just like all our other instincts? (Lewis (1), p. 20)

As presented, these critics run together two claims: that the moral law has developed from the herd instinct and that it *is* the herd instinct. On the face of it the two claims are quite distinct.

There is more to be said, however. Clearly the bald formula quoted above is invalid. We cannot argue that because a hen comes from an egg a hen *is* an egg. That would be nonsense. Yet sometimes there does seem a serious question to be raised about how something's origins relate to what, essentially, it is. In fact, the question of morality and herd instinct is a good case in point. The nineteenth-century German philosopher, Friedrich Nietzsche, argued for just such an identity of morality and the herd instinct in his book *Beyond Good and Evil*:

Inasmuch as ever since there have been human beings there have also been human herds (family groups, communities, tribes, nations, . . .), and always very many who obey compared with the very small number of those who command . . . the need for [obedience] is by now innate . . . If we think of this instinct taken to its ultimate extravagance there would be no commanders or independent men at all; or if they existed, they would suffer from a bad conscience and in order to be able to command would have to practice a deceit upon themselves: the deceit, that is, that they too were only obeying. (Nietzsche, p. 120)

So, according to Nietzsche, the need to obey becomes so strongly implanted in people that even those who give orders feel the need of something to obey, namely, the moral law. We do not have to sub-scribe to Nietzsche's story of how conscience and the notion of moral laws take root. Yet anyone who did accept this story would naturally express their view by claiming that morality *is* (really or essentially) nothing but the herd instinct. On Nietzsche's view, morality has not only developed out of an original herd instinct, it exists as a modi-fication of the herd instinct. It has developed, but it has not changed its fundamental nature.

The same sort of issue—how far development changes the nature of something—surfaced in debates in Britain in the 1960s about whether the Keynesian, mixed economy which prevailed at that time was 'really' capitalist. Marxist critics tended to say 'yes', while its liberal defenders tended to argue that a mixed economy was differ-ent from capitalism. What was at stake was partly the importance of words in setting attitudes. Capitalism had acquired something of a bad name because of its association with the harsh working envir-onment and grim social conditions of Victorian times. Marxist critics of the mixed economy labelled it 'capitalist' in part because of its negative overtones and defenders of the mixed economy resisted the label for the same reason. Underlying this superficial fight about attitude-setting words, however, there was a more serious issue.

Marxists argued that the forces operating in a mixed economy were essentially the same as in Victorian times. They held that to regard the differences as anything other than superficial would prevent a proper understanding of the ways in which society would develop. Hence they maintained that the mixed economies of the time were essentially capitalist.

It does not matter for our purposes whether that claim was correct or not. The point is that it is simplistic to regard the critics as arguing: 'Mixed economies developed out of capitalism, so they are a form of capitalism.' Their claim is that how societies are labelled will—if the labelling is correct—direct our attention to the forces at work in society, rather than simply evoke attitudes. Interesting issues are often concealed behind the disputes about whether or not *X* is 'really' *Y*.

Exercises

Assess:

8.4 There is no such thing as a third alternative. This is true grammatically. It is also true politically.

8.5 Psychologists say that some people are introverts and others extraverts. But I don't believe it's possible to divide people into two groups in this way. Everybody wants to enjoy people's company on some occasions and wants to be on their own at other times.

8.6 SPEAKER: If you think a foetus is the same thing as a human being you shouldn't have an abortion. But most people do not think that a foetus is the same as a human being.

REPLY: Nobody here denies that if you leave a foetus it will grow into a human being.

How is the reply best interpreted? Section 7

8.7 A cell has life. Any cell: of a cabbage, or a horse's ear, or a worm. Ah, but they aren't human cells. No; and it makes sense to differentiate between your own species and another. Or does it? At what point do the cells in a transplanted pig's liver join the club, become human cells? (*Observer*)

9 'All' and 'Some'

I

In this chapter we extend our formal study of arguments, turning to the syllogism, a type of argument first systematically examined by Aristotle in the fourth century BC, and to which we turn now. Two examples of this type are:

Every mammal is warm-blooded. No reptile is warm-blooded. So no reptile is a mammal.

Every cat is carnivorous. Some cats are tame. So some carnivores are tame.

The forms of valid argument considered in Chapters 3 and 4 do not capture the structure of arguments like those above, and we need to find a way of treating them. The first step towards a formal treatment is once more the introduction of letters. But whereas previously we introduced letters in place of whole statements ('It is raining', 'The game is off', and so on), in this case more is needed. Replacing statements by letters, a new letter for a new statement, would bring out both the above syllogisms as:

$p, q; \therefore r$

—invalid, and plainly inadequate to capture the internal complexity of the two arguments. We must try again; and in this case we need to introduce letters not to represent different statements but different types of thing: mammals, reptiles, carnivores, and so on. As before, letters help us to see more clearly the structures of the different arguments. Here the convention is to use capital letters from the beginning of the alphabet.

In the first example above, with A for 'mammal', B for 'warm-blooded (thing)', and *C* for 'reptile', we can present the argument as follows:

Every *A* is a *B*
No *C* is a *B*
∴ No *C* is an *A*.

In the second example above, we have a different form of argument. Putting *A* for 'cat', *B* for 'carnivore', and *C* for 'tame (thing)', we get:

Every *A* is a *B*
Some *A*s are *C*s
∴ Some *B*s are *C*s.

Both these forms of argument are in fact valid. At present we have no way of showing this except by appealing to examples of each and 'seeing' that the conclusion follows. However, we can develop a simple way of testing syllogisms for validity. In what follows the diagrams should be studied carefully.

2

Syllogistic logic depends on the concepts 'all', 'some', and 'no'. We begin by considering four basic sorts of statement involving these notions.

Suppose we want the contradictory, the exact denial, of the claim that every cat is a carnivore. We have already encountered one way of contradicting the claim; we can say 'Not every cat is a carnivore'. But there is another fairly common way of forming the contradictory, which is to say 'At least one cat is not a carnivore' (or, more briefly, 'Some cat is not a carnivore'). Similarly, if we required the contradictory of 'No cat is a carnivore', we could get it by asserting 'Some (at least one) cat is a carnivore'. We can summarize this by a diagram in which contradictory statements are joined by diagonal lines:

Every cat is a carnivore   No cat is a carnivore

Some cat is a carnivore   Some cat is not a carnivore

Instead of writing 'Every cat is a carnivore', we could have put 'All cats are carnivores'. In place of 'Some cat is a carnivore', we could write 'Some cats are carnivores', as we did in the previous section. (Strictly speaking, this suggests more than one carnivorous cat, and is stronger than we want or need. However, in most cases it would be pedantic to insist on the distinction, and we shall not remark on it, except here.)

The table which we drew up for 'cat' and 'carnivore' can be generalized. By putting letters in place of the two nouns we turn our square of statements into a square of dummy-statements:

Every A is a B No A is a B

Some A is a B Some A is not a B

(The statement-forms joined by diagonal lines are contradictory.)

A word of warning. 'Not every cat is a carnivore' does not mean the same as 'Every cat is not a carnivore'. The first says that there is some non-carnivorous cat, and the second that all cats are non-carnivorous. The former is possibly true. The latter is certainly false.

3

We turn now from statements to possibilities.

To aid our explanations we shall use diagrams. These diagrams (devised in the last century by the mathematician John Venn) will be familiar from school to some readers, although perhaps in a slightly different form from the way they are used here. Those who have not encountered them before will, I think, find them self-evident. They give us a map of the logical relations between classes. They picture logical possibilities.

Suppose we are considering two sorts of thing, As and Bs. We represent each sort by a circle, and the sorts can be existing things, such as cats, or imaginary, such as unicorns. By overlapping the circles we can show different possibilities. Put A = 'cat' and B = 'carnivore'. Then by overlapping the circles as shown we represent three possible sorts of object. Reading from left to right we have (1) As which are not Bs (cats which are not carnivores); (2) things which are both

As and Bs (carnivorous cats); and (3) Bs which are not As (carnivores which are not cats). By enclosing the circles in a box we create a fourth possibility: (4) things which are neither *A* nor *B* (neither carnivores nor cats). Our four areas show only possibilities, so far. We are not saying that there *are* any non-carnivorous cats—or even that there are any carnivorous cats, come to that. We are showing only what might be; providing a framework for positive assertions about what does or does not exist.

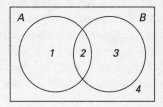

4

Now we return from possibilities to statements, thus linking the two previous sections.

Suppose we have the assertion 'Some *A* is a *B*' (in our example, 'Some cat is a carnivore'). In terms of the following diagram what we are saying is that there is something in the area of overlap between *A* and *B*. This is signified by putting a tick in the area of overlap. A tick signifies existence.

Similarly, we can represent 'Some *A* is not a *B*' by putting a tick inside the *A* circle but outside the *B* circle, as shown in the second diagram. We are asserting that there is at least one thing which is *A* but not *B*; hence we tick the appropriate area in the right-hand diagram.

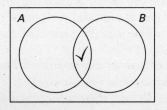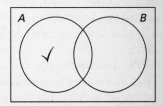

Just as a tick signifies existence, so we show non-existence by shading. Consider the statement 'No *A* is a *B*'. In terms of the diagram, the claim is that there does not exist anything which is in both the *A* circle and the *B* circle. We show as much by shading out the area of overlap between the two circles as in the left-hand diagram below.

So far we have dealt with three of our four basic sorts of statement. The remaining one, and the one most likely to cause difficulty, is 'Every *A* is a *B*'. We interpret this as saying 'There is nothing which is an *A* but not a *B*', or 'If anything is an *A* then it is a *B*'. That interpretation perhaps seems surprising and unduly complicated; in appendix 2 are indicated some of the factors which lead logicians to adopt it. For the present we shall take on trust the need for this analysis, and try to make clear just what it involves.

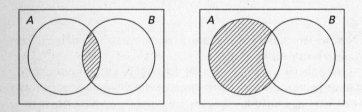

Put *A* = 'cat' and *B* = 'carnivore'; then a statement such as 'All cats are carnivores' becomes 'If anything is a cat then it is a carnivore', or 'There are no non-carnivorous cats'. Both expressions are equivalent and both are represented in the right-hand diagram by shading out the space for non-carnivorous cats. It is obvious that the diagram represents the second sentence, but what of, 'If anything is a cat then it is a carnivore'? The diagram shows are much, because the only place where *A*s (cats) can exist—the only unshaded part of the *A* circle—lies within the *B* circle; if anything is in *A* it must be in *B* as well.

If the four basic types of statement are set out in juxtaposition their relations are the more easily seen:

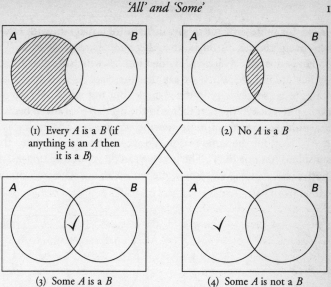

(1) Every *A* is a *B* (if
anything is an *A* then
it is a *B*)

(2) No *A* is a *B*

(3) Some *A* is a *B*

(4) Some *A* is not a *B*

Logic maintains that (1) and (4) are contradictory statements, and
similarly (2) and (3). The diagrams confirm this. Of each pair of contradictory statements one ticks what the other shades; where the one
asserts existence the other exactly denies it.

Fix the diagrams in mind before moving on. If in doubt reread
the section.

5

We can use the diagrams to say other things too. Suppose we want
to say 'There are no *A*s'. This can be shown on our diagram by
shading out the whole of *A*. Notice that we are not committed to
the existence of what we talk about. Drawing a circle is not the same
as asserting that there is anything in the circle; only ticking indicates
existence. So, for example, we can draw a circle for unicorns and go
on to say, in terms of our diagram (below, left), that there are no
unicorns.

It is a bit more difficult to say, in terms of a diagram with circles representing *A*s and *B*s on it, that there are *A*s, that *A*s exist. The problem is this: the *A* circle is divided into *A*s which are also *B*s and *A*s which are not *B*s. When we say that there are *A*s we know that a tick has to go somewhere in the *A* circle, but not where. We do not want to put a tick in the part that is in the overlap of *A* and *B* because that would be to make a more specific statement ('Something is *A* and *B*'). Nor, for the same reason, do we want to tick the area that lies inside *A* but outside *B*. The best we can do is put question-marks in both areas. A tick goes somewhere within *A*, but where we cannot say (below, right).

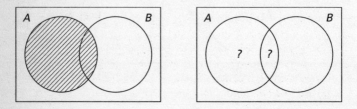

6

The diagrams are, as we saw, capable of representing our four basic statements, and more besides. There is one major variation which can be sorted out by means of the diagrams. This is the difference between 'All *A*s are *B*s' and 'Only *A*s are *B*s'.

First, an example: 'Only conservatives wear ties.' This is not the same as saying that all conservatives wear ties. Some may have thrown them away, some may never have possessed them. However, what we are saying is 'All who wear ties are conservatives.' If only conservatives wear ties then nobody else wears a tie; all who wear ties are conservatives. In general, if only *A*s are *B*s then every *B* is an *A*. We can show this on a diagram: Every *B* is an *A* = Only *A*s are *B*s. If we examine the diagram it is apparent that only *A*s are *B*s, for nothing is in *B* which is not in *A* also.

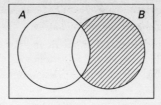

Exercise

9.1 *Draw diagrams to express:*

    (1) Something is *B* and not *A*.
    (2) Only *B*s are *A*s.
    (3) Nothing is *B* and something is *A*.
    (4) Something is both not *A* and not *B*.
    (5) Nothing is both not *A* and not *B*.
    (6) Everything is either a *B* or an *A*.
    (7) Everything is either a *B* or an *A*, and nothing is both.
    (8) All and only *A*s are *B*s.

7

This completes what we have to say on the diagrams of two circles. In assessing the various forms of syllogism we need to extend the diagrams to deal with three sorts of object: *A*s, *B*s, and *C*s. This time the diagram has three interlocking circles, giving eight distinct areas and eight corresponding divisions, numbered in the next diagram.

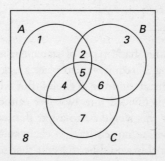

Exercise

9.2 *Complete the table for the diagram above.*

　　(1) Things which are *A*s, but not *B*s and not *C*s.
　　(2) Things which are *A*s and *B*s and not *C*s.
　　(3) Things which are *B*s but not *A*s and not *C*s.
　　(4)
　　(5)
　　(6)
　　(7)
　　(8)

Given a three-circle diagram as above, how would one say 'No *A* is *B*'? Well, we simply ignore the *C* circle and continue as if we had only two circles on our diagram. This makes good sense. If nothing is *A* and *B* then nothing is *A* and *B* and *C*; nor is anything *A* and *B* and not *C* (below, left).

Similarly, in representing 'Every *A* is a *B*' we ignore the *C* circle entirely. There are no *A*s except the ones which are *B*s, and it is irrelevant whether in addition they are *C*s or not *C*s.

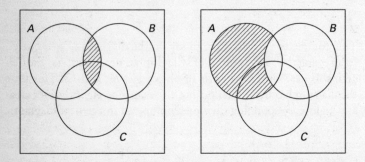

However, the other basic types of statement are less straightforward. 'Some *A* is a *B*' requires us to place a tick in the area of the overlap between the *A* and the *B* circles. But where in the area of overlap? The area is divided into two. We cannot confidently tick the lower part, for this would be to assert that some things are *A*s, *B*s, and *C*s, and we are not entitled to claim this. Nor can we tick the upper part, for this would be to assert that some things are *A*s,

*B*s, and not *C*s, and we were not told this either. There is a tick somewhere in the area of overlap, perhaps in the upper part, perhaps in the lower, perhaps in both. We put a question-mark in both parts of the area, to signify our hesitation (below, left).

Similarly, 'Some *A* is not a *B*' raises a problem and again we put question-marks to signify that we cannot determine in which subdivision—perhaps both—the tick should be placed.

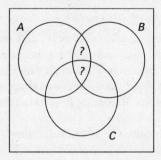 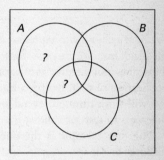

Exercises

9.3 *Draw three-circle diagrams (A, B, C) to express:*

(1) No *C* is a *B*.

(2) Every *B* is a *C*.

(3) Some *A* is a *B* and a *C*.

(4) Only *C*s are *A*s.

(5) Some *A* is a *B* or a *C*.

(6) Nothing is not *A*.

9.4 None but the brave deserve the fair (i.e. . . . are people who deserve the fair).
Represent on an appropriate diagram.

9.5 *We have seen how the diagrams look for two sorts of object, A and B, and for three sorts of object. What about for just one sort of object, As?*

9.6 Everything which is not *A* is *B*.
No *A* is *B*.
Are these two statements equivalent? Hint: 'Everything which is A is B' is equivalent to 'Nothing is A and not B'. Use diagrams.

10 Arguments with 'All' and 'Some'

I

We have seen how to represent statements with 'all', 'some', and 'no' on diagrams. We can use those same diagrams to test arguments. This does not involve the learning of any new material; only the application of what has been learned already in the previous chapter. We will work through several arguments illustrating how to use the diagrams to test for validity.

The first example is the one we looked at at the beginning of Chapter 9:

Every mammal is warm-blooded. No reptile is warm-blooded. Therefore no reptile is a mammal.

Put A = 'mammal', B = 'warm-blooded (thing)', and C = 'reptile'. The argument then becomes:

Every A is a B
No C is a B
∴ No C is an A.

We test by means of a three-circle diagram. The technique is simply to draw in the premisses. If we find that we have drawn in the conclusion at the same time then the conclusion follows, and the argument is valid.

The first premiss above is 'Every A is a B'. We draw it in (diagonal shading) on the diagram, in the way shown on page 116. (Remember that 'Every A is a B' means 'If anything is an A then it is a B', or 'Nothing is A and not B'.) The second premiss is that 'No C is a B'. Nothing exists in the area of overlap between B and C, so we shade out (vertical shading) the entire area of overlap between them, as shown earlier.

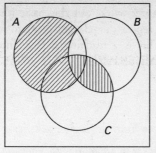

All *A* is *B* (diagonal shading); No
C is *B* (vertical shading)

Having transcribed what we were given in the premisses on to the diagram, we can, as used to be said at school, lay down our pens. If the argument is a valid one, our drawing in of the premisses should have drawn in the conclusion as well. Has it? We look and see. The conclusion is that no *C* is an *A*. In terms of the diagram, this is so when the overlap between the *C* circle and the *A* circle is fully shaded out. The area (heavily outlined) is fully shaded out, so the argument is valid.

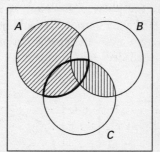

No *A* is *C* (heavily outlined)

Résumé

To recap: the technique is to draw in the premisses on the diagram, then look and see whether we have *ipso facto* drawn in the conclusion. If we have, then the argument is valid; if not, then it is invalid.

The rest of the chapter works out this basic idea in various cases. Throughout I shall repeat the relevant diagram with the conclusion heavily outlined. This is a teaching device, intended to help the reader, but not strictly necessary.

2

A traditional example from the logic books is:

All Greeks are men; all men are mortal; therefore all Greeks are mortal.

Put A = 'Greeks', B = 'man', and C = 'mortal (being)'. The argument becomes:

Every A is a B
Every B is a C
∴ Every A is a C.

The first premiss is shown in the usual way by shading the A circle lying outside B (diagonally). By a parity of reasoning the second premiss, 'Every B is a C', is shown by shading (vertically) the part of B lying outside C.

The conclusion is 'Every A is a C'—'Nothing is A and not C'. If it follows, then all of A lying outside C should be shaded. We look and see that the relevant area—the heavily outlined crescent in the second diagram—is shaded out completely. The argument is valid.

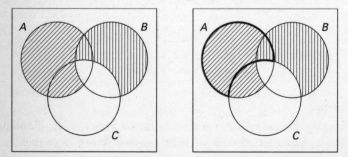

All A is B (diagonal shading); All B is C (vertical shading) It follows that All A is C (outlined crescent)

3

These arguments can be contrasted with the following invalid one:

All journalists are writers. Only writers are intellectuals. So all journalists are intellectuals.

Put A = 'journalist', B = 'writer', and C = 'intellectual'. Then the form of the argument is:

Every A is a B
Only Bs are Cs (= Every C is a B)
∴ Every A is a C.

We depict the first premiss by shading all of the A circle outside B (diagonal shading). We depict the second premiss by shading (vertically) all of the C circle outside B. Notice that the area of shading overlaps, in part. Now the conclusion is 'Every A is a C', 'Every journalist is an intellectual'. Does this follow? If it did we would expect to find all of the A circle which lies outside the C circle to be fully shaded. But when we inspect the right-hand diagram the relevant area—heavily outlined—is not fully shaded; part has been left blank. The conclusion, therefore, does not follow, and the argument is invalid.

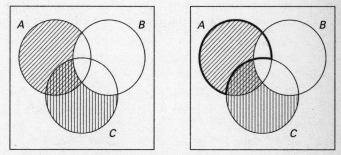

All A is B (diagonal); Only B is C (vertical); It does not follow that all A is C (outlined area)

Exercises

Test for validity.

10.1 All success involves much thought, and all thoughtful people are patient. Hence only the patient are successful.

10.2 All vitamins are cheap. Only cheap things are nutritious. Therefore all vitamins are nutritious.

4

Another example:

Since all wealthy people are independent, and yet several wealthy people are miserable, it follows that some independent people are miserable.

Ignoring stylistic variations and putting A = 'wealthy person', B = 'independent person', and C = 'miserable person', we get:

Every A is a B
Some A is a C
∴ Some B is a C.

We draw in the first premiss 'Every A is a B' in the usual way, shading out all of the A circle lying outside B. The second premiss is of a different kind, asserting existence. It tells us that there is something which is both A and C. To represent this on the diagram we must put a tick in the area of overlap between the A circle and the C circle. Part of the area of overlap has already been shaded out, as can be seen from the first diagram below. Part is left blank, and that part must therefore carry the tick. (Obviously, if something lies in the

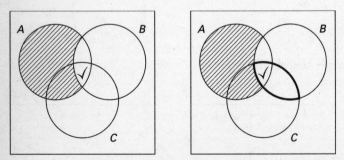

All As are B (shaded); Some A is C (ticked)
∴ Some B is C (outlined)

area of overlap between *A* and *C*, but not in the one part, then it must lie in the other.) The conclusion is that some *B* is a *C*; that there is something in the area of overlap between *B* and *C*. Does it follow? We look and see that there is a tick within the overlap of *B* and *C* (outlined in the second diagram). The argument is valid.

5

Our next example is perhaps a bit more difficult:

Some self-satisfied people are liars. For only fools are self-satisfied, and some liars are undoubtedly fools.

The first essential is to identify correctly the conclusion. The word 'for' gives us the clue: the conclusion comes first, not last. What we have is:

Only fools are self-satisfied
Some liars are fools
Therefore some self-satisfied people are liars.

And now we put *A* = 'fools', *B* = 'self-satisfied people', and *C* = 'liars', to get:

Only *A*s are *B*s (= Every *B* is an *A*)
Some *C* is an *A*
∴ Some *B* is a *C*.

We now show the argument to be invalid. The first premiss is 'Only *A*s are *B*s' which is equivalent to 'All *B*s are *A*s', and accordingly we shade the whole of the *B* circle which lies outside *A*. The second premiss tells us that some *C*s are *A*s—that the area of overlap between *C* and *A* is not empty. In terms of our diagram it tells us to put a tick somewhere in the area of overlap. But this area is divided into two. At least one of these sub-areas is inhabited, but since we do not know which we cannot definitely tick either. The best we can do is put a question-mark in each part to show that somewhere in the area of overlap between *A* and *C* a tick must go.

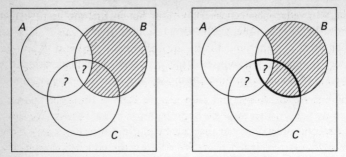

Only *A*s are *B*s (shaded); Some *C* is *A* (queried)
It does not follow that some *B* is *C* (outlined area)

The conclusion of the argument is 'Some *B* is a *C*'. This *could* be true because part of the overlap between *B* and *C* has a question-mark within it. It does not *have* to be true, however. The tick might lie outside this area, in *A* and *B* but not *C*. The doubt is enough to render the argument invalid, for the acceptance of the premises does not drive us to accepting the conclusion. Valid arguments do not admit of 'maybes'.

Exercises

Test for validity. Make sure you identify the conclusion properly.

10.3 Some intelligent people do not make good parents. For no selfish people are good parents and some intelligent people are selfish.

10.4 Only mechanisms with feedback devices are purposive, and some feedback mechanisms are not complicated. So some purposive mechanisms are not complicated.

10.5 Some tenants are not ratepayers. For no tenant is entitled to vote, and some of those entitled to vote are not ratepayers.

6

Rather similar to the syllogisms considered previously are arguments involving reference to particular individuals. Such an argument is the following:

No American is a believer in Shintoism. Don is an American. Therefore Don is not a believer in Shintoism.

Put A = 'American', B = 'believer in Shintoism', and * = 'Don'. We represent the first premiss in the usual way. The second premiss cannot be represented by a relation between circles because circles show classes of things, and Don is not a class of things but himself a thing (a particular person). Represent him by an asterisk. We show the second premiss in our diagram by placing the asterisk inside the A circle, or what is left of it. We read off the conclusion from the diagram. The argument is shown to be valid, as the asterisk lies outside the B circle.

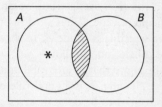

As well as proper names, phrases which denote an individual, such as 'The first man on the moon', can be treated by the device of the asterisk.

7

In some cases, finally, an argument can be ruled out on inspection; in such cases a short cut is possible and there is no need to test the argument for validity.

No syllogism can be valid if both its premisses begin with 'some'. The reader can experiment and satisfy himself that this is so. One example may suffice:

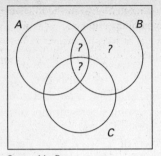

Some *A* is *B*
Some *B* is not *C*
∴ Some *A* is not *C*.

There is a tick in the *A–B* overlap, but we do not know where. There is a tick in *B* and outside *C*, but we do not know whether in the part of that area which falls inside *A*. In short, nothing is definite enough for the conclusion to follow.

It follows from the above that in any valid argument at least one premiss must involve shading. It is a good rule of thumb to shade before ticking if both need to be done. It saves adjusting diagrams as one goes.

Again, if both premisses are negative—of the form 'No . . .' or 'Some . . . are not . . .'—then no valid syllogism is possible. The reader can confirm the fact by experimenting with diagrams. The nearest he or she will get is:

No *A* is *B*
Some *B* is not *C*
∴ Some *B* is not *A*

—which is valid, but unlike a normal syllogism in that *B* occurs in every line.

Exercises

Test for validity:

10.6 All weak people are tempted to lie; and Bill's being tempted to lie shows that he is no exception.
   How are names represented? See section 6.

10.7 Some of the brightest children in the town were not offered a place at the High School. For nobody who was offered a place there accepted a place at St Joseph's and yet some children who accepted a place at St Joseph's are amongst the cleverest in town.

10.8 Kant's philosophical writings are undeniably difficult, and only difficult writings are profound. It follows that Kant's philosophical writings are profound.

10.9 It cannot really be argued that the press treated all the delegates as irresponsible. Quite the opposite. For not all the delegates voted for a one-day stoppage; and only those who did were branded as irresponsible.

Here the claim is that the opposite of a certain conclusion follows from the premises. Test, and see whether this is true.

11 Groups and Individuals

I

People can be led into error by the belief that what holds true of a group must hold true of the individuals who comprise the group, or vice versa. This assumption can be quickly shown to be highly suspect. To take a rather extreme illustration, if a football team is a hundred years old it does not follow that each member of the team is a centenarian (though each may play as if he is). And, conversely, a team of centenarians need not be in its centenary year. However, despite the fact that the principle cannot be relied upon, it fairly often underpins arguments.

John Stuart Mill argued last century that because it is true of each man in a community that he desires his own happiness, therefore it is true of all that they desire the happiness of all. In fact, of course, if Bill desires the happiness of Bill, Mary that of Mary, John that of John, and so on, there is no reason to conclude that anybody desires the happiness of all.

This century I. A. Richards, beginning roughly where Mill began, reached roughly the same conclusion, making roughly the same mistake. He associated value with the satisfaction of desire:

In other words, the only reason for not satisfying a desire is that some more important desires will thereby be thwarted. Thus morals become purely prudential, and ethical codes merely the most general scheme of expediency to which an individual or a race has attained. (Richards, p. 48)

Here Richards speaks as if it is of small moment whether it is the expediency of the individual or of the race which is involved. But what is expedient for an individual—what satisfies or benefits him—

may damage the group, and the good of the group may demand sacrifices from an individual.

Finally we take an example from Winston Churchill's *History of the Second World War*. Summarizing the doctrines of *Mein Kampf*, he wrote:

Man is a fighting animal; therefore the nation, being a community of fighters, must be a fighting unit. (Churchill, p. 61)

The claim that man is a fighting animal means, I take it, that all men have aggressive instincts. Whatever the truth of this, it does not follow that any group of aggressive animals must unite in acting aggressively. The simplest way of showing this is to reflect that his way of reasoning would make the Pontypool Male Voice Choir a fighting unit.

These are all examples of the fallacy of going from a claim about the individuals to a claim about the group, traditionally known as the 'fallacy of composition'. For an example of a fallacy running in the other direction, going from a truth about the group as a whole to a truth about its members—the 'fallacy of division'—the following will suffice:

America will be made richer by a free-trade zone, so if some Americans fail to welcome the removal of tariff barriers either they fail to realize that they will benefit or they do not want to benefit.

Clearly, it can be true that America as a whole will benefit without its being true that each individual American will benefit.

2

It is possible to go a little more deeply into the sort of statement that can be made about groups.

First, there are things which are said of a group in its own right. Mainly one thinks here of how big the group is and how long it has been in existence. The same questions can be asked of the individuals in a group, and the same words applied to individuals. But there is no way of arguing from the age or size of the group to the age and size of its members, or vice versa. We saw this in the case of 'a hundred years old'; but it is also true that, for instance, a small group of people is not necessarily a group of small people.

We can also extend this class of words to include group activities. A group, as well as an individual, can make a pleasant noise or act self-interestedly, for example. Again inferences from group to individuals and conversely from individuals to group are not valid. If a group makes a pleasant noise this may be a blend of individually unpleasant noises; while if the individuals all make pleasant noises the resultant collective sound may be a cacophony.

Second, there are things which can be said of a group derivatively, but which apply primarily to the individuals in the group. Thus a group of people can be described as healthy when enough of its members are healthy; more precisely, it is a healthy group when the general health of its members is average (if the population at large is healthy) or above average. Similarly, a group is intelligent when enough of its members are intelligent. In these cases, the inference from individual to group carries through, but not vice versa. A healthy group of people need not be a group all of whose members are healthy, but if every member is healthy then it is a healthy group.

Third, there are some words which can be applied to individuals but cannot be applied to groups even derivatively; words like 'married', which imply a relationship to an individual. A group of predominantly healthy people is a healthy group of people, but a group of predominantly married people is not a married group of people. There is not even a temptation to argue from group to individual or vice versa in these cases.

No doubt the rough-and-ready classification above could be improved upon. Its point is to sort out those cases where inferences from individuals to groups are possible—those of the second type— as opposed to cases where the inference is not reliable.

3

We can talk of group preferences, as well as of individual preferences. When we do, I think we talk derivatively; to say that a group prefers X to Y is to say that most of its members prefer X to Y. Hence, if every member of a group prefers X to Y then the group prefers X to Y. To talk of group preferences is to talk within the second category of the previous section.

Not all group decisions are the outcome of group preferences. Partly this is because not all groups are democratic (in the sense of striving to reflect the views of the majority in the group). But even when decisions are attempts to reflect the preferences of the group, it is not always possible. Although every member of a group may have a clear preference, the group may lack one—if members are evenly divided over a proposal. Whatever rule is then adopted to reach a decision, the outcome will not reflect a collective preference.

Moreover, it would be wrong to suppose that group preferences have all the properties of individual preferences. If an individual is rational and prefers X to Y and Y to Z, then he must prefer X to Z. But for a group preference no such inference holds. A group can prefer X to Y and Y to Z, but nevertheless prefer Z to X. For a group's preferences, remember, are determined by what the majority prefers.

Suppose we have a group of just three people, John, Mary and Bill. Their individual preferences are given in the table below:

	John	Mary	Bill
Order of preference			
1st:	X	Z	Y
2nd:	Y	X	Z
3rd:	Z	Y	X

Each individual can order his choice: first, second, third. John, for example, prefers X to Y and prefers Y to Z; hence he prefers X to Z. Mary prefers Z to X and X to Y; so she prefers Z to Y. But the preferences of the group are not so accomodating. The reader can verify that John and Mary—a majority—prefer X to Y, so that the group as a whole prefers X to Y. A majority (John and Bill) also prefers Y to Z. But nevertheless the group prefers Z to X, because Bill and Mary prefer Z to X.

It is not always possible to rank group preferences, even when individual preferences can be ranked.

There are other features of group preference which must not be taken for granted. When a group alters its preference, we cannot conclude that most of its members have altered their preferences. This may be the case, but it may be that the group has altered some or all of its membership. A group can retain its identity even though its membership changes, considerably or even completely. This will affect the degree to which we can hold a group responsible for decisions made previously. The current membership may be in no sense responsible for past sins. Again, an individual who chooses one course of action at one time and reverses his decision later has changed his mind. This is not necessarily a vice; only a fool holds his views intact for ever. But anyone who changes his mind frequently can be regarded as either fickle or rash. It is doubtful if the same can always be said of a group which reverses its decisions. I once heard a university senate roundly condemned for its inconsistency in reversing a decision it had previously made. 'Previously' was in fact many years previously and membership of the senate had altered in the meantime. 'Senate' had changed its mind although perhaps no member of Senate who had voted on both occasions had changed his or her mind.

These facts about groups have a clear reference to the things we are entitled to say about nations. A. J. P. Taylor writes about the mood between the two world wars:

Hence the study of war-origins had an urgent and practical importance. If the peoples of Allied countries could be convinced of the falsity of German 'war-guilt', they would relax the punitive clauses in the treaty of Versailles, and accept the German people as victims, like themselves, of a natural cataclysm. Alternatively, if the Germans were persuaded of their war-guilt, they would presumably accept the treaty as just. (Taylor, p. 33)

Taylor depicts people as reasoning about Germany very much as they would about an individual: if an individual has done wrong he should accept his punishment and if he has been unjustly condemned his punishment should be set aside wholly or in part; and the same for a nation. Maybe this is how people did (or do) think, but it is over-simple. Those who suffer the burden of reparations do not do so in proportion to their responsibilities for the outbreak of war. Thus, during the fifteen years or so that the punitive clauses of the Treaty of Versailles were in operation, a whole generation not old enough to have fought in the First World War suffered the punishments inflicted because of Germany's fighting that war.

One might be inclined to shrug and say, 'The sins of the fathers are always visited on the children—that's the way it goes.' This response misses the point, for it is the *justice* of war reparations that is in question; not what usually happens, but what ought to happen. If an individual has done wrong then he ought to make reparation for his misdeeds. There is a case for saying the same of aggressor nations (it may deter aggression). However, on grounds of justice, it is to countenance the punishment of many people who are innocent, especially if reparation takes a long time.

Similarly, there are problems in blaming a nation for dishonouring its pledges. If the pledges were made by one government, it is not clear how far another government is morally bound by them. Obviously there is a case for a government not lightly disregarding pledges given by its predecessors. Honoured pledges oil the wheels of international co-operation and avoid giving rise to resentment. But there is a difference between this case and the one where individuals who give a pledge themselves break it. The difference is obscured by talk of a nation breaking its pledges.

4

Parallel to the examples involving groups and individuals are arguments involving parts and wholes. One famous philosophical example is the argument that blood is not really red because, seen under a microscope, the parts of blood—the corpuscles of which it is made up—are straw-coloured. If the parts are not red then the whole cannot be red. This is another example of the so-called fallacy of division—just the same as arguing that if a group is large then its members must be large. There seems, though, no reason why the parts should resemble the whole, or vice versa: a square building can be made of rectangular bricks. There are some properties which carry through—if the whole is tiny the parts will be so too, and if all the parts are metal then the whole will be metal. In general, however, such inferences must be regarded with suspicion.

Exercises

Assess the following arguments involving part and whole:

11.1 Everything in the universe, so far as we can tell, ceases to exist eventually. At the one extreme, stars exist for millions of years; at the other extreme, high-energy particles for millionths of a second. They all have their allotted spans. Can we doubt, then, that the universe itself has its allotted span, and must eventually cease to exist?

11.2 The British are far more interested in public affairs than the people of any other nation. One Briton in two buys a daily newspaper, but for the rest of the world the figure is one in ninety.
The buying of a newspaper may not be good evidence of interest, nor the failure to buy a newspaper evidence of lack of interest—but these are not the main points.

11.3 Science tells us that the wall is made up of electrons in incredibly rapid motion. It is wrong to believe, then, that the wall is stationary, as we all suppose.

5

There is another sort of argument involving part and whole which should be considered here. This does not involve an inference from what is true of the whole to what is true of the parts, or vice versa. Rather it involves a failure to make clear whether something is asserted of whole or of part, and equivocation between these possibilities. Here is an argument against euthanasia—compulsory euthanasia—for the old and infirm:

The maternal instinct, originally directed to the care of one's offspring, later becomes directed to any helpless object.
The instinct is, then, sublimated into activities like that of nursing the sick . . .
The maternal instinct, necessary to the continuance of the race, is that which compels us to keep alive the aged and the sick.

Suppose, then, in the interests of a virile race, you killed off the sick and the old. You cannot destroy the unfit without doing violence to the maternal instinct upon which the fitness of the race depends. If you killed off the sick you must first have stifled the maternal instinct, and if you stifle the maternal instinct you would kill off the race. If we killed off the sick, far from having a virile race we should have no race at all. (Hadfield, p. 109)

It would be pleasant if it could be shown that compulsory euthanasia is a policy destructive of society. Unfortunately it cannot. The Inuit and other peoples have practised essentially this policy in the past without disastrous consequences.

Hadfield's argument fails because it is unclear whether he is saying that killing off the old and sick would destroy in part the maternal instinct, or whether he is saying that killing off the old and sick would wholly destroy the maternal instinct. He seems entitled to claim only the former, but in order to establish the conclusion that the human race would be endangered he needs to establish the latter.

The same mistake occurs in arguing that Tom knows American history so Tom will know where the first battle of the Civil War was fought. Only if Tom knows the whole of American history can this be spoken other than in hope.

A document concerning salary negotiations in universities went like this:

It would be absurd for the association to press for further reductions in differentials. For it is quite certain that the reduction of differentials cannot be a continuing process unless it leads to the same salary for everyone. Nobody seriously suggests this as an objective, and so we must recognize that the lowering of differentials in itself is a blind alley policy.

The conclusion is that to press for further reductions in differentials would be absurd (because nobody wants equality of salary). But what would be absurd would be the elimination of the whole of the difference in pay between different groups, not the elimination of a part of the difference. Because nobody wants the whole of the difference eliminated, it does not follow that they want no part of the difference eliminated. It is this sentence which largely powers the move:

'the reduction in differentials cannot be a continuing process unless it leads to the same salary for everyone'. This is, as the mathematicians might say, the limit of the change. But differentials can continue to narrow for some time without equality resulting. Cutting down on food cannot be a continuing process unless it leads to death from starvation; nevertheless, my present consumption of calories might still be too high.

6

Finally, there is an argument which somewhat resembles those with which the chapter began, and which are sometimes incorrectly treated as identical with them.

Whoever we take, if his income increases then he is better off. But it does not follow that if everyone's income increases then everyone is better off. For an increase in income all round may simply lead to inflation without more wealth being generated. That is to say, we cannot argue 'If anybody has his income increased then he will be better off; therefore if everyone has his income increased then all will be better off.'

Or again—another example from economics—if one farmer increases his output he can expect to make more money. But if every farmer increases his output then it does not follow that all their incomes will rise. How so? Let us suppose that one farmer works harder and produces more. Because he is a relatively small-scale producer he can sell his extra produce at the market without depressing the market price. Now suppose that every farmer did the same. In this case there would be a flood of produce on to the market, the price would drop and the increase in the quantity of goods sold would probably not compensate for the drop in price per unit.

It is tempting to regard this as one more case where what is true of every individual is not true of the group. If so it would be a straightforward fallacy, like arguing that because every member of a group is making a pleasant sound the group must be making a pleasant sound; every farmer can increase his income by increasing his yield, therefore the group can increase its income by increasing its yield. A familiar fallacy.

And yet, this cannot be the answer. For if every member of a group is better off under certain conditions, surely the group is better off. That is to say, 'better off' is one of those words which is applied to a group derivatively, like 'healthy', and true of the group when it is true of all or most of its members.

What has gone wrong in the above argument is that the premiss implicitly assumes a condition which the conclusion violates: that other things remain the same. Thus, a person whose income is increased is better off so long as money incomes remain steady. The same goes for the farmer who raises his output; he is better off so long as other farmers do not do the same.

There is a story of a new recruit to the army who complained that there was not enough hot water for everyone to shower. He was told: 'Then make sure you get there early.' Good advice, so long as few people follow it. But if many get there early, the situation does not stay the same and arriving early achieves nothing.

Exercises

Assess the following arguments:

11.4 Criticism of the House of Lords rumbles on. But we should pause to consider whether the Commons is much more credible. MPs are elected by voters who need have no special qualifications or even an interest in making a judgement. For my part I would rather keep a second chamber of largely hereditary peers who, in striving to safeguard their heritage, must necessarily be concerned to safeguard their country.
Section 1.

11.5 People talk as if joblessness were a necessary feature of our society. What nonsense. Anybody can get a job if he's prepared to do a harder day's work than anyone else.
Section 6.

11.6 The need for a 'head' in any marriage follows from the idea that marriage is permanent. As long as both the husband and wife are agreed, no question of a head need arise. But when there is disagreement which cannot be settled by discussion, what can be done? They cannot decide by a majority vote, for there are just two of them. One

or other must have power to make the decision. Hence the possibility of disagreement necessitates a permanent decision-maker. (Lewis (1), p. 99)
What other ways could be found of resolving the problem? Section 3.

11.7 The prime purpose of international politics is to prevent war. But war was not prevented. So each and every statesman must accept that he failed in his chief function.
Section 1.

11.8 —I agree we need to look at our defence needs. But whether that requires spending £15 billion on a jet fighter designed for the cold war is another question.
—I think national safety must always come first.
Section 5.

12 Probability, Evidence, and Causes

I

When we consider general statements, such as:

All mammals are warm-blooded
No birds have teeth
Most reptiles lay eggs

—we may wonder how it is possible to be really sure of their truth. General statements are assumed as premises, conclusions are drawn from them, but how is their truth established?

A natural answer is that these statements are established by observation. But it is impossible to observe all birds, mammals, and reptiles, for the individual animals are changing constantly; new members are being born and old ones dying. Also our observations are severely limited. We study comparatively few members of comparatively few species. We are inevitably confined to a narrow basis of observation, but we extrapolate to make statements about the whole class of animals involved. We thereby assume that the known is a guide to the unknown.

The case is similar when we take past experience as a guide to the future. We expect the sun to set because within our experience it always has done so. We expect that if we jump in the air we will fall back to earth rather than float on upwards. These seem to be rational expectations, firmly based on past experience. Basic laws of science, such that every action has an equal and opposite reaction, are relationships which have always held within our experience and which we expect to hold universally.

Over 250 years ago the Scottish philosopher David Hume wrote:

there can be no *demonstrative* arguments to prove, *that those instances of which we have had no experience resemble those of which we have had experience.* We can at least conceive a change in the course of nature; which sufficiently proves that such a change is not absolutely impossible. (Hume, p. 136)

What Hume meant by a demonstrative argument was a logical proof. It could not strictly be proved that the future resembles the past, the unknown the known; for there is no contradiction in supposing otherwise.

Hume went further and challenged the rationality of extrapolating from experience. If we do assume that the future resembles the past we have no warrant for doing so. It is a natural belief, a sort of instinct we all possess, but at root unjustified. There is thus no difference between a rash inference from experience and one which is well grounded. All alike are flawed.

Hume's challenge is known as the *problem of induction*, and such inferences from experience are also known as inductive inferences. Many philosophers would argue that Hume's mistake lies in measuring inductive inferences against the standards of deductive inference. This is to use an inappropriate yardstick, and it is then no wonder that inferences from experience are found wanting. Looked at in their own terms, there are good as well as bad inductive arguments. This may not be a complete answer to Hume, but we shall cut short debate and assume that there are legitimate inferences from experience.

However, at this point three brief comments are in order. First, it is possible to predict events unlike any which have happened in our experience. For example, scientists predict that eventually the sun will massively expand and destroy this planet. How can Hume account for the prediction of a radically new sort of situation? Hume would reply that scientists are not strictly justified in any predictions they make, but that here as elsewhere the prediction is in fact ultimately relying on experience. The sun is a star, and from our experience of physical forces and our observations in astronomy we assume that stars have life-cycles, and that our own star, the sun, will develop like other stars of the same mass.

Second, it is tempting to brush Hume's problem aside with the remark that our expectations 'work'; it is rational to expect the future to resemble the past because experience teaches us that it does. But this response begs the question. In the past the future has resembled the past, but what right have we to suppose that in the future it will continue to do so? Our expectations have worked to give success previously, but what reason is there to expect that they will continue to work to give success? This is Hume's initial question in a slightly different form.

Third, another fairly natural response to Hume, and one directly relevant to the theme of this chapter, is to say that inferences from past to future are only probable. This is not very satisfactory. To begin with, it runs counter to common sense. Hume himself remarks:

One would appear ridiculous who would say that it is only probable that the sun will rise tomorrow, or that all men must die. (Hume, p. 174)

But in addition, given Hume's doubts, it is not clear that we are justified even in claiming that the sun will 'probably' rise tomorrow. Why should it be rational to incline cautiously towards belief rather than towards disbelief in the matter? Normally we make cautious claims about the future—'Probably it will rain'—because such evidence as we have (black clouds, cows lying down in fields, and so on) is not conclusive. And we reckon the evidence to be inconclusive because in the past it has mostly, but not invariably, been followed by rain. We use past experience as a guide to the future here, too. The inference from known to unknown underpins our cautious claims just as much as our confident ones. And it is this inference that Hume was calling into question.

2

The two sorts of inference, deductive and inductive, can be contrasted in this way:

Deductive inference (demonstration)	*Inference by extrapolation (inductive inference)*
The conclusion cannot be denied without inconsistency.	The conclusion can be denied without inconsistency.
The content of the argument is irrelevant; the form is what counts (sometimes the meanings of terms).	The content is important; it matters what we are arguing about.
The conclusion is deduced from the premiss(ess).	The conclusion is in varying degrees supported by the premiss(ess).

Consider one of the examples we took at the start of this chapter, the claim that no birds have teeth. The evidence for this comes from observation—no observed birds have teeth—but not entirely so. It is unusual to draw a conclusion solely by extrapolating from observation. There is often some element of theory lying behind an inductive inference. In this case one element of theory is that having a light skeleton is important for animals which fly, and the weight of jaws with teeth is likely to be greater than that of a beak. To the extent that this theory is well established it increases our confidence that our inference was justified.

If the above is right then we cannot expect to assess inductive arguments by a simple formula, as we can many deductive arguments. 'All observed *A*'s are *B*'s, so all *A*'s are *B*'s', is a step whose soundness cannot be assessed in the abstract. Obviously we need to know: (i) how many *A*'s were observed; (ii) the range of observations—whether, in our example, lots of different sorts of bird were observed, from many parts of the world, or just a few similar species from one country; and (iii) whether the observations fit in with previously well-established theories, or are 'stand-alone'—if the latter, then we will require more observations, drawn from a wider range, before we can be confident in our conclusion. Even (i)–(iii) are vague. We have not said how many observations are needed, nor how to measure whether a range of observations is wide enough.

3

In our discussion of Hume above we touched on statements of probability, and noted Hume's comment that it appears ridiculous to claim that *probably* all men are mortal. We turn now to consider claims such as 'Probably that man's a sailor', 'Almost certainly that man's a sailor', 'Quite possibly that man's a sailor', and the like.

To claim that something is probably the case, or fairly certainly the case, or quite possibly the case, is both to make a statement ('That man is a sailor') and at the same time to indicate the quality of the evidence on which it is made. If a thing is 'probably' the case there is good evidence for it; if it is 'quite possibly' the case then the evidence for it is not negligible; and if it is 'almost certainly' the case then the evidence for it is very strong indeed. There are very many such phrases indicating the strength of evidence for a statement at the same time as making the statement.

The claim 'He is probably a sailor' can thus be challenged in one of two ways. We can challenge its truth by saying, 'No, that's not so. I happen to know he's never been to sea.' Alternatively, we can challenge the evidence for it by asking, 'Is there good reason to suppose he's a sailor?'

The sense of probability which we have begun to discuss above, and which will be discussed further in this chapter, is not the only one in common use. Statements of mathematical probability, such as 'The probability of drawing the Ace of Hearts is one in fifty-two', are related, but do not work in quite the same way. Someone saying this is not claiming, however cautiously, that the Ace of Hearts will be drawn, but is rather giving the basis for predicting how often it will be drawn from a properly shuffled pack in the long run. We shall return to this sense of probability later (in Chapter 13), but for the present concentrate on the less formal sense of probability.

For many purposes our ordinary statements are enough. Imperfect evidence leads to cautious claims. Black clouds are imperfect evidence of rain; they are not always followed by rain. Hence, on the evidence of black clouds, we make the cautious claim, 'It will probably rain.' Here we leave everything vague, and are content to do so.

How sure we are that it will rain depends on how dark the clouds are and how much of the time clouds of this darkness are followed by rain. But we don't keep any figures on the matter. Not enough hangs on it.

If we contrast this with an insurance company trying to predict how much it will pay out in claims, the need for precision quickly becomes apparent. Suppose Mr Smith, aged 60 and in reasonably good health, wishes to insure his life for the next five years. It is no good the insurance company arguing that most people who make it to 60 also make it to 65, so Mr Smith will probably live for the next five years. It will want to know how many healthy 60-year-olds survive to 65. For this reason actuarial tables are drawn up showing the numbers who die at each age. Then the company can calculate that, say, seventeen out of every twenty 60-year-olds survive to 65. Then they are likely to have to pay out on average three such claims out of every twenty 60-year-olds insured, and they have a better idea what premium to charge in order to cover their costs and make a modest, or immodest, profit.

Of course, all this is based very firmly on past experience. We need to say how likely it is that such a man will live for the next five years, and we look at what has happened in the past. Watching the figures over a few years we may notice changes. Perhaps better medicine is keeping a higher proportion of elderly people alive; perhaps less-healthy life-styles are increasing the mortality rate. An insurance company may have to guess that a trend will continue, and fix its premiums according to what it thinks the rate will be in the future rather than what it has been in the past. Even so, ultimately past experience will be the guide. And, of course, the vague 'probably' and 'possibly' of ordinary language will give way to something more precise.

4

Statements of the form 'Probably p', 'Almost certainly p', or 'Quite possibly p' are closely related to inductive arguments by virtue of the fact that they implicitly appeal to evidence. Where such statements occur as the conclusion of arguments, more of the evidence on which they are based becomes visible. For example:

That man over there has an anchor tattooed on his arm; most men with anchors tattooed on their arms are or have been sailors; so probably he is or has been a sailor.

Here we have two explicit premisses and a probable conclusion. Given the premisses, how acceptable is the conclusion? Well, we should enter a note of warning. The argument assumes that nothing else is known about the man which might undermine the conclusion. For example, suppose he has red hair, and due to superstition red-haired people are never allowed to work at sea. In that case the premisses would be true but the conclusion that the man is a sailor would be certainly false. The conclusion is probable relative to all the available evidence, not to some restricted part of it. If there is no reason to think that countervailing evidence is available then we can put trust in the conclusion.

Many arguments are less explicit and more complicated than the one above. Here is an argument from *Scientific American*, arguing that a group of Minoan people inhabited the city of Miletus in ancient times:

From the type of clay used it is apparent that the pottery in Miletus was made locally. It is also clear that these Linear A [Minoan] symbols were inscribed before the pot on which they were written was fired, . . . these facts . . . suggest that Minoan speakers must have been there—probably as members of a Minoan colony. (Schneider, p. 14)

Two facts serve as premisses: the clay was local to Miletus, and the Minoan symbols were written on it before it was fired. Two conclusions are drawn inductively from these initial premisses: that Minoan speakers were at Miletus in ancient times, and that a Minoan colony was there. The second is regarded as less certain than the first.

We can think of competing hypotheses which would also explain the initial facts. For example, clay might have been exported from Miletus to the Minoans in Crete, made into pots there, and shipped back to Miletus. In that case Minoan speakers need not have been at Miletus at all. Again, a Minoan refugee might have set up a pottery at Miletus using local labour, rather than there being a Minoan colony at the city. The author does not discuss these possibilities, but we can take it they are less likely than the ones suggested. As is often the case, the structure of the argument, and the range of competing hypotheses, are not fully displayed.

Earlier (Chapter 3, section 5) we looked at arguments of this sort:

If Einstein's theory is true then light rays passing close to the sun are deflected. Careful measurement reveals that they are deflected. Therefore Einstein's theory is true.

The argument is apparently of an invalid form:

If p then q
q
$\therefore p$.

Nevertheless, it would be widely regarded as sound. We suggested at that time that if such an argument is acceptable it is so because it is advanced against a background of competing theories; p follows from q because q eliminates p's competitors.

Arguments with a cautious conclusion often need to be approached in the same manner. They are advanced against a range of competing theories, often not made explicit. So in assessing the argument about Minoan pottery above, we have to consider the conclusions which the author draws as preferred to any competing suggestions. No rival explanation is mentioned, but they lie in the background.

An argument in which more of the background structure is revealed is to be found in the following passage:

It may seem as though we are assuming too much in supposing that Jesus was brought up as an Essene. But he was certainly not brought up as a Sadducee; and in view of his hostility to the Pharisees, he is not likely to have been brought up in that sect either. So it was an Essenic sect or nothing. As Jesus obviously knew the scriptures well, it is impossible that he had not been schooled. We cannot believe, then, that he belonged to no sect at all. Thus, even by a process of elimination, we see a strong probability that his education was Essenic, and as we know from previous sections, his teaching and his entire outlook relate him to the Essenes. (Powell Davies, p. 111)

The conclusion is that very probably Jesus was educated by the sect of the Essenes.

Powell Davies considers four competing theories:

(1) Jesus was educated by the Essenes.
(2) He was educated by the Pharisees.
(3) He was educated by the Sadducees.
(4) He did not receive an education.

The fourth he rules our from the fact that Jesus knew the scriptures well. The third he rules out for reasons which are not specified in the passage quoted. The second, he says, is not likely, given the fact that Jesus was hostile to the Pharisees. Hence, by elimination, we arrive at the first view. It cannot be asserted with complete confidence because the second theory cannot be eliminated with complete confidence.

There are particulars of the case which could be challenged. For example, the fourth suggestion may have been too quickly ruled out: it is not unknown for people to learn scripture without the benefit of teachers. However, for our purposes the importance of the example lies in what it reveals of the structure of arguments of its kind.

All the arguments in this section have offered evidence for a conclusion. The bending of light was evidence for Einstein's theory; symbols on the clay pots were evidence for a Minoan colony; Jesus's knowledge of the Scriptures was evidence for his being educated by the Essenes: in every case, unless the rival theories are completely ruled out, the evidence does not support a firm conclusion but at best a probable one.

Exercises

12.1 All *A*s are *B*s. Most *B*s are *C*s. Therefore most *A*s are *C*s.
       Valid?

12.2 There are no signs of a forced entry at any of the windows and both doors are locked. So the burglar probably had an accomplice inside the house.
       What competing theories could account for the facts as presented?

12.3 *Which 'most' statement lies behind each of the following?*
    (1) James is Irish, so he'll probably wear a shamrock on St Patrick's Day.
    (2) James wears a shamrock on St Patrick's Day, so he's probably Irish.

12.4 We have hundreds of man-years' operating experience of nuclear reactors so we have a shrewd idea how great the risks are.
    Explore the notion of a man-year's operating experience.

12.5 Of course we should go ahead with this new product. There's a risk that we'll lose money, but there's a risk in everything. There's even a risk in sitting in the garden sunning yourself.
    Convincing?

5

There is a fallacy traditionally classified as '*post hoc ergo propter hoc*' (literally, 'after this, so because of this'). We are tempted to argue that the incidence of skin cancer is greater amongst sunbathers than amongst those who don't sunbathe, and therefore sunbathing causes skin cancer. Or we argue that the number of sex offences has risen since the greater availability of pornographic films, therefore the viewing of pornographic films causes a rise in the number of sex offences. These particular examples may or may not be correct. However, it is certainly not the case that merely establishing a correlation is enough to show a causal connection. There is no doubt a good correlation between the sale of hot drinks in Britain and that of cold drinks in Australia, but it is not true that an increase of hot drinks in Britain causes an increase of cold drinks in Australia. There is an indirect causal link, of course, because Britain's winter coincides with Australia's summer, and there are geophysical causes of that. But a correlation is not the same as a causal connection. Similarly, in Britain the rise in the number of school-exam passes over recent years has gone along with a rise in the number of marriage breakdowns; but we cannot regard either as causing the other.

The dangers of jumping to conclusions are well recognized by medical researchers. When a new drug is tested it is often found that a number of patients will report an improvement in their condition even when it subsequently turns out that the new drug is ineffective. They are responding to the fact that they are being treated, rather than to the treatment itself. They expect to feel better, and this fact alone brings it about that some patients do feel better. This problem is normally met by dividing the patients at the testing stage and putting half on the new treatment and half on a substance which looks and tastes the same but is known to do neither good nor harm. Such substances are known as placebos. No patient, of course, knows which group he is in. In this way it is hoped to separate the genuinely medical effect of the new treatment from the purely psychological effect, for the expectations of those on placebos will not differ from the expectations of those on the real treatment.

There is another factor which needs to be considered when changes are introduced involving people, and this we might term the *novelty effect*. It is well known that when new systems of business management are set up there is a tendency for output to increase for a while, even when the systems turn out to be no better in the long run than those they replaced. The workers are being asked to do something different from normal, and often they respond positively to the change in routine.

It is not only in business management that a novelty effect can emerge. Traffic experiments might well be subject to this effect. Drivers are being asked to do something different, or are being confronted by unusal road markings, and for this reason alone they might drive more alertly and less routinely than usual. Their increased alertness might be what leads to a reduction in accidents, rather than any new instructions.

6

One might wonder, in view of all the cautions and caveats of the preceding remarks, just when one is justified in passing from a correlation to a causal connection? However, before coming on to this we must consider the notion of cause more fully. It is a fairly vague notion, and several distinctions need to be drawn.

First, we talk of the cause of specific things—the window breaking, the bridge collapsing—as well as of the cause of widespread phenomena such as legionnaire's disease, which occurs at many times and places. We can ask what causes house fires as well as what caused this house fire.

Secondly, one must distinguish between asking for *the* cause and *a* cause. If we seek the cause of foot-and-mouth disease in cattle we might reasonably hope to establish a single factor. If we seek the cause of household fires we shall get nowhere. They are caused in a variety of ways, some by faults in electricity circuits, some by unattended chip-pans, some by smouldering cigarettes. Some phenomena are caused by one thing, some by a multiplicity of things. Even when we are talking of a single event it is often impossible to pick out a single cause. We talk happily enough of the cause of the window's breaking, but historians tend to talk in terms of multiple causes—the causes of the French Revolution, for example.

Thirdly, one must distinguish between seeking an event as cause and seeking a standing condition as cause. For example, we might identify an earthquake—an event—as the cause of one building's collapse. But the cause of another building's collapse might be identified as bad design, or weak concrete, both of which are standing conditions, in the building from the time it was built. If we identify design or materials as causing the collapse then we ignore any trivial event—a slight gust of wind, or a car's horn—which might have set off the collapse. In such a case we tend not to pick it out as the cause. The notion of cause is strongly driven by practical concern. From all the factors surrounding an event we tend to pick out as the cause or causes those things that strike us as unusual or which we hope to do something about. Houses should be built to withstand slight gusts of wind and the disturbance of a passing car, so we pick out the condition of the house as causing the collapse.

Finally, we sometimes pick out one type of event as causing another type of event when there is a connection but not an invariable connection between the two. For example, medical researchers say that smoking causes lung cancer, even though not all smokers get lung cancer. Smoking increases the risk of getting lung cancer.

Exercise

12.6 People claim that unemployment causes crime. Nonsense. Lots of
people can't get jobs, but most of them remain perfectly law-abiding.
Assess.

7

Suppose, however, that the notion of cause is clear enough for our
purposes. Even so, it seems unlikely that general rules can be given
for discovering causes.

Attempts have been made to lay down such rules. The most
famous occurs in John Stuart Mill's *System of Logic*, written in 1843
and subsequently running to many editions. Mill discussed the
methods of experimental inquiry and tried to lay down general rules,
or canons, for going from observed outcomes to their causes. Characteristically, Mill himself pointed out many of the main problems
his account faced.

There are five canons, of which only the three most important will
be stated (fairly informally), and some objections to them.

- The 'method of agreement':
  Suppose we observe several instances of a phenomenon and in all those
  instances we find some common factor. Then that factor is the cause of
  that phenomenon. (Strictly, Mill says the instances should have only
  one factor in common, but I suspect we could always find more than
  one, if we looked hard enough.)

Problems. If there is a plurality of causes the inference will fail. For
example, the phenomenon of cratering on the moon could have been
caused by now-extinct volcanoes or by meteorites hitting the surface.
Perhaps some were caused one way and some the other. If so, then
although the craters would have things in common (e.g. being cir-
cular), these common factors would be irrelevant.

Even if there is a single cause, it need not be the common factor
picked out. An invented example may make the point most clearly,
although there is no shortage of factual examples. Suppose some
people are afflicted as follows: their hair turns green and shortly after-
wards their toes drop off. I doubt if we would be content to say that

their hair going green was the common factor which caused their toes to drop off. Rather we would regard green hair as a further symptom of a strange disease or poison and look for some other as-yet undiscovered common factor in the bloodstream of the individuals concerned. Some theory as to the sort of thing which might be responsible will guide our search.

- The 'method of difference':
  We are investigating some phenomenon. We have a case, *A*, in which the phenomenon occurs and a case, *B*, in which it doesn't. In other respects the two cases are exactly alike. Now we find that in addition *A* has some further property which *B* lacks. Then that further property, says Mill, is the cause of the phenomenon in question.

Problem. Suppose we are investigating the exotic chain of events which was considered above. We come across identical twins, one of whom has had his toes drop off, while the other is unaffected. We find that the first has also recently suffered his hair turning green. On Mill's account we have to regard the hair turning green as the cause of the toes dropping off. I do not think we would so regard it. As in the first example, we would look for some further factor causing changes.

- The 'method of concomitant variations':
  Whenever one phenomenon varies in a regular way as another varies, they are causally connected.

Problem. If the two phenomena vary together (and we are satisfied that this occurs too regularly to be simply chance) then there is some connection between them, although it may be a remote one. We cannot conclude that the one causes the other; perhaps both are the result of some further chain of causes. As we noted earlier, the sale of hot drinks in Britain and cold drinks in Australia vary together, not because one causes the other, but because both stem from remoter causes.

Mill's contemporary William Whewell rejected Mill's canons and argued instead that science proceeds by forming hypotheses (making guesses) and testing them against experience. Mill thought this too indirect and casual a procedure, and hoped his 'methods' would provide a logical short cut to the true causes of things. Time has favoured Whewell's approach. Many philosophers and scientists would nowadays argue along similar lines—that there are no simple inferences to be 'read off' from experience but that all our observations are guided and directed by theories. We are unlikely to be satisfied that a change of hair-colour to green can cause toes to drop off. We approach the facts with preconceptions, even in so bizarre a case as this. We conjecture that chemical changes in the body might cause both kinds of phenomena, even if we have no idea yet which specific chemical changes might do so.

The lesson to be drawn from this is not that Mill's methods are worthless. Far from it. Suppose that it occurs to Angela that the last couple of times she has eaten trifle she has suffered indigestion. She will suspect that some ingredient in the trifle is affecting her. She is likely to eat some trifle again, just to confirm that trifle and indigestion go together (method of agreement). If so, she may try the ingredients—eggs, cream, and so on—separately (method of difference). She may even vary the amount of trifle and see if the indigestion varies in severity (method of concomitant variations). But behind all these procedures lie common-sense ideas about what sorts of things cause one to feel unwell. For example. Angela will not use the method of agreement to argue as follows: 'Until recently I ate trifle without getting indigestion, so trifle is not a common factor and cannot be the problem.' She knows that over time people's tolerance to different foods varies, and this and other background knowledge will affect the way in which she applies Mill's methods.

Exercises

12.7 The cause of war is man's aggressive nature.
   What sense of 'cause' is this (Section 6), and how good is the explanation?

12.8 More-recent groups of immigrants to the USA do less well on IQ tests than older-established immigrant groups do. This shows that the innate intelligence of the newer arrivals is lower.
   Are there alternative hypotheses?

12.9 Most people convicted of motoring offences are men; which ought to do something to dispel the popular myth that women are poorer drivers.
Assess.

13 Probability: Statistics

I

Arguments involving numbers are sometimes too sophisticated for the layman to follow. They can require a better grasp of mathematics than most of us possess, or they can raise subtle points in experiment design and interpretation. For the average person statistical arguments are a minefield without a map. One unfortunate response to this is to dismiss arguments involving statistics as all alike invalid. It is a common complaint that you can prove anything with statistics; which is tantamount to saying that statistical arguments really prove nothing. This sentiment can be a generalized expression of despair (in which case one can sympathize but not agree). It can also be a rhetorical trick in debate, and there it is more harmful.

Some years ago there was a broadcast discussion between two eminent historians on the causes of the Second World War. The first claimed that in 1939 France was better prepared for war than Germany, and quoted figures showing that France had more tanks in 1939 than Germany. The second historian replied, 'I'm dealing with facts, not figures.' This may score a point, but to oppose facts and figures in this way is quite wrong. These figures were, or were claimed to be, facts. Perhaps the figures came from unreliable sources; perhaps, even if true, they give a misleading picture of preparedness for war (if, for example, the French tanks were older and worse). To attack the figures on such grounds as these would have been reasonable, but to attack the very use of statistics is unfair. For very often, as in this case, figures provide evidence for a claim. Figures also render a claim more precise. Instead of being told that most *A*s are *B*s or that few *A*s are *B*s (vague statements, in all conscience) we are told how many; which is more informative and often more useful to know.

There is nothing very complicated about the way such information is given. Suppose we know that sixty out of 150 *A*s are *B*s. We can express that figure baldly as it stands, but more often it will be convenient to express it in one of three ways: as a simpler fraction, by cancelling down (two-fifths of *A*s are *B*s); as a decimal (0.4 of *A*s are *B*s); as a percentage (40 per cent of *A*s are *B*s). These three ways enable us to state the proportion in a way which lends itself to easy comparison, so that we can compare proportions using a common base. For this reason it is often valuable to round off numbers. Fifty-nine out of 150 is as near as no matter 40 per cent. There may be cases where the difference is important; more often than not, it will not be.

Numbers reduce some people to panic, but a bit of common sense plus a lot of caution can help one to avoid the most glaring errors, even where there is no natural aptitude for mathematics.

2

We saw earlier that it is wrong to argue from a statement of the form 'Every *A* is *B*' to one of the form 'Every *B* is *A*'. If every human being is a mammal it does not follow that every mammal is a human being. The same point holds for 'most': if most cats are black it does not follow that most black things are cats. And the same goes for 'few': if few human beings are playwrights it does not follow that few playwrights are human beings. The same is equally true when these imprecise assertions are rendered more exact by numbers. If 78 per cent of cats are black it does not follow that 78 per cent of black things are cats. And if one in a thousand human beings is a playwright, it does not follow that one in a thousand playwrights is a human being.

These points are so straightforward that it is hard to conceive of being led astray by failure to attend to them. But not so. At one point in the mid-1960s, when the controversy about cannabis smoking was at its height, it was claimed by a British government spokesman that

95 per cent of heroin addicts began by smoking cannabis. The statistic was presented as an alarming one, showing how dangerous a habit cannabis smoking is. Yet I suspect that much of the alarm was generated by the confusion we have just been considering. If 95 per cent of heroin addicts began by smoking cannabis it does not follow that 95 per cent of those who smoke cannabis will go on to become addicted to heroin. The two claims are quite distinct. If they are not clearly distinguished and kept distinct, however, then it does look as though those who smoke cannabis are either ignorant of its effects or tired of life. To repeat, knowing what proportion of heroin addicts previously smoked cannabis tells us nothing about what proportion of cannabis smokers go on to become addicted to heroin. In fact, the latter proportion will be relatively small.

A second source of error in the use of statistics is what we might term the *snapshot danger*: we determine the proportion of *A*s which are *B*s at one moment and assume that this gives us the true proportion of *A*s which are *B*s. There are at least two dangers here. The more obvious is that if the proportion of *A*s which are *B*s is changing then we cannot extrapolate to the future.

To illustrate, let us tell the tale of Mr Glum, who has just inherited a business growing orchids. Mr Glum's name currently reflects his mood because he has just discovered that stem wilt is affecting some of the orchids. He counts up and finds that ten out of 490 are affected. He calculates that this is approximately two in a hundred, and plans for the future on the basis of that figure. This is an example of an inductive inference, as discussed in the previous chapter. However, it may well be a rash inference. We know in general that plant diseases can fluctuate, and if the stem wilt is spreading then his finances will be thrown into confusion. It would make sense for Mr Glum to do future counts and see whether or not the proportion of affected plants stays the same before extrapolating the figure.

Apart from this there is a less obvious trap associated with the snapshot approach. Even if the rate of infection is constant, Mr Glum might have got it wrong. This would be the case if orchids with stem wilt do not live as long as healthy plants. What Mr Glum hasn't counted and cannot count are the orchids already killed by stem wilt.

To aid our explanation we shall make some simplifying assumptions: Mr Glum inherits his business in the year 2004; the rate of infection is in fact 4 per cent, not 2 per cent; all orchids affected by stem wilt get it within a year and die within four years; the healthy orchids are sold after four years. On these assumptions we would expect the situation to be just as Mr Glum found it, but the rate of infection is *twice* what his snapshot count revealed. The way the situation developed as Mr Glum found it is shown in the table below.

Year	Number of new orchids planted in year	Number getting stem wilt within the year	Number of these alive in 2004	Number of group planted still alive in 2004
2000	100	4	0	96
2001	100	4	1	97
2002	100	4	2	98
2003	100	4	3	99
2004	100	4	4	100

Notes: Population after fourth year: 490; number of these plants suffering from stem wilt: 10; number of plants having died during the period: 10.

The figures are of course too neat to be realistic, but they make it easier to understand what is going on. Each year a hundred new orchids are planted and four of them contract stem wilt. After a year one of the four dies, another at the end of the second year, and so on. At the end of the period only around 2 per cent of total existing stock are infected, but during the period death from stem wilt has also reduced the stock of orchids by ten. Mr Glum has still to realize the full extent of the problem. He has been misled by the snapshot perspective.

Exercises

How good are the following arguments?

13.1 More people suffer from mental illness than any other serious form of illness in Britain. That is clear from the fact that at any time a third of all hospital beds are occupied by mentally ill patients, and no other illness approaches that proportion.

13.2 In the country three-quarters of those who contracted whooping cough had been inoculated. This seems to show pretty clearly that inoculation has absolutely no value, whatever its supporters say.

3

In the previous chapter we considered statements such as 'That man is probably a sailor.' It was claimed that this sort of statement plays a dual role. It makes a claim ('That man is a sailor') and indicates the confidence with which the claim is put forward ('There is good but not conclusive evidence'). In this chapter we shall look at a slightly different application of probability.

'The probability of a person in Britain having red hair is one in twelve.' This is not like the statement above, because it is not in itself put forward cautiously. There is no hedging. In this kind of probability statement the concentration on the second (evidential) role is complete. We have a more precise specification of the weight of evidence for or against an assertion (in this case the assertion that a randomly selected Briton will have red hair).

This sort of probability statement gives a measure of rational confidence. The higher the probability of an event or state of affairs the greater the confidence we are justified in having that it will come about. If there is conclusive evidence in favour of an event it is assigned the number 1; if there is conclusive evidence against, it is given the number 0. Between these points, the stronger the evidence, the greater the number attached. Thus the probability of a person's some day dying is 1; the probability of someone's running a mile in thirty seconds is 0; the probability that someone, randomly selected, who lives in Britain also lives in Scotland is about one in nine, or

0·11 recurring; the probability that someone who lives in Britain does not live in Scotland is about eight out of nine, or 0·88 recurring.

These probability estimates are ultimately based on experience. A claim such as, 'The probability of those who take cannabis going on to heroin is one in a hundred' involves an extrapolation from past to future. We know what will happen to a proportion of cannabis smokers, based on what has happened before. The probability could change, so that we could say, 'The probability used to be one in a hundred but now it is one in ninety.' Still we rely on past experience; having noted the change to the new ratio, we expect it to continue.

4

There is some contrast between the kind of case discussed above, involving extrapolation from experience, and that involving games of chance; coin-tossing, for example, or drawing cards from a pack. Again we use numerical estimates: 'The probability of a coin falling heads is a half (one in two)', 'The chance of drawing a spade from a shuffled pack is a quarter (one in four)'. Yet these estimates do not seem to be based on past experience of coin-tossing or card-drawing. Typically they are made by academics who must be assumed to have better things to do with their time than toss coins and shuffle cards for long hours. What happens is that mathematicians take it for granted that tossing pennies approximates very closely to producing an entirely random series containing two sorts of sign (call them heads/tails, Hs/Ts, 1s/0s, or whatever you will). Mathematicians are interested in random series and random selections, not in tossing coins and shuffling cards. But in fact these operations are close enough to true randomizing procedures for the mathematical results to apply. So we can ignore for practical purposes the remote possibility of a penny balancing edge-uppermost, and say that the probability of a coin falling heads uppermost is a half, and the same probability holds of its falling tails uppermost. Between them these exhaust all the possibilities: $^1/_2 + ^1/_2 = 1$.

We assume that the coin falls randomly; that we cannot predict which way the coin will fall. In effect, this is to say that we cannot find any pattern in a sequence of throws, although we can predict that in any long sequence of throws the number of heads will be very close to the number of tails.

What is the probability of throwing heads on two successive tosses of a coin? Mathematicians appeal to what they call the 'multiplication law': if two events are independent, then the probability of both occurring is the probability of the first multiplied by the probability of the second. The probability of heads on the first throw is $^1/_2$, and the probability of heads on the second is also $^1/_2$. So the probability of heads on both throws is $^1/_2 \times ^1/_2 = ^1/_4$. We could set out a table showing the rationale of this. There are four independent and equally likely outcomes, so each has one chance in four of arising:

	Possible outcomes			
	(1)	(2)	(3)	(4)
First throw:	H	H	T	T
	or	or	or	
Second throw:	H	T	H	T
	$^1/_4$ +	$^1/_4$ +	$^1/_4$ +	$^1/_4$ = 1

(One of the four outcomes is certain to occur.)

The probability of three heads occurring in three tosses is $^1/_2 \times ^1/_2 \times ^1/_2 = ^1/_8$. In this case there are eight possible outcomes, each as likely as any other.

Exercise

13.3 *Draw up a similar table of possible outcomes for three throws of a coin.*

5

So far, then, we have looked at the very first steps in the arithmetic of probability. Even here there are dangers. Suppose, for example, that a coin which is known to be unbiassed and fairly tossed—I stress that these things are known—falls heads ten times in a row. What are the chances of its falling heads on the eleventh toss? Our arithmetic tells us that if the coin falls randomly its chances of falling heads is a half. But there is a common and fallacious mode of thinking which says that there must be a better-than-even chance of getting tails on the eleventh toss. The reasoning is that if the series is deviating from a parity of heads and tails then it must move back towards equality at some stage. There must be a compensatory principle at work, otherwise we could not end up with equal numbers of heads and tails. To argue in this way is to commit what is known as the 'Monte Carlo fallacy' (presumably because gamblers are prone to bet heavily on a tail following a sequence of heads).

This line of thought can perhaps be disentangled by pointing out that there is no finite point at which the number of heads has to balance the number of tails. Over a large enough sequence of throws an 'extra' ten heads would be of vanishingly small significance. Over, say, a million throws we might very well expect to find that the number of heads and tails did not exactly match; and an extra ten heads would certainly not excite comment.

Furthermore, over a long enough sequence of tosses we would expect occasionally to get ten heads in a row. We can calculate the probability of ten successive heads by the method we used earlier. It is $1/2 \times 1/2 \times 1/2 \times 1/2 \times 1/2 \times 1/2 \times 1/2 \times 1/2 \times 1/2 \times 1/2$, which is $1/1024$. A sequence of ten tosses can turn out in 1024 different ways. We could list these ways, as we did for two tosses and three tosses earlier, but life is short. Of these 1024 outcomes, all equally likely, just one consists of ten heads. In other words, we could expect a sequence of ten heads to occur once in about every thousand sequences of ten throws.

Finally, while it may seem very remarkable and unusual to get ten successive heads, it is no less remarkable and unusual to get nine successive heads followed by a tail; there is one chance in 1024 of getting that also. Indeed, any quite 'ordinary' sequence of heads and tails, such as

HTTTHHTHTH

is just as rare as ten successive heads. There is only one chance in 1024 of that particular sequence occurring, too. Only we do not notice whether it occurs or not, because it is completely unremarkable.

This form of the Monte Carlo fallacy occurs in some cases when lotteries take place. People will sometimes avoid a draw ticket numbered 1000, on the grounds that it has less chance of coming up than an 'ordinary' number such as 1217 or 846—undistinguished numbers. But of course most numbers are undistinguished, so we would expect an 'ordinary' number to be drawn more often. The probability of any particular 'ordinary' number being drawn is just as remote as the probability of 1000 being drawn.

Then again, there is the common superstition that because a national lottery number has come up once it is less likely to come up on the next occasion that the lottery is held (or the equally common superstition that if it has come up on one occasion it is lucky and therefore more likely to come up again). If the lottery involves a truly random device for generating numbers it is utterly irrelevant whether a number has come up before or not: each draw is independent of all previous draws.

Exercises

13.4 In two throws of a coin there are just three possibilities: two heads, two tails, or one of each. So if all are equally likely there's a one-in-three chance of getting two heads in two throws of a coin.
What's wrong with the reasoning? (Section 4.)

13.5 The numbers of my lottery tickets are more spread out than hers, so I have a better chance of winning.
Assess.

6

I stated—indeed, emphasized—that when we know a coin to be unbiased and fairly tossed it is irrelevant that we have a sequence of ten heads; the eleventh toss is just as likely to produce a head as a tail.

On the other hand, can we really be so confident that a coin is unbiased and fairly tossed if the first ten tosses come down heads? We might well be inclined to think that the coin is weighted or the tossing 'fixed'. If we are dealing with a biassed coin or an unfair mechanism it is rational to expect heads to continue to predominate.

What we have, in fact, is a rather delicate balancing job to do. The chances of a truly random procedure turning up ten heads in a row is rather remote ($^1/_{1024}$). If we are very confident that the tossing mechanism is fair and the coin true we will incline to shrug aside the sequence as just one of those things. If we already had doubts about the procedure we will tend to regard the sequence as confirming our doubts. But we may be content to reserve judgement for the next few throws. If heads continue to be thrown we will be strongly inclined to reject the procedure or suspect the coin.

What we do here is ask ourselves how likely it is that the result came about by chance. If the result would not have come about by chance except very infrequently then we look for some other explanation. This technique of testing results against what one would expect by chance has become a very important technique in science. It is usually known as testing against a *null hypothesis*.

7

One area where the null hypothesis is crucial is in the investigation of claims of extra-sensory perception (ESP), the power to perceive things without the use of the senses; or, at any rate, the usually accepted senses.

In the most common kind of experiment, the person being tested—the subject—is seated behind a screen. The experimenter turns over cards at intervals, signalling whenever a card is turned, and the subject has to try to say which card has been turned over. Special cards are used, with five different symbols. As well as screening off the subject, elaborate precautions are taken to try to ensure that the test is stringent. The experimenter does not call out when he turns over a card in case his tone of voice enables the subject to guess which card was turned. Mathematical tables of random numbers are used to determine the order in which the cards are turned over, for a person asked to turn cards over at random will almost certainly fail to do so; he will unconsciously hit a pattern, and if the subject guesses according to a pattern which happens to coincide then results can be artificially inflated. The experimenter who turns over the cards will not himself record the results, because it has been found that experimenters sometimes unconsciously mis-record in the subject's favour.

What typically happens then is that the subject makes twenty-five calls. Since there are five different symbols he or she would be expected by sheer guesswork to call correctly about one-fifth of the time; to score around five correct calls in twenty-five guesses. Suppose a subject scores eight correct calls in twenty-five guesses. That may be just lucky guessing. But if further trials continue to give scores at that kind of level we shall have to think again. There is food for thought. In 1941, for example, Dr Soal and Mrs Goldney carried out a series of experiments with a subject called Basil Shackleton. Over a very long series Shackleton tended to average eight correct calls where chance alone would have led us to expect five. Over one trial such a proportion of correct guesses would not be significant; over so many trials it would arise by chance once in many billion times. In Chapter 11 we argued that our judgements are made against a background of theories. This result runs so flatly counter to our everyday knowledge of the world and our scientific theories that we may not want to rule out the possibility that it is just an amazing freak of statistics. The other possibilities are that there was some flaw in the experiment, or collusion (which would not have been easy), or that Basil Shackleton had some means beyond the normal of telling what cards were showing on the other side of the screen (a rather fitful talent, since correct calls didn't 'feel' any different to him from incorrect ones).

Testing against chance has value in rather more mundane fields, too. Suppose we are trying out a new treatment for dandruff. Let us suppose that 100 people are given the old treatment and thirty-five cured, whereas 150 are given the new treatment and sixty-five cured. If we are cautious we will ask ourselves whether the differences could have arisen purely by chance, and whether the new treatment is really any better than the old.

If the two treatments were equally effective, we would expect them to be successful in the same proportion of cases. Taking both treatments together, 100 out of 250 cases were successfully treated, two-fifths of all cases. If both treatments were equally effective, then two-fifths of those treated in the old way should have been cured, and two-fifths of those treated in the new way. Instead of the expected forty cures under the old treatment we get thirty-five. Instead of the expected sixty cures under the new method we get sixty-five. Is the difference significant?

This is not so easily solved as cases involving cards or coins, but mathematicians have various techniques for solving this sort of problem. In fact, the difference from the expected result could quite easily have arisen by chance in this case. (Those who are interested in following up the mathematics involved should consult M. J. Moroney, *Facts from Figures* or Derek Rowntree, *Statistics without tears*.)

Exercises

13.6 I remember an American said there is more upset to the ozone layer by cows breaking wind in fields than by a whole fleet of supersonic transports flying simultaneously. (Sir Archibald Russell, designer of Concorde)
Is this reassuring, even if true?

13.7 The cost of insurance rose by 10 per cent last year and is forecast to rise by 10 per cent again next year. That will mean a rise of 20 per cent in two years.

13.8 The chances against what happened to the nuclear reactor at Harrisburg were astronomical. People get irrationally alarmed because they forget that very occasionally the very unlikely happens.
Section 6 is relevant; is the arguer correct?

13.9 There are 5 billion people in the world, and China produces 4 billion pairs of shoes a year, so roughly 80 per cent of the world's population wears Chinese-made shoes. (Chinese official, quoted by *Time* magazine)

14 Analogies

1

Analogies are resemblances between things of different types. Such resemblances are often drawn explicitly, as in the rather startling claim of Tom Lehrer that, 'Life's like a sewer; what you get out of it depends on what you put into it'. In many cases the resemblance is not spelled out but is left implicit. Robert Burns wrote 'My love is like a red, red rose', but left it to the reader to fill out the respects in which the likeness held. Some authors restrict the term 'analogy' to cases where the points of comparison are made explicit, but I shall use the term more widely to embrace cases such as the one from Burns. Furthermore, I shall not distinguish between using similes—likening one thing to another—and using metaphors, which apparently identify different things. 'All the world's a stage' will be regarded as saying that the world is *like* a stage. In some contexts this might be misleading, but for our purposes the wider usage is more convenient.

Analogies are employed for a number of reasons: to help a listener or reader understand, to evoke attitudes, or even simply to indulge the desire for vivid expression. Analogies are also used in argument, in attempting to justify a conclusion or an action. But arguing from analogy is a suspect business.

2

We can range analogies along a scale, with elucidatory uses at one end and evocative or poetic uses at the other.

This attempt to explain the physics of sub-atomic particles seeks to elucidate by means of analogy:

If we know that an electron is at a certain point in space, we cannot specify exactly the speed with which it is moving—nature . . . knows nothing, apparently, of absolutely exact measurements. In the same way, if we know the exact speed of motion of an electron, nature refuses to let us discover its exact position in space. It is as though the position and motion of the electron had been marked on the two different faces of a lantern slide. If we put the slide into a bad lantern, we can focus half-way between the two faces, and we shall see both the position and motion of the electron tolerably clearly. With a perfect lantern we could not do this; the more we focussed on the one, the more blurred the other would become. (Jeans, p. 39)

The author goes on to say that physics before quantum theory was rather like the old lantern.

The point of the example is to help the reader grasp something of the import of the uncertainty principle. No doubt it gives only a partial understanding, but the comparison with a familiar object gives the reader something to grasp on to and test the new ideas against. Ultimately he or she may come to grasp what is involved directly. If the comparison can be dispensed with, it has done its job. The analogy of the two kingdoms which was employed in Chapter 8 is intended to serve the same function, providing a model to help clarify certain claims about word meanings.

At the other end of the scale are uses which are mainly evocative. In the novel *Moby Dick*, Captain Ahab talks of his pursuit of the great white whale:

The path to my fixed purpose is laid with iron rails, whereon my soul is grooved to run. Over unsounded gorges, through the rifled hearts of mountains, under torrents' beds, unerringly I rush! Naught's an obstacle, naught's an angle to the iron way! (Melville, p. 177)

The thought is straightforward: that Ahab's purpose cannot be changed, it is beyond his control. As it is spelled out, the comparison to a railway engine proceeding unswervingly along its track makes vivid and emphasizes the overwhelming, obsessive nature of Ahab's pursuit.

Somewhere in between lie examples in which elucidatory and evocative elements are mixed.

Consider the following passage:

It seems to me that defenders of air travel are sometimes very muddle-headed. Some of them have suggested that the people who stand to benefit from a reduction in aircraft noise, those who live near airports, are the ones who should bear most of the costs. But that is like saying that if a neighbour throws rubbish in my garden I should have to bear the costs of cleaning up the mess. Why shouldn't he?

Here the suggestion that those who gain from the reduction of noise should be the ones to bear the costs is answered in the form of an analogy. The point being made could be expressed without analogy: those who cause a nuisance, rather than those who suffer it, should bear the expense of removing it; and aircraft noise is a nuisance. The analogy probably makes the relevance of the reply easier to grasp than a bare enunciation of the principle being appealed to. More than this, however, it probably has the effect of rather deflating the original suggestion, by picking a parallel case where what is being suggested looks outrageously cheeky. The example has elucidatory as well as evocative force.

Exercise

14.1 *Consider the following analogy*:
When normal channels of expression are blocked, emotional energy must find an outlet somehow.
What things are being compared? How appropriate is the comparison, do you think?

14.2 Harold is behaving like a real dog in the manger. He never takes his boat out to sea any more, but he won't let anyone borrow it and he refuses to contemplate getting rid of it.
Find and explain the analogy here. Suggest circumstances consistent with the information above in which the analogy would not be appropriate.

3

Analogies can shade over into literal truth. Consider the frequently drawn analogy between a cloud of gas and a very large number of very tiny balls in rapid, random motion. Molecules, the particles of which the gas is made up, are very tiny and in random motion. They do not deform on contact with other molecules. They rebound as if they are spherical. At one time the analogy must have seemed more than that; it must have seemed the literal truth, or a good approximation to the literal truth, about molecules. As more became known about molecules they turned out to have properties which did not fit the simple picture. It became clear that after all the model of a tiny, hard ball was just an analogy.

Conversely, in many cases words are applied by analogy and become so firmly established in the language that nobody thinks of them any longer as analogical. They become what are called 'dead' metaphors. Thus we talk of *high* and *low* musical notes, of the *hands* of a clock, of being *dogged* by misfortune. Particularly when describing feelings and sensations, analogies are adopted which become established and later are accepted as the literal truth. When we talk of a sharp or a throbbing pain, or of anger welling up inside someone, when we describe a person as coming out of his shell or as being hot-tempered, the expressions are so natural and appropriate that we rarely think of their origins.

4

Analogies can go wrong in various ways.

The most obvious source of failure is that at some point the analogy will simply fail to hold. This does not necessarily involve its wholesale rejection; there is nothing wrong with an analogy which holds only partially.

Consider the problem of the nature of light. Ever since Huygens wrote his *Treatise on Light* in 1690, scientists have been aware that many of the salient features of light can be explained on the assumption that it is a type of wave motion. Huygens conjectured that just as water-waves are pressures transmitted through water, and sound-waves are pressures transmitted through air, so light is a sort of wave pressure transmitted through a substance more pervasive than air, which he called the Ether:

And I do not believe that this motion of light could be better explained than by supposing that . . . the sun and the stars are composed of particles which float in a much more subtle matter . . .

Now if we examine what may be this matter in which the movement which comes from luminous bodies is propagated—which I call Ether— we see that it is not the same as that which serves for the propagation of sound. For we find that the latter is indeed the very air which we feel and which we breathe; when this is removed, the other matter which serves for light is still to be found there. (Wolff (tr.), pp. 211–12)

Huygens is arguing that since sound cannot travel in the absence of air, but light can, air cannot be the carrier of light. The matter which carries light-waves must be finer than anything else, for it flows through the walls of a vessel from which all air has been extracted.

Not until the beginning of this century did scientists surrender belief in such a luminiferous Ether, after all attempts to detect its presence had failed. What until then had seemed a good analogy between light and sound had broken down in respect of a medium of transmission. In other respects the analogy still has attractions, and physicists believe today that light has wave as well as particle characteristics in its fundamental nature.

We have here what is apparently an argument from analogy which comes unstuck: sound consists of pressure waves in air; light resembles sound; therefore there must be a medium in which light waves travel. But if arguments from analogy can come unstuck in this way, are they ever justified?

If we think in terms of deductive arguments, clearly not. This is because analogies are in essence comparisons between different sorts of thing. We can set out the general form of reasoning by analogy as follows:

One thing, X, resembles another thing, Y, in certain known respects: X has certain properties and Y has the analogous properties. X has some further property, P. Therefore Y has the analogous property, P'.

Thus, we know that sound radiates spherically from its source and that light radiates spherically from its source; sound can vary in loudness, light in brightness, and so on. Now we argue that sound travels in a medium (air), therefore light also travels in a medium (Ether).

There would clearly be no contradiction in accepting the premisses and concluding that light does not travel in a medium. That is what science discovered to be the case. If we are to give any credence to an argument from analogy, then, it must be considered in terms of inductive arguments, based on experience, as discussed in Chapter 12 above. We argued there that it is legitimate to extrapolate from the known to the unknown. Although going from known to unknown cannot logically entail a conclusion, it can support confidence in it to various degrees. So we are now faced with the question, How acceptable are arguments from analogy, regarded as a type of inductive argument?

There is a general problem with extrapolating from experience by means of an analogy. Something we know from experience is that the two things being compared are similar in some respects but are not the same. Since they are not the same sort of thing they will have many different properties. (In our example light is electromagnetic radiation, sound is not, and so on.) Therefore in all such cases experience fails to point all one way. The effect of this is to make arguments from analogy fairly weak inductive arguments at best. On their own they cannot support great confidence in their conclusions.

In the passage quoted above, Huygens says plainly that propagation through the Ether seems to him the best explanation of the nature of light. He is not attempting to infer the existence of Ether, but saying that this is the best bet. (He thought it more likely that a wave could travel at the colossal speed of light than a particle.) Analogy is important in advancing knowledge, but as warranting suggestions rather than firm conclusions.

5

Other sources of failure are more serious. Elucidatory analogies can fail to elucidate, either because they are in their own right impossible to understand or because they are inappropriate.

Both failings can be found in successive passages in *The Problem of Pain* by C. S. Lewis. Lewis is trying to defend the traditional Christian doctrine of Hell, as a place of everlasting punishment. He admits that the concept is unpopular, but he believes that it is both true and just. He grapples with the following criticism:

Another objection turns on the apparent disproportion between eternal damnation and transitory sin. And if we think of eternity as a mere prolongation of time, it is disproportionate. But many would reject this idea of eternity. If we think of time as a line—which is a good image because the parts of time are successive and no two of them can coexist; i.e. there is no width in time, only length—we probably ought to think of eternity as a plane or even a solid. (Lewis (2), p. 111)

It is important to get straight the structure of the passage. The criticism is that Hell involves everlasting punishment for a finite lifespan of sinning, but the idea of punishment without a fixed term seems unfair. Lewis concedes this, so long as 'eternal' means what it is traditionally taken to mean. But he offers us an alternative account of 'eternal'. The trouble is understanding it. The usual comparison, as Lewis says, is between time and a line. Of a line running across the page we can say that one point is to the left of another, as we can say in time that one moment precedes another. Of any two different points on the line, one must be to the left of the other; of any two different moments in time, one must be before the other. Suppose now we compare eternity to a plane. Then time (presumably eternity is still some sort of time) will be measurable in two directions, corresponding to left/right, as before, and up/down. It will then be necessary to say of some events that one is before another in the first direction and after it in the second direction. I find it impossible to conceive of any happenings that one would want to describe in that way. It may be that after death experience will be so strange that this way of talking will convey something. But at present, in default of some more concrete account of what it would be like in actual experience if eternity were like a plane rather than an endless line, we can make nothing of the claim. Lewis has failed, I think, to elucidate a meaning of 'eternity' which supports his case. His reply to the objection comes to this, that perhaps eternal punishment can be seen to be legitimate, so long as 'eternal' is given a new meaning. He does not help us to see what that meaning is.

An example of an inappropriate analogy can be found in the same chapter of the same book. Lewis examines the criticism that it is unfair to condemn a sinner to everlasting punishment without giving him a second chance. He replies to this as follows:

I believe that if a million chances were likely to do good, they would be given. But a master often knows, when boys and parents do not, that it is really useless to send a boy in for a certain examination again. Finality must come some time, and it does not require a very robust faith to believe that omniscience knows when. (Lewis (2), p. 112)

The analogy is a dramatic rendering of a point which could have been made without reference to schoolboys, schoolmasters, or examinations. It is that God knows that there is no point in giving a sinner a second chance because the sinner would not improve his performance a second time round. The analogy does not help in making the point, though. Indeed, it rather interferes with it. It is true that sometimes a schoolmaster can know that it is useless to put a boy in for a certain examination again. These are the cases when the boy is incapable of passing the examination because it is beyond him. And these are the cases when we would not think it right to punish the boy for failure. If a boy is punished for failure it is normally at least partly in the belief that he can improve his performance sufficiently to pass. On the analogy, God would be like a schoolmaster who punishes a boy for failure, knowing that success was beyond him. In fact it is not God's foreknowledge that is the problem, but the reason for such a massive scale of punishment.

Exercises

How appropriate are the following analogies?

14.3 I am surprised to see the clergy making such heavy weather of reconciling the Bible story with modern scientific and historical knowledge. If you are the recipient of a message which cheers your heart and fortifies your soul, why should you worry about the shape and colour of the envelope, or whether it is stamped and dated?

14.4 In old age people get resistant to change, prone to treat new ideas as a threat. In youth, on the other hand, people tend to be rash and impetuous. And we can expect to find a somewhat similar thing among nations, the older ones resisting change, the younger tending towards rash adventurism.

6

When they are used to justify an action or recommendation, analogies can in effect beg the question. This is illustrated by the famous story concerning Menenius Agrippa. The patricians of Rome had levied new taxes on the plebeians, and a discontented and rebellious crowd gathered. Menenius Agrippa confronted them and recounted the fable of the Stomach and the Limbs:

The limbs were tired of working constantly for the good of the stomach, and one day decided to go on strike. But they soon found that they were harming themselves by refusing their help to the stomach. Deprived of the nourishment provided by the stomach, the limbs grew weak, and came to realize that every organ of the body has its part to play in the flourishing of the whole.

Agrippa pointed the moral:

Then patricians and plebeians must form one body, strengthened by the activity of all its members.

Thus silenced, the crowd dispersed.

Although the speech achieved its desired effect, logically it is not compelling. The comparison between the body and the state—the body politic—provides the basis for arguing that the plebeians should co-operate, accepting the larger tax-burden. To the extent that one endorses that conclusion, one will find the analogy acceptable. To the extent that one finds the conclusion uncongenial, one will not accept that the analogy is a good one. Karl Marx, predictably unsympathetic, commented that the Roman patricians, far from providing nourishment, withdrew nourishment from the rest.

Even if Agrippa was right in thinking that the tax was justified the analogy does not provide independent support for that conclusion.

The patricians are likened to the stomach because (1) they don't seem to do much, but (2) they are allegedly vital to the well-being of everyone else. There isn't any *independent* reason for likening them to the stomach rather than, say, to the appendix.

Our next case is rather more complicated but essentially no different:

It is none of our country's business how other countries are governed, any more than it is the shopkeeper's business to investigate the private morality of his customers.

Here the comparison is between on the one hand the shopkeeper selling to his customers and on the other hand a country trading with other nations. The analogy is familiar and obvious in some degree. Nations, like people, can amass wealth, spend beyond their means, and so on (although it should be said that these things do not always have the same implications for states as for individuals). The comparison between nation and trader is extended a little. A shopkeeper should not concern himself with the private morality of a customer, therefore a nation should not concern itself with the way another nation is governed. The private morality of a citizen is compared with the internal government of a nation.

We have first to ask what 'private' morality is. The distinction between public and private morality is roughly between those things which are felt to be the proper concern of the law and those actions which, however much we may disapprove of them, we feel to be best left to the individual to decide. So theft, vandalism, and violence are questions of public morality; while sexual relations between consenting adults, gambling, and non-rowdy drunkenness are usually regarded as questions of private morality. The distinction is by no means uncontroversial, but let us suppose for the sake of argument that it can be drawn along these lines.

If it can then a parallel distinction could be drawn for nations as follows: acts of war, treaty violation, and the like correspond to public transgressions, and how a government treats its own people corresponds to private morality. It is wrong for a shopkeeper to concern himself with the private morality of his customers. Hence it is wrong for a nation to concern itself with the internal government of other nations.

If we consider extreme cases it is hard to take the comparison seriously. Suppose some foreign government were systematically exterminating a minority racial group. It would not seem at all appropriate to say that it was none of our business what went on in that country. To that extent it does not seem appropriate to compare what a government does to its nationals with the private morality of a citizen. It appears to be far more like a matter of public morality, as it would be if a citizen were murdering his own children.

If we are thinking of less extreme cases the analogy may well strike one as appropriate. We may disapprove of benign dictatorships, or of governments dedicated to the propagation of a particular religion, or of strongly hierarchical societies, but not think that our government should try to change things: each nation must work out its own destiny. Again, though, the analogy is not doing any work. If we think in some particular case that non-interference is the correct policy then we will accept the comparison as appropriate in that case. If not, the comparison will seem inappropriate.

Exercises

Consider the following analogies carefully.

14.5 Freedom of speech is obviously vital in any civilized community. But when a community is at war, and the basis of its civilization threatened, then freedom of speech has to be curtailed. We are a nation at war, and the war is the more insidious for being fought with words rather than bombs. Our most cherished institutions, church, family, monarchy, and private property, are under open attack.
Section 5.

14.6 We can justify a system based on markets as essentially democratic. What determines how the resources of the country are distributed is how people vote to spend their money every day on the goods they purchase.
Section 5.

14.7 It is suggested that terrorist outrages are made worse by the prominence given to them in the news. This is rather like blaming weather forecasters for bad storms.
Section 5.

14.8 But while [the author] shows how affirmative action has been botched in practice, he never completes the book's main task: convincing the reader that all affirmative action programs should be junked. If something's not working right, after all, you don't throw it away. You fix it. (*Washington Post*)

15 Indirect Proofs

I

When we discussed proofs in Chapter 2, we said that a proof is a valid argument going from true and mutually acceptable premisses to a conclusion previously doubted or denied by the opponent. This is true of direct proofs, but we now have to consider a more complicated strategy sometimes known as that of indirect proof.

Suppose one wishes to prove that some statement, p, is false. It may be that one cannot find a direct proof of the falsity of p. Nevertheless the following procedure may be possible:

- Assume for the sake of argument that p is true.
- Find something which follows validly from p but which is obviously, and agreed to be, false.

  Now p cannot be true since it leads validly to a false conclusion, and we can never get validly from a true premiss to a false conclusion.
- Conclude that p is false.

We have given an indirect proof of not p. To set out the procedure slightly more formally, we introduce the sign $p\rfloor$ to indicate the assumption of p, and an arrow to show where it leads:

$$p \rfloor$$
$$\searrow$$
$$q$$
Not q
$\therefore$ Not p.

There are clear connections between this pattern of argument and the valid form of argument known as 'denying the consequent' which we looked at in Chapter 2:

If p then q
Not q
∴ Not p.

The difference between them is that in the first case we show a connection between p and q, while in the second case we *state* a connection. But in an ordinary, informal bit of prose the difference is often none too clear.

Let us flesh out the bones with a couple of examples—both, as it happens, taken from astronomy. Our first example concerns pulsars, star-like objects giving out radio pulses:

The conclusion that pulsars—or at least their radio transmitting regions—are also small comes from the sharpness of their pulses. Suppose a pulsar were as big as the Sun, and once a second it shook all over its surface and pumped radio noise into space. After a short interval, the radio noise from the nearest part of the Sun (the centre, as we see it) would arrive at the Earth. But the radio waves from the edge of the Sun, having an extra distance to travel, would arrive more than two seconds later. In other words, the signals from different parts of the Sun would smudge one another, and instead of sharp pulses there would be a continuous rumble of radio noise. From the rate and clarity of the pulses astronomers deduce that pulsars, or their active areas, must be a good deal smaller than the Earth. (Calder, pp. 28–9)

The author makes an initial assumption; for the sake of argument he assumes that pulsars are as big as the sun. Then follows a chain of argument designed to show that on this assumption we would not get sharp radio pulses from them. But we do get sharp signals from pulsars. Our initial assumption, then, since it leads by valid steps into error, must be wrong. The passage is a very clear example of an indirect proof.

Our second example comes from Galileo, who attempted to account for the fact that, at the new moon, as well as a bright crescent of light there is a dimmer light illuminating the remainder of the lunar surface—the 'old moon in the new moon's arms'. In fact the dim light is light reflected from the surface of the earth, as Galileo correctly surmised. What interests us is Galileo's argument against a rival theory.

Apparently it was suggested that the pale light emanates from the moon, rather than being reflected. Galileo argues against this as follows:

Some would say it is an inherent and natural light of the Moon's own . . . But statements of this sort are refuted and their falsity evinced with little difficulty. For if this kind of light were the Moon's own, or were contributed by the stars, the Moon would retain it and would display it particularly during eclipses, when it is left in an unusually dark sky. This is contradicted by experience . . . (Drake (tr.), pp. 42–3)

This is a direct proof 'denying the consequent'. Galileo does not assume or suppose for the sake of argument that the pale light is the moon's own; he does not go on to show the consequences of making that assumption. Rather, he simply asserts that if the light belongs intrinsically to the moon then it will show up more clearly in an eclipse. Thus he does not show a connection between these two facts: he states it.

The response is likely to be: Well, both get there in the end, so why fuss about which method is used to get there? In informal, ordinary arguments it may not be easily decided which of the two methods is being used, anyway. However, the point is that sometimes a bald 'if . . . then' statement will not be convincing. If the author in the first passage above had simply asserted that an object the size of the sun would not give a clear radio pulse, then we would either take his word for it or remain sceptical. Instead he offers us grounds for the claim. The more complex the chain of argument in the background the greater the need for bringing it out in an indirect proof.

Exercises

Consider the following indirect proof, taking the italicized phrase as introducing an assumption for consideration.

15.1 It is a widely held belief that people are perfectly happy living on social security benefits. *If that were right we would find very few people prepared to work for less than they could pick up on social security.* In fact we find a great many people working whom it would pay to stay at home. The layabout happy to scrounge off the state is something of a myth.

15.2 *Is the following argument of the same form as 15.1?*
Let us assume that the Universe is expanding. If it were then the spectrum of the furthest stars should show a shift towards red. This red shift is precisely what we do find. So we can assume that the Universe is in fact expanding.

2

Indirect proofs are sometimes known as proofs by *reductio ad absurdum* ('reducing to absurdity'). I prefer to reserve this term for a special form of indirect proof where it is shown that some statement, p, is false by showing that adopting it actually leads to a contradiction. The assumption leads not just to a false statement but to a self-contradictory one, and therefore must be rejected.

It is likely that the best examples of this will come from mathematics, and our example involves simple algebra. Suppose we are given that n^2 is even; can we show that n must be even as well? We argue by *reductio ad absurdum*:

- Assume the opposite of what we are trying to prove: assume that n is odd. That is to assume that n has the form $2k + 1$.
- Then n^2 has the form $(2k + 1) \times (2k + 1)$, which is $4k^2 + 4k + 1$.
- So n^2 is clearly odd (since it is divisible by two, remainder one).
- But we were given that n^2 is even. Our assumption that n is odd has led us into a contradiction, and must therefore be rejected.

Non-mathematical examples are less easy to find, but here is one quite straightforward example:

In the seventeenth century the French philosopher Descartes gave a new direction to philosophy. Trying to establish knowledge on a firm basis he set out to doubt everything that could possibly be doubted. Only what resisted all possible doubt could be truly known. In the course of expounding his programme of doubt, Descartes writes that he is prepared to follow his method whithersoever it leads, even if it leads him to maintain that the only thing he can know for certain is that nothing is known for certain.

Let us consider this claim, that it is known for certain that nothing is known for certain. Assume this to be the case:

- If it is known for certain that nothing is known for certain then it is true that nothing is known for certain (for whatever is known for certain must be true).
- If it is known for certain that nothing is known for certain, then something is known for certain (it is known for certain that nothing is known for certain).

The assumption leads to the claims that nothing is known for certain and that something is known for certain. It leads to a contradiction, and hence must be rejected. It cannot be known for certain that nothing is known for certain.

We showed, where $p =$ 'it is known for certain that nothing is known for certain' and $q =$ 'nothing is known for certain':

$$p \dashv \atop \searrow \atop q \qquad \text{and} \qquad p \dashv \atop \searrow \atop \text{Not } q.$$

Putting both together gives:

$$p \dashv \atop \searrow \atop q \text{ and Not } q.$$

But we cannot accept a contradiction or anything which leads to a contradiction. So p must be rejected:

$$p \dashv \atop \searrow \atop q \text{ and Not } q \atop \therefore \text{Not } p.$$

A more immediate form of *reductio ad absurdum* is sometimes possible. Its lynchpin is that any assumption which leads to its own negation must be given up; in symbols:

$$p \dashv \atop \searrow \atop \text{Not } p \atop \therefore \text{Not } p.$$

Consider the following claim:

Nothing in this book is true.

If nothing in the book is true then at least one thing in the book, the claim above that this is the case, is true. So it cannot be that nothing in the book is true.

What leads to its own negation must be surrendered. For if we insisted on holding it as true we should be committed to holding it and its negation; our beliefs would be inconsistent.

Exercises

15.3 *Given that* n^2 *is odd, show by reductio ad absurdum that* n *is also odd.*
     Section 2.

15.4 'Martians never tell the truth, and I am a Martian.'
     What follows?

3

A statement, *p*, can occur in different ways according to context. It can be:

(a) asserted straightforwardly;
(b) asserted cautiously ('Probably . . .');
(c) put forward as an assumption to see where the argument leads;
(d) uttered as part of a conditional statement ('If . . .').

In the first two cases we are committed to the truth of the statement, *p*, albeit in different degrees. In (c) there is no commitment, no sense in which the person putting *p* forward has lent authority to the claim. In (d), *p* is not being asserted at all, and may indeed be uttered in the full conviction of its falsity. 'If smoking's good for you then I'm a Dutchman'—here the statement 'smoking's good for you' is not advanced as true, and in essence the claim is being made that smoking is *not* good for you.

The different ways in which *p* can occur help to make clear some otherwise puzzling features of conditional statements.

What is the relation between the following two statements?

• If it rains then the match will be cancelled

and

• If it rains then the match will not be cancelled.

The natural instinct is to say that the two are flatly contradictory. Yet if we symbolize them in the usual way we have respectively:

• If p then q

and

• If p then not q.

These are not contradictory. (The contradictory of 'If p then q' is 'It is not the case that if p then q.')

First, consider the occurrence of p, not in mode (d) but in mode (c). Given

p ↓ and p ↓
q . Not q.

What should we conclude? Putting the two together, we see that p leads to q and not q. Since p yields a contradiction, and a contradiction cannot be tolerated, p must be denied. The same is true when the two occurrences of p are in mode (d) rather than (c) above. The two claims, 'If p then q' and 'If p then not q', can be true together, but together they rule out p. In the example we take it for granted that rain cannot be ruled out. We build in to the example more than we are strictly given. That accounts for the discrepancy between our instincts and what logic dictates.

Exercise

15.5 *The detective spoke*:

We know that just one of the three, Austin, Brown, or Chambers is guilty. We also know that Brown gives Chambers a good alibi; so if Brown is innocent then Chambers is innocent. This is all we need to establish the guilt of Austin. Suppose for a minute that Austin is not guilty. Then we're left with a contradiction: that if Brown is innocent then Chambers is innocent, and if Brown is innocent then Chambers is guilty—they can't all be innocent. So the supposition that Austin is innocent leads us into a contradiction. So we must conclude that Austin is guilty.

Does it follow? What can we say about Chambers?

4

We saw earlier that the following form of argument is valid:

$$p$$
$$\downarrow$$
$$\text{Not } p$$
$$\therefore \text{Not } p.$$

However, what if one could show of some statement both that it and its negation each led to their own denial? Suppose we could show, that is, that both:

$$p \qquad\qquad \text{Not } p$$
$$\downarrow \qquad\qquad \downarrow$$
$$\text{Not } p \quad \text{and} \quad p$$
$$\therefore \text{Not } p \qquad \therefore p \,(= \text{Not not } p).$$

In such a case we would be committed to holding both p and 'not p'. By the first stage we would be committed to holding 'not p' and by the second stage we would be committed to holding p.

There are examples of alleged contradictions established in this fashion. Perhaps the clearest example is the riddle of the village barber.

There is a barber in a village who shaves all the men and only the men who do not shave themselves. The riddle is, Does the barber shave himself?

- Suppose the barber does shave himself. Then, since he shaves only those who do not shave themselves, it follows that he does not shave himself.
- Suppose, on the other hand, he does not shave himself. Then, since he shaves *all* those who do not shave themselves, it follows that he does shave himself.

If our barber shaves himself then he doesn't, and if he doesn't then he does. A contradiction indeed. But how do we avoid these snares, and what is the answer to the riddle?

It seems clear that as defined the barber cannot exist. So long as the barber is not himself counted as amongst the men in the village, then there can be a barber who shaves all those and only those who do not shave themselves. But if that qualification is not made then the barber is effectively defined out of existence: nothing could fulfil the definition, any more than a thing could fulfil the description 'round square'.

The paradox may appear trivial. But paradoxes similar to that of the barber have assumed considerable importance in the philosophy of mathematics this century—see, for example, chapter 7 of Bertrand Russell's *My Philosophical Development*.

5

The final example of an attempt to derive a contradiction, held to be inherent in our self-reflective reasoning, brings in an argument from the writings of the theologian Reinhold Niebuhr, alleging that human thought about human nature is irretrievably shot through with contradictions:

[If man takes his uniqueness for granted] he is immediately involved in questions and contradictions on the problem of his virtue. If he believes himself to be essentially good and attributes the admitted evils of human history to specific social and historical causes, he involves himself in begging the question; for all these specific historical causes of evil are revealed, upon close analysis, to be no more than particular consequences and historical configurations of evil tendencies in man himself. They cannot be understood at all if a capacity for, and inclination towards, evil are not presupposed. If, on the other hand, man comes to pessimistic conclusions about himself, his capacity for such judgements would seem to negate the content of the judgements. How can man be 'essentially' evil if he knows himself to be so? (Niebuhr, vol. i, pp. 1–2)

The passage is a complicated one, having arguments within arguments. The only way of making sense of something like this is to begin with the tediously familiar question, What is the passage aiming to show? The conclusion that Niebuhr is trying to establish comes in the first sentence: that man is involved in contradictions on the question of his virtue. The rest of the passage is taken up with spelling out the contradictions.

There are two sub-arguments, one beginning from the assumption that man is essentially good, the other that he believes himself essentially evil ('If, on the other hand, man comes to pessimistic conclusions about himself'). Perhaps it would be simpler to begin with the latter.

The argument is that a completely evil being would not judge itself to be evil. Presumably the argument turns on the idea that anyone who judges himself to be evil makes an unfavourable judgement about himself; and a thoroughly evil being would be wholly satisfied with his own character.

The other sub-argument begins from the assumption that man regards himself as essentially good. But any account of the origin of the evil in man which blames it on, say, social conditions will have left unaccounted for an evil tendency in man to exploit those social conditions. So man cannot be essentially good.

Each of the judgements, then, 'Man is essentially evil' and 'Man is essentially good', is untenable. If we believe that we are good then we cannot account for the evil in the world; while if we believe that we are evil then the mere fact that we believe it shows it is not so. Surely we must be one or the other; yet neither belief is really tenable—hence, it is claimed, a contradiction of the Barber type.

The main weakness of the argument seems to me to lie in the alternative—either we believe ourselves to be essentially good or we believe ourselves to be essentially evil. Niebuhr implies that so long as we think at all about the nature of man we must choose between these alternatives. But they are not exhaustive alternatives, and we can reject them both. This is not obvious, because we are inclined to suppose that the choice lies between saying that man is 'on the whole' good and saying that he is 'on the whole' bad. Really it is not this at all. What Niebuhr presents is the choice between saying that man is 'entirely' good and that he is 'entirely' bad. Thus man is not essentially good if he has an inclination towards evil; and he is not essentially evil if he has self-knowledge. But there is a lot of territory between these extremes. People may have inclinations towards evil which they manage largely to hold in check—if they are partly but not wholly good; and people may judge themselves truly to be very bad though not perhaps completely evil.

Exercises

15.6 It is often said that if there is unemployment then businessmen are happy. There is a lot of unemployment now, but the business world is not in the least happy about it. So the generalization is just not true.
   What is the assumption that is argued against? How does the argument against it go? Chapter 3, section 6.

15.7 *A barber shaves only those (but not necessarily all those) who do not shave themselves. Does he shave himself?*
   Section 2, end.

15.8 Belief in free will is an illusion. In every situation that we come across we are already committed, by heredity and by the habits of past experience, to the way we will act. But because we know that behaviour is determined we can learn how to alter it as a matter of deliberate policy.
   Section 2.

16 Authority and Repute

Light travels at 300,000 kilometres a second. Einstein said so.

Above is an appeal to authority. To appeal to authority is to offer in justification of a claim the fact that an acknowledged expert advanced or supported (and, if living, still supports) that claim. Such appeals are often necessary, despite the fact that throughout the history of philosophy they have been regarded at times with deep suspicion. Unless we are geniuses—even if we are geniuses—we have to rely on facts which we have not personally established or verified. We accept as truths about physics, for example, the claims which we read in books written by physicists. If in doubt we check one author against another. What we can very rarely do is dispute with an authority on his own subject, unless we have read up corners of that subject. Even then we will have taken for granted the work of past generations of scholars, and we will not have reduplicated crucial experiments. The experts themselves are in the same position; they, too, take a great number of facts on trust (as Einstein did the measured velocity of light).

Scepticism about the correctness of appeals to authority is understandable when one considers how much the history of scientific thought was hampered during the Renaissance by the immense prestige of Aristotle. The deference which his writings were accorded even prevented appeal to experiment because orthodox opinion was so convinced that the truth was already known. Clearly that is unreasonable; in the last resort the test of experience is vital. What had happened, if the popular histories are correct, was that Aristotle's writings had become almost holy writ and an obstacle to truth.

His opinion had become decisive, rather than simply worthy of respect.

That kind of deference seems today archaic and unattractive. But there persists a shadowy form of it which is very much alive and unlikely to appear ridiculous. This attitude manifests itself in the notion of the wise individual, the person whose opinion on any subject must be valuable. Against this I would say that outside his or her subject an authority loses authority. Eminence in one subject is not evidence of omnicompetence. A fine physicist may or may not be a sound historian. Prestige built up in one area cannot legitimately be transferred to an area which is unrelated.

There is implicit in the remarks above a policy or principle: that in the absence of other information we should go along with established voices in a field, we should give acceptance to the consensus of the experts. This is a policy which, like any other, can lead to error. It is a cautious, conservative policy, which will minimize mistakes but cannot eliminate them. It may be that the consensus among the relevant authorities is that one man's theories are 'wild' and the evidence for them slender; yet the academic outsider may on this occasion romp home ahead of the field. Or it may be that the experts are on occasion gullible, and accept a theory without submitting it to proper examination. The work of Sir Cyril Burt on the degree to which intelligence is inherited was, it now seems, too readily accepted by psychologists. Experts can be presumed to have both expertise and a critical attitude to new claims, but in this case the experts seem to have failed.

Nevertheless, the policy of putting trust in the consensus of authority is rational; the layperson is not in any position to adjudicate on theoretical novelty without having mastered theoretical orthodoxy, and betting on outsiders is in the long run a recipe for losing. If the authorities are sceptical about some new, exciting theory—ley lines, pyramid-building spacemen, telepathic plants—their scepticism is probably, though not invariably, justified.

The matter becomes more complicated when expert opinion is sought as a guide to policy rather than to truth. For on occasion it might be entirely reasonable to act on an outside chance of something coming to pass. Suppose, for example, expert opinion is unanimous that there is a reasonable chance of finding oil off the Irish coast; it is not probable that oil will be found, but there is some chance of discovering it, and if it is found the rewards to the economy will be great. In such a case, assuming a strong economy to be desirable, the sensible thing to do would be to act on the improbable assumption that oil is present. One has to balance the probability of exploration being in vain—with all the costs in time and money that this entails—against the high rewards if oil turns out to be present after all.

The most extreme case in which the pursuit of long odds is to be commended is when some disaster is predicted as inevitable. While it would be silly to ignore the consensus of expert opinion, it would not be silly to refuse to accept the inevitability of what was forecast, just so long as any course of action seemed to offer any hope, however remote, of averting it. Any way out, no matter how desperate, is better than doing nothing. To believe that the experts might be wrong is to clutch at straws; but if there is nothing else to hand a drowning man is fully justified in clutching at straws. So, for example, the person who refuses to accept reputable medical opinion that his or her illness is terminal cannot be blamed for turning to less reputable opinion. The costs of treatment in time and money will not weight heavily if there seems no better use to put them to, and if the fringe medicine fails one will not be any the worse off. (Of course, out of the desperation of the very ill comes a host of opportunities for swindlers and cranks to cash in. A market in medicine needs very strict control, because a bargain struck between a desperate individual and one with nothing to lose is too likely to favour the latter disproportionately.)

2

Suspicion of appeals to authority in general is also given credence by the fact that in some areas it seems inappropriate to appeal to authority at all. Morality seems to be such an area. For all of us there are occasions when we are unsure how we ought to act. Sometimes these cases will resolve themselves into questions of consequences; what will the probable effects of alternative course of action be? There may be people particularly good at answering this kind of question because they have more relevant information than most of us. They will not be moral authorities, but authorities in the relevant areas of expertise: economic, psychological, and so on. If, for example, we want to know whether hanging is a deterrent to would-be murderers there are criminologists whose statements on the matter can be accepted as authoritative: they have access to the relevant statistics here and abroad. They can answer the factual question we put to them. But only if we have decided already that the question of the rightness or wrongness of capital punishment turns on whether or not it is a deterrent does this answer the question whether capital punishment is justified. As criminologists they may be able to tell us whether it deters, but no more.

We might seek moral experts, who would attempt to apply to particular cases general moral principles and techniques, rather as mathematicians apply general principles and techniques to the solution of mathematical problems. However, there is no consensus about what techniques and principles should apply in general to morality. Different societies, religions, and philosophies advance different principles for the guidance of actions. Ethical codes vary, from those which put the emphasis on warrior virtues to those which demand complete pacifism from their advocates; from those which assert the inalienable rights of property to those which assert that property is theft. Adherents of a moral code may treat some person as an expert or authority in moral matters—whether priest, rabbi, elder, or guru. But their authority is acknowledged only within their code. When the variety of codes is taken into account, it becomes less clear that there are moral experts comparable to experts in science and mathematics. Moreover, an appeal to moral authority could be used to avoid serious thought about moral questions. The relationship between authority and conscience would need to be considered.

Exercises

How legitimate are the following?

16.1 As Descartes said, appeals to authority are never really reliable.

16.2 That so brilliant a scientist as Einstein advocated pacifism is surely an indication that it is the course which politicians should pursue.

3

We have have seen that appeals to authority can be used to bolster one's case; legitimately by showing the basis of a claim, or illegitimately by falsely attaching prestige to an opinion. The other side of the coin is the attempt to refute an opponent's case by denigrating the opponent. Traditionally this is known as arguing *ad hominem* ('at the man'). Like appeals to authority, such attacks are sometimes justified. For example, in the history of psychical research several of those who have claimed extraordinary powers have at some time been detected in cheating. R. H. Thouless describes in *Experimental Psychical Research* how towards the end of the nineteenth century two sisters called Creery claimed powers of thought transference, involving card-calling. It was discovered upon investigation of these claims that occasionally the one sister signalled to the other enabling her to know which card had been turned up. The sisters confessed to cheating but subsequently claimed that they had obtained their most successful results by fair means. They were not believed, and not really surprisingly. Here is a case where an argument *ad hominem*, that the Creery sisters are known to have sometimes practised fraud, would seem to cast real doubt on their claim to have genuine extra-sensory powers.

A common use of *ad hominem* argument is where a critic is met by the response, 'You, too.' Consider that much replayed occasion when the government of the day raises taxes and the opposition howls its disapproval. It is surely reasonable for a government to point it out if the opposition have also raised taxes in the recent past. It casts doubts on the sincerity of the disapproval if those who disapprove have only recently done the same themselves.

On the other hand, such *ad hominem* arguments can be purely diversionary and seem at best a preliminary shot. If the opposition is arguing a case against a raise in taxes then a reminder of their own past actions is not an answer to their criticisms. They may reply that they were wrong before (a rare admission in politics), or they may try to show that circumstances have changed since. Either way the *ad hominem* argument is bypassed and becomes irrelevant.

The background of the speaker can obviously play a part in determining how much credence we give his claim. Many branches of industry as well as firms within those branches employ spokesmen on their behalf. The pronouncements of these people on the product or industry in question inevitably raise suspicions once their connections become known. They are not impartial; they have a vested interest in extolling the efficiency or environmental harmlessness of their industry, or the novelty or range of their products. This does not mean that we can discount their statements automatically. Paid spokesmen may be telling us untruths or (more likely) misleading us in what they leave out; but they may not. We are more suspicious of what the paid spokesman tells us. The authority with which he speaks is weakened, and we will be more inclined to seek confirmation of his claims from other sources. Yet this is only the most obvious source of doubt. People's enthusiasms extend beyond their direct source of income, and we cannot suppose that an economist arguing the case for the railways, for example, is not swayed by a strong antipathy towards cars.

What makes *ad hominem* arguments dangerous is that they can serve to prevent the proper examination of a claim. Just as the prestige attaching to Aristotle's name meant that at one time no critic of Aristotle could get a fair hearing, so the opprobrium attaching to certain speakers because of their commitments (industrial, political, etc.) may mean that nothing they say will get a fair hearing either. We have to walk a fine line between gullibility and a closed mind, trying to detect partisanship, but not letting suspicion of the arguer obstruct the fair assessment of the case.

4

The most extreme form of argument *ad hominem* is to attack the motives of a speaker simply because of the views which are being advanced. For example:

Certainly we have to suspect the true aims of all those who offer . . . programmes of wholesale and irreversible social change. For the more extensive and irreversible such a programme is, the more difficult or even impossible it must become, either to determine how far it is actually achieving its stated objectives, or to make the corrections required by discoveries of where and how far it is in fact falling short. (Flew, p. 116)

That is to say, that because wholesale changes are difficult to monitor, we must suspect the motives of anyone who advocates them. Now when someone tells us what ends he thinks wholesale changes will bring about, why should we immediately doubt his sincerity? True, there would be a problem in monitoring widespread changes to see how far they actually achieve their ends. But perhaps the advocate of wholesale change has never even considered that problem; or perhaps he has considered it and believes (rightly or wrongly) that it can be solved. He may be naïve or mistaken rather than insincere. There is no reason to suppose in advance that the radical reformer has some sinister aim which is being concealed from us. That way lies political paranoia.

Exercises

How acceptable are the following arguments 'ad hominem'?

16.3 It is perhaps significant that among those who advocate greater worker participation in British industry are a number of Communists, whose commitment to this country and its industrial system is very slight.

16.4 How seriously can we take the economic theories of a man who in the sixties was a confirmed Keynesian, in the seventies a staunch monetarist, and who now tells us that only a programme of zero growth and import controls can save the country?

5

So far in this chapter we have considered appeals to authority and attempts to discredit an opponent (even, as in the last example, attempts to discredit his authorities). We must not forget that the speaker himself can carry authority. His qualifications to speak on a subject may be known to his audience, and if not there is no harm in his informing them. We are all acquainted with speakers who are quick to remind us of their authority to discourse on the topic to hand:

Speaking as one who has taught for many years at one of our oldest universities, I think I can modestly venture the opinion that . . .

This rather hackneyed opening gambit is not in itself wrong. The background information may be known already or irrelevant to the point at issue, but that is all. There is, however, the familiar danger that the audience will respond uncritically to what is said, being impressed by who is saying it. To some extent the danger is always present. Even if a speaker lacks particular authority in some areas and claims none, to the extent that he is prepared to speak out and seems relaxed and confident he will suggest authority. The manner can override the matter, even when the matter is slight.

The following argument against the British Race Relations Act says little, but can sound impressive if spoken boldly:

It is foolish to assume that some act of Parliament can change the way that people think; not so. It is naïve in the extreme to suppose that mere legislation can override attitudes. And when we talk of freedom of speech we must remember that that includes not only the freedom to pay people compliments and sing their praises. It must also include the freedom to attack and insult them. Freedom is one and indivisible.

Here we have a doubtful claim (that legislation can never change attitudes) advanced as if it were self-evident, and repeated rather than defended. Then the main question is begged: why must freedom of speech include the freedom to attack and insult on racial grounds? The reason offered, that freedom is one and indivisible, though at first glance it seems like a factual claim, is really a claim about how we ought to act, and adds nothing. Nevertheless, the passage may be made to sound weighty and carefully thought out.

Here we cross the boundary which divides logic—the study of good and bad argument—from rhetoric—the study of success and failure in argument. The two do not always match. The outcome of an argument will often depend on how well it is presented, both when trying to persuade an individual and perhaps even more when arguing a case to a committee or before an audience. Arguments can be 'sold', rather like encyclopaedias; and the personality of the sales-man is as important in the one case as in the other.

An argument in cold print can be analysed in a detached way because it is an argument held in suspension; there is no pressure of time and less emotional charge than in debate or conversation where, if you cannot see at once what is wrong, the moment for challenge is gone. An emotional atmosphere creates pressure, and so do one's own emotions—anger at the line the opponent is taking, fear of being made to look foolish in opposing it, irritation at being unable to formulate properly what one wants to say. Most people (I include myself) are probably not very good at spotting faulty reasoning in conversation or discussion. Or, to be more precise, they may have a shrewd idea when a mistake has been made but need time to detect just what the mistake is. Added to this is the difficulty of concen-trating on the details of an opponent's reasoning rather than simply reacting to the issues raised, for or against. It is difficult to remain detached and dispassionate when emotions are running high. One cannot be surprised that discussions often fail to go to the heart of the disagreement, and that the presentation of a case counts for so much.

The value of elementary logic is that by encouraging a concen-tration on validity and invalidity, on identifying conclusions and the premises they rest on, it can teach us to listen better, even if we are not blessed with razor-sharp mental reflexes. We will get attuned to listening for the important things. There may be supplementary techniques which can help us to overcome the aura of prestige attach-ing to a speaker, whether by virtue of his academic qualification or of a confident manner. R. H. Thouless suggests at one point in *Straight and Crooked Thinking* that since much of the prestige of a speaker depends on the clothes he is wearing we should try always to deflate that prestige in our minds by picturing the speaker without his clothes. Entertaining as it may prove, the obvious objection to this supplementary technique is that it distracts attention from what the speaker is saying. More prosaically, the really important trick is to listen for the argument, the reasoned case behind the verbal flourishes. The question we ought to be pondering is, Would this argument, would these reasons, convince the sceptic? At the time the task of disentangling the thought from the wrappings may be one which fully occupies our attention, so that we cannot think critically. That is no matter. We can recall the argument and think about it critically at our leisure. Having made it our business to listen for the argument, we will find it easy to recall. And I am convinced that listening for the argument is the single most important way of dealing with any tendency to be overawed by the prestige, manner, or verbal facility of the speaker. In many cases the fine wrappings will be found to conceal banal thoughts ill-defended; but if, after all, these skills contribute to the presentation of a well-argued case, our respect will be thoroughly deserved.

6

Traditionally lists of logical fallacies included some which were no more than rhetorical tricks. For example, the argument *ad populum* ('to the people') and the argument *ad misericordiam* ('to pity') were appeals to popular prejudice and compassion, respectively. I will not attempt to explore rhetorical techniques in any detail. What seems to me the case is that they often rely on the fact that people are affected by a desire to conform.

When a speaker addresses his audience with the words 'We here tonight can surely agree . . .' there is the suggestion that speaker and audience form a group and are at one. Anyone who disagrees risks being the outsider. This can generate a powerful pressure inhibiting criticism in some circumstances. It seems likely that a speaker who is skilful at employing words can create a rapport between himself and his audience and inhibit those who dissent from expressing their doubts or even from formulating them clearly to themselves.

Exercises

Assess:

16.5 The tone of the book is one of violent abuse, characterized by frenzied attacks on his opponents and extremity of language. All of which leads me to conclude that the underlying argument is thin. If there is a case to be made it can be made calmly; but this author simply antagonizes the reader.

16.6 Why do our adversaries argue for drab equality all the time? The simple answer is that they are full of envy for those who have more than themselves.

17 Practical Reasoning

It is tempting to head this chapter 'Political Ploys', although that would be to use 'political' in a broad sense. There is a lot of argumentation directed towards getting things done or preventing things getting done. It is often difficult to know how to argue directly for or against a proposal; its consequences may be not clear-cut or even when clear-cut not clearly good or bad. And in the welter of words surrounding a proposal there are certain bad arguments which tend to recur, and which deserve a close examination. They are heard in debating chambers, heard on the radio, and read in newspapers. Few of these arguments are subtle, but their popularity suggests that they are capable of persuading people nevertheless.

Some bad arguments for change are considered first, then a larger group of arguments opposing change or favouring delay, and finally arguments concerned with doing the right thing, whether or not it involves change.

I

One argument, if indeed it can be called an argument, in favour of change is simply to brand the change 'progress'. We saw in Chapter 6 that Muggeridge and Russell both defined 'progress' as 'desirable change'. That fits with the dictionary definition, 'improvement'. If this is how we define 'progress', then it is simply begging the question to describe a contentious change as progress. For some people, however, 'progress' suggests little more than novelty, particularly technological novelty. For example, those who are critical of supersonic transport are sometimes told, 'Well, that's progress.' It is undoubtedly novelty. Whether or not it is a desirable novelty is precisely what the argument is about. Failure to separate the correct meaning from the popular usage can make it seem as though anything new is desirable. Regardless of what the advertisers would have us believe, this is not self-evidently so.

The identification of novelty with progress often goes along with a tendency to regard criticisms of a novelty as unworthy of serious examination. The argument often goes like this:

There were people who objected to trains. There were people who objected to aeroplanes. Every invention beneficial to mankind has had its critics. No doubt somebody objected to the wheel. So those who object to Concorde (atomic power plants, genetic engineering, etc.) should think again.

It is tempting to see the argument as embodying a simple fallacy:

All beneficial inventions were opposed. Concorde is opposed. Therefore Concorde is a beneficial invention.

It may be, however, that this is to misinterpret the case that is being put forward. Perhaps the argument relies on the principle that the future resembles the past. Because in the past many critics have been unnecessarily alarmist, they are probably just being alarmist in this case too. Even at best, this is a dangerous argument because it encourages us to turn a deaf ear to the case the critics are making. The only safe course is to treat each criticism on its merits. Even if other critics have been wrong in the past we cannot be confident that these critics are wrong now.

2

A second argument in favour of change starts from dissatisfaction with the *status quo*:

Since one man has to work overtime to earn £95, and another man with the same commitments gets £98 from the state for doing nothing, it is clear that social security payments are just too high.

This kind of argument might be called the 'one-way fallacy'. It goes from the premiss that there is something wrong with the *status quo*—

in this case it is wrong that a person who is not working gets more than one who is—to the conclusion that the man who is not working ought to receive less. It would be equally possible to argue from the same premiss that the man who is working should receive more. It is wrong to assume that there is only one way of righting the present wrong; hence the nickname, the 'one-way fallacy'. To repeat: from the premiss that some people out of work receive more than some people in work (assuming this to be the case) we cannot immediately conclude either that those in work are underpaid or that those out of work are overpaid. The present wrong could be righted in more than one way, and which way requires further consideration.

The one-way fallacy occurs surprisingly often. During the Vietnam war America committed troops and arms, but periodically found herself unable to contain the Communists. According to one's source, the response varied. The 'hawks' argued: 'We are failing to contain the Vietcong, so we should commit more troops and arms.' The 'doves' argued: 'We are failing to contain the Vietcong, so we should admit defeat and withdraw.' In each case the inference was too quick. Both sides agreed that the *status quo* was thoroughly unsatisfactory. The mistake was to assume that agreement thus far led naturally to the one obvious way of proceeding. There was no one obvious way of proceeding. There is normally more than one way of transforming a present wrong. The argument is about which is the best way.

3

The third and last argument in favour of change that I shall consider is the argument that everyone is doing it; so that if we do not do it we'll be out of step. At first glance this is a very weak basis for any proposal, for why assume initially that there is any obligation to march in step?

Perhaps the appeal depends in some measure upon the unspoken fear that not to change is to be left behind. But this in turn relies on a tacit assumption that the change in question represents progress. As we saw, this is normally an assumption that needs arguing for.

Isn't there, though, a desire for conformity? Perhaps the appeal to keep in step is not so silly, because people who are out of step feel uncomfortable or even unhappy. Consider fashion in clothes. People can feel so uneasy at not conforming that they will buy clothes they do not need or even much care for, simply to be in fashion. Indeed, high costs are involved and the only benefit obtained is the knowledge that one is wearing the sort of thing that everyone else is wearing.

The difference between group and individual is important in this case. An individual who is out of step with other members of the group is likely to feel some pressure to conform. But the urge to conform is less likely to motivate a group to fall into line with other groups. Constrast the position of an individual following fashion with that of a country contemplating changing its monetary system—Britain and the other EC countries moving towards a common currency. Exporters favour it because it will save time and money; apart from that there is little pressure for change. People within a community who do not conform in some matter are constantly made aware of it; but people in a community which has its own way of doing things belong within that community and need not be constantly aware that its way of doing things is not the way of others. Even if they are aware, they may take pride in belonging to a distinctive group.

The argument that 'we'—a group—must keep in step is, then, a weak one. There is rarely a need to conform to the practice of others, and very often little pressure to do so.

Exercise

Assess the following arguments:

17.1 There is no doubt that if we support this measure we will be acting in accordance with the trend of history. There has been a steady growth in home ownership over the years, and this measure will help to consolidate that growth.

17.2 Everybody admits that the health service needed reform. We have carried out a programme of far-reaching reform. But still our opponents complain. Nothing satisfies them.

17.3 The case for the present 'welfare reform' is that, despite many flaws, it would disrupt the existing system . . . [We] may discover what works and what doesn't. (*Washington Post*) Section 2

4

Turning now to arguments against change, the first consists in representing the proposed change as the first step on a slippery slope. Plainly this is an appeal to analogy, and obviously the comparison will in no way deter people from change unless they see the bottom of the slope as bad. This is the first test of the analogy. Those who cite the slippery slope are saying, essentially: 'If you agree to this change then you will be unable to deny that further change, which you assuredly do not want.'

Thus spelled out, the claim looks at first sight dubious. One is inclined to say that if the group or individual responsible for making decisions wishes to permit the first change but not further changes then only the first change will occur. If, for example, a dictator or an elected government wishes to give an allowance for a first child but not for subsequent children, there is no reason why that should not come about. There is no inexorable force equivalent to gravity, driving the legislators on to extend the measure to all children. The slippery slope is really a stairway: we can descend just as far as we like and stop just where we want.

The response is too facile, however. It can happen that making a change generates pressure for further change. Let us suppose that Parliament is poised to give the police a large pay rise. If it does, it is clear that other workers will regard themselves as unfairly treated and demand large pay rises too. It may be that the government would be unable to resist these further demands although it regarded them as highly undesirable. In this case giving the police a rise would be describable appropriately as the first step on a slippery slope. Whether or not a change is so describable will depend on whether making it will generate uncontainable pressures for further change, and whether that change is undesirable. If a change will not generate pressures for more change then there is a stairway rather than a slope; and, however odd or irrational a stopping-place looks, there is no necessity for any further shift.

The disappointing thing is that the analogy of the slippery slope often goes unchallenged. Those who use the analogy should be prepared to support it: to say in clear terms why agreement to the change will mobilize irresistible pressure for more change of an undesirable sort.

5

This change is not necessary. There is no demand for it.

So runs an objection to change which is frequently heard and which was discussed in *The Book of Fallacies* by Jeremy Bentham in the early nineteenth century. Bentham analyses the argument in these words:

The argument amounts to this: nobody complains, therefore nobody suffers. It amounts to a veto on all measures of precaution or prevention and goes to establish a maxim in legislation, directly opposed to the most ordinary prudence of common life;—it enjoins us to build no parapets to a bridge till the number of accidents has raised an universal clamour. (Bentham, pp. 190–1)

We must be cautious about this analysis, because in some circumstances the absence of demand for a change is crucial. Suppose that the proposal is to repaint all city corporation buses some new and hopefully more attractive colour. It may be that there is no demand for a change in colour, and that the change will cost money. It is fair enough to cite the lack of demand as a very important consideration, and even an overriding one.

However, when a proposal is made to alleviate undoubted difficulties and bring about clear improvements, Bentham's criticisms seem to me well merited. People will sometimes not complain, because they are unhopeful that their complaints will be attended to, or because they have learned to take for granted things which they would want altered if they saw an opportunity to change them.

Absence of complaint is not always good evidence for the absence of just cause for complaint. People are sometimes apathetic; that may be regrettable, but it is understandable. Complaining takes time and effort, and involves the risk of failure, which can be more upsetting than a placid acceptance of one's lot. So a decision-maker who works solely to the principle 'no complaint—no necessity for change', as well as ruling out acts of legislative foresight, disregards the possibility that people suffer in silence. Either he overlooks it or he believes (implausibly) that only changes wrung from a government are desirable.

One refinement of the principle which makes it even more conservative, but which Bentham did not consider, runs as follows:

Either this proposed change is unnecessary because none demands it, or it is undesirable because to bow to clamour is a sign of weakness.

Either there is clamour for change or there is not. Whichever is the case, any legislator who argues in the manner above is determined not to bring about change. That degree of intransigence can be dangerous.

A final comment on this section. All the arguments expressed have been put in terms of whether change is necessary rather than whether it is desirable. That suggests a built-in reluctance to disturb the *status quo*. This talk contrasts sharply with that of those who tend to talk of change in terms of 'progress'. Contrasting attitudes to change are reflected in contrasting vocabularies.

6

Why disturb a system that we all know works, in pursuit of something which may be all very well in theory but which probably won't work out in practice?

This pragmatic appeal strikes a responsive chord in all of us at times. We all know that schemes which look promising can come unstuck. But there are a couple of points about this argument which should give us pause.

The first is the vagueness of the claim that the present system 'works'. We all know what it is for a machine to work, because there is a clear opposite; we know what it is for the machine not to work. But to say 'Our way of doing things works' is really to say nothing. If it did not work it would not be a way of doing things. The question really is how well a way of doing things achieves its purposes, and whether those ends which it achieves are the ends we should be aiming at. The claim that the present system works can make it seem as though the question of ends is settled in advance, as though we all agreed what ends we are aiming at.

The second problem in the example above is that if a scheme will probably not work in practice then it is not all right in theory. A scheme may look perfectly all right in theory, yet in practice throw up all sorts of unsuspected problems. But if we are entitled to assert that it will 'probably' fail in practice then there must be some grounds for our suspicions. We must have some reason for supposing that it will prove not to work, and this will be a reason for suspecting that it is not satisfactory in theory. The argument is a lazy man's approach—an attempt to plant seeds of doubt about the measure without providing any grounds for doubt.

7

Attempts are sometimes made to forestall action to put right a wrong by pointing out that there are greater wrongs to which the critic might be directing his or her attention. This is a version of the *ad hominem* argument—the appeal to the 'greater evil'.

An example:

Must you continue to publish these venomous letters from people complaining about dogs? Fouling pavements is nothing compared to the way man is fouling the earth, seas, and beaches with his sewage. Nobody complains about the dirty habits of other humans.

There is some overstatement in the complaint, since not all of the critics are unconcerned about human pollution. But some are, and the complaint is that they are being unselective in their target. Even if this is a fault in the critics, however, it does not show their complaint to be unfounded. It shows that some other problem should be attacked as well as, not instead of, the one they are concerned with. Quite possibly the attack on the one problem would not compete in any way with the attack on the other; if this is the case the two campaigns can proceed together. Even if the two campaigns would compete (for funds, say), it could well be legitimate to tackle the lesser evil before the greater. What immediately affects people, even if only a relatively minor problem, will often move them to action more than greater problems that they only read about; and campaigners need to attract people to a cause if it is to prove successful. But obviously where there is competition it is better if possible to tackle the greater evil first. Unfortunately, the appeal to the 'greater evil' is rarely a clarion call to action, but an attempt to put a damper on action instead.

A rather similar argument is the 'fallacy of false consolation', a response to compliant which runs 'Why do you complain? Others suffer worse conditions.' Like the previous argument it assumes that the fact that there are greater evils elsewhere is a reason for taking no action on the evil that is here. Bentham, who discussed the argument (Bentham, pp. 194–7), pointed out that those who employ the argument employ it selectively. If cheated out of half a sum owing him, nobody would be much consoled by the news that others were cheated of the full amount.

What should not be confused with the above is a reasonable plea for inaction which says this:

To deal with your complaints now would mean a delay in dealing with the complaints of others who suffer worse conditions.

Obviously it is right and proper for legislators to order their priorities. If ignoring the lesser evil is a necessary condition of tackling a greater, then there is a good reason for no action on the lesser evil. But an idle reminder that in distant parts others suffer more is not a good reason for doing nothing in these parts now.

8

The last argument against change that I shall discuss is the argument from tradition. This states that within the group in question a thing has been done in a certain way for a long time; that such and such a proposal would mean the end of that tradition; and that therefore the proposal in question should be turned down.

In some ways this is the counterpart of the argument for a change that 'everybody's doing it'. In neither case is there any attempt to determine whether the change would be for the better or not. The one way points to the practice of contemporaries to justify a change; the other points to the practice of previous generations. Neither approach leads to any consideration of the merits and demerits of the change proposed. And just as there are good and bad contemporary practices, so there are good and bad traditions. Also, there are traditional ways of doing things which, while not in themselves very bad, could be improved. The appeal to tradition dismisses a case for change without a hearing. Those whose function is to make judicious changes shirk their responsibilities by ruling out proposals in this manner.

Those whose job is not to make but to interpret tradition—a priest or rabbi, for example—would clearly be correct to point out that a proposed change would represent a break with the past. The same goes for the English judge citing precedent, whose task is to interpret and uphold, not improve, the laws of the land. Those whose job it is to make laws, though, have no right to block a change by the appeal to tradition.

Exercises

Examine the following:

17.4 You complain about clocking in and say the management has broken an agreement by insisting on it. But surely it is true that hundreds of thousands of workers in Britain don't complain about it; are glad to have a job in fact.
Section 7.

17.5 If you allow students to attend as observers, where will it end? They'll be wanting the right to speak, next; then the right to vote; and pretty soon they'll be agitating for a majority of places on all the committees.

Section 4.

9

Finally, I turn to arguments which are not unambiguously for or against change, but may be used in defence either of the *status quo* or of a proposed change.

One such argument is the appeal to human nature: what is natural is right and what is contrary to nature wrong. We met earlier (exercise 6.3) the claim that space exploration could be justified because it is part of man's nature to seek adventure. We discussed (in Chapter 7) Robert Ardrey's claim that territorial behaviour is natural and that patriotism, by implication, is a good thing. Others have attacked moves towards international pacifism on the ground that it is unnatural; man is by nature aggressive. The argument can be deployed in favour of change—an increased expenditure on space exploration—by presenting the change as in accordance with human nature. It can be deployed against change—against a reduction in defence expenditure—if the change is presented as contrary to human nature.

Such arguments are, it seems to me, characteristically flawed in two ways. The first has already been pointed out. It is that those qualities which the authors purport to find in human nature are rather general characteristics—aggression, the seeking of adventure, the urge to protect territory. But what are being defended are particular ways in which these characteristics find expression. Even if individual men are prone to act aggressively that does not explain why nation states must do so. Even if all people have an urge to defend territory there is no obvious reason why there should be an urge to defend territory thousands of miles away as 'one's own'. And if man is by nature adventurous there is no reason why this desire should be satisfied vicariously, by reading about a handful of people putting their lives at risk in space. In each case there seems to be a gap between pointing out a general trait of human nature and defending the particular form in which it shows itself.

The second weakness in appeals to human nature is that one is often left in the dark as to whether these general traits are supposed to be present in all individuals or only in some. This is often disguised by what might be called the *Reader's Digest* use of 'man'; for example, 'Man by nature seeks adventure'. I rather suspect that while this may be true of some men and women it is unlikely to be true of them all, and certainly not true of the vast majority for the vast part of their lives. It would seem just as true, in the spirit of these daunting generalities, to say 'Man by nature seeks a quiet life'. What is the case is that some human beings seek excitement and fresh fields and many more like hearing about those who do; adventure by proxy. To describe this state of affairs by saying that man by nature desires adventure is to try to claim legitimacy for seeking excitement and fresh fields. In this particular case in our sort of society it is not a difficult task. We may regard someone's seeking adventure as risky and imprudent, even dangerous, but we are likely to have a sneaky admiration. In other cases there is more controversy. Is man, as one sometimes reads, naturally grasping and acquisitive? Well, these characteristics are more obvious in some people than in others in our society, and in addition anthropologists tell us that there are nomadic tribes who live by hunting and gathering who have no use for possessions beyond bow or spear. But it would be naïve to divorce such a claim from the context in which it is made. More often than not it will be found that the claim is made in defence of some practice, proposed or already in vogue, which is likely to encourage acquisitiveness: if it is natural, let it flourish. It may be, let us suppose, that 'human nature' is acquisitive, that there is a widespread tendency among people towards acquisitiveness. Whether it then needs encouragement, and in what directions, is an altogether different question.

At the risk of exaggeration, I would maintain that the claim that something is in human nature is, in the broad sense, a political claim, a grand and large-scale justification for particular measures.

10

Suppose the claim is made that it is wrong to sell arms to repressive governments. This may occur as an argument for change (if hitherto arms have been sold indiscriminately), or as an argument against change (if hitherto the policy has been to deny arms to repressive governments). Now what I am concerned with is the reply 'If we don't do it somebody else will': 'If we don't sell them arms then some-body else will.' This has been described as the 'dope pedlar's defence'. Its advocates would prefer to regard it as a defence of tough-minded realism.

What does the defence amount to? The claim that some course of action is wrong is met by an attempt to show that the moral scru-ples in question will (a) change nothing, and (b) involve a missed opportunity (normally an opportunity to make money). If that were an acceptable defence then the dope pedlar could indeed plead it in justification of selling heroin. By refusing to provide the drug he will not prevent the addict getting his 'fix', and he will forfeit the chance of making a lot of money himself. This seems to me enough to show that the defence is misconceived: there are some things which are wrong and which we should not do, even if not to do them costs us money, and even if others will do them anyway. The alternative policy, the one suggested by the dope pedlar's defence, is to follow self-interest unless one is the last source of supply—essentially, to set one's standards by the lowest that prevail. This alternative policy is certainly viable, but I doubt if many who resort to the dope pedlar's defence would really want to subscribe to it. Mostly, I think, they appeal to the argument because they do not think that the course of action proposed is really all that bad. For example, many people do not care whether we sell arms to repressive governments or not. Quite obviously, then, the gesture of denying arms will not seem worth the loss of money involved. It is easier to adopt a cynical atti-tude towards moral gestures than argue the pros and cons of the par-ticular case. But in other cases, I think, these same cynics would forgo the chance of gain: they would not, for example, construct gas cham-bers for a Nazi regime, even if others were willing and the rewards high.

Well, perhaps there are some hard cases who would do even that; consistent advocates of the dope pedlar's defence. What can one say to them? The first thing to be said is that a policy of following self-interest does not always lead to the best outcome. A simple case of this is panic buying when a commodity is in short supply. Each person is anxious to secure his or her supply and purchases more of the commodity than usual, which increases the shortage and drives up the price. A second point against self-interest is that moral gestures can have some effect. If enough people refuse to supply heroin its purchase may prove difficult if not impossible. It would be wrong to pretend that these are complete answers to the egotist. One may well suspect than an individual moral gesture will have no effect. Does it then have value? For the egotist it does not. For most people it does, to the extent that they are often prepared to say 'Others may feel no scruples about this, but I will not do it'. I do not know how to argue for this view, but I share it.

II

Finally there is the objection 'If you support (oppose) this change then logically you must support (oppose) that': for example, 'If you support easy abortion then logically you must support euthanasia', or 'If you oppose free housing then logically you must oppose a free health service'. On pain of inconsistency, those who sanction one change must sanction another which they would not wish to see; those who oppose one measure must oppose another which they favour.

Arguments of this kind involve unstated premisses. Adopting an attitude to the one measure is held to entail the same attitude to some further measure, but the connection is not obvious and depends upon hidden assumptions. Hidden assumptions were discussed in Chapter 5, with a warning of the danger of attributing implausible assumptions. Implicit beliefs must be dragged into the open, and the critic should be challenged to make explicit the connection which he thinks he sees. Only when this is done can we say whether the hidden belief has been fairly attributed; or if not, on what principle the original measure was supported or opposed.

Thus, to take the first example above, we must ask what principle is supposed to connect support for easy abortion with support for compulsory euthanasia. It is possible to guess that the principle the critics have in mind is the following: it is permissible to take a human life if the person involved is dependent on, and a burden to, others. On that principle, support for euthanasia would be connected with support for easy abortion; but if that is the principle then it begs the question of how far a foetus is to be treated as a full human being.

The important point is that it is not possible to examine an objection while everything remains in a state of conjecture. Alleged connections, if they are not clear, must be made clear.

Exercises

17.6 The people of Britain will not endure it. If so, it is idle to argue whether they ought or ought not to do so.
Fair comment? Section 9.

17.7 It is true that the new syllabus restricts choice more than some critics would like. But I don't see how logically they can really object to it, since none of them was prepared to allow complete freedom of choice.
Section 11.

18 Being Rational: Final Remarks

1

A rational attitude is necessarily a somewhat sceptical attitude. It is an attempt to apportion belief on the basis of evidence, withholding belief in the absence of evidence. If this sounds straightforward it should not. There are problems in this line of approach, and it would be wrong to blur its edges in exposition.

2

It is rational to hold beliefs, not in proportion to the evidence that one can cite, but in proportion to the evidence which one has reason to believe can be cited. For example, I believe that the Milky Way is an edge-on view of the galaxy on whose outer limits the sun lies. I cannot cite evidence for that belief but, so far as I can ascertain, it is regarded by astronomers as an established fact. So it is rational to believe it on good authority (Chapter 16). I cannot prove to anyone that the Milky Way is in our galaxy, because I cannot cite facts from which it follows. But it is an established fact, and it could be proved to a rational and honest doubter who had the time and ability and took the trouble to master the evidence and arguments for its truth. This seems to be essential to complement the notion in Chapter 2 of proving something to someone; there exists a proof of the conclusion which would satisfy any honest doubter.

In science, of course, most of our knowledge rests on the authority of experts. So, too, in history. Historians cannot see for themselves; they have to take on trust contemporary accounts and on their basis put together an account of what actually happened. Of course, historians do not approach their sources with complete credulity.

They will be prepared to reject scientific impossibilities. The monk Aelfric, writing in the eleventh century of the death of King Edmund, tells how he was beheaded and the head separated from the body and thrown in a briar; later the head guided searchers to itself by calling out 'Here . . . here', and when the head was placed back on the body the two rejoined, leaving the corpse intact. No historian will for a moment accept this part of Aelfric's narrative as true because it makes mockery of established natural sequences. On other occasions Aelfric's testimony may be sufficient basis for belief. Such cases aside, the historian may also be inclined to reject an otherwise completely plausible account because he suspects that the author is grinding an axe, writing for propaganda purposes. In such cases historians will try to compare this source with other contemporary accounts. Where possible they will search for archaeological or other evidence to test it. Historians are not the helpless victims of their sources, though in many cases they might find it hard to confirm their suspicions. In this respect scientists have the advantage: if in doubt they can often repeat an experiment.

3

People sometimes cheerfully admit to holding beliefs which cannot be proved, to believing what is not an established fact.

Evidence may incline strongly, though not yet conclusively, in a certain direction; and where certainty is not to be had, probability should be our guide. We can admit to holding beliefs which cannot be proved but which are probable. It is rational policy to apportion belief to the evidence, and there may be evidence which is strong but not compelling.

What is to be resisted is this sort of attitude to the evidence:

No, I don't suppose anyone can prove it, but so what? Where, outside mathematics, do you find real proof?

This appeal to a high redefinition of proof avoids the burden of providing evidence or citing authority for a belief. It might be possible to so raise the standards of proofs that only in mathematics will certainty be found. But it should not follow that below this all other beliefs are on a par, and it does not free us from the maxim that probability should be our guide where certainty cannot be had.

An analogy may help. Some people are inclined to offer a high redefinition of 'footballer', so that it turns out that the only 'real' footballers that the world had ever seen are a select few such as Pele, Best, and Matthews. Let us accept the redefinition. Even so, it does not follow that below this peak of perfection we cannot distinguish good from bad. In the same way, even if mathematical statements can alone be termed certain, it does not follow that we can place equal confidence in—or be equally sceptical of—all the rest.

4

Apportioning belief to the evidence means refusing to place any credence in a claim for which there is absolutely no evidence.

Suppose that somebody tells us—people occasionally make such claims—that the world will end on 5 June next. He offers no evidence for the claim: a voice told him. The rational thing to do, I would maintain, is to refuse to treat the prediction seriously. It is a claim for which there is no evidence, so it merits no credence.

But surely it's possible for the claim to be correct, and if it's possible how can we be justified in refusing to treat it seriously at all?

It is possible in the sense that there is no way of disproving the conjecture in advance. The claim is that some force unknown to us will bring life on earth catastrophically to an end on that date, and there seems no way of knowing that there is no such unknown force. Nevertheless, this is just a formal possibility and not to be taken seriously; just because someone has uttered one date for destruction does not mean that that date has any reason for being rated as more likely than any other for unknown forces to come into play. If we were trading in the unknown, relying on unknown forces and merely formal possibilities, then an infinite number of conflicting predictions would have to be given equal weight. The historian would not then be justified in dismissing Aelfric's story of the death of Edmund:

perhaps Edmund's vocal chords were activated in some unknown way by unknown forces in his severed throat. Nor could we be justified in taking any fact as established, for perhaps in some unknown way our perceptions were distorted when we thought we had established it.

Contrast these purely formal possibilities with a real possibility: the possibility that there will be another bad earthquake in San Francisco in the next fifty years. This is a real possibility because San Francisco lies along a fault-line in the earth's crust. Geologists have good reason for supposing that there is a risk, and perhaps on the strength of this evidence they can even give some estimate of the size of the risk. An earthquake in San Francisco is a real possibility; there is some evidence for it, even if an earthquake there is on balance less likely to happen than not.

The problem of belief and evidence becomes rather plainer if we consider another example. It is sometimes said that even if one could show that all the arguments for the existence of God were bad ones and all the alleged evidence no real evidence at all, nevertheless atheism would not be rational; instead, the rational position would be agnosticism. For although nothing would lead one to suppose a God existed, neither would a disproof of God exist. So it would still be possible for there to be a God.

My answer to this is that, in the case envisaged, the possibility of a God would be only a formal possibility. There would be no reason, if there was an absence of evidence and good argument, to do other than dismiss as false the claim that there is a God. One would be apportioning one's degree of belief to the evidence—zero in both cases.

If, on the other hand, one could show that some evidence existed for a God, but not enough to reach a decision either way, then in that case agnosticism would be rational. One would be undecided on the basis of the evidence. If there were absolutely no evidence for a God then it would be as perverse to be agnostic about a God as it would be to be undecided about the destruction of the world next June on anybody's unsupported say-so.

5

The problem with this stern reliance on rationality and the balancing of evidence is that everyone believes things which are in fact difficult to justify.

Of course, there are beliefs which are merely probable and which cannot be conclusively established; say, the belief that St Paul was an epileptic. In cases of this sort we may hope that the matter will be settled one way or the other, given further evidence. But further evidence is not always easy to acquire, and the matter may have to remain unsettled. Rationality is not threatened, because such confidence as we feel is related to the strength of the available evidence.

More difficult, from the rational standpoint, are those beliefs which are so fundamental that they set the framework for any justifications. A case in point is the belief, discussed in Chapter 12, Section 1, that past experience is a guide to the future. This belief underpins all our reasoning about the world, but if we are asked to justify it we are disorientated. In assembling evidence for it we would be assuming what was supposed to be shown—that the evidence assembled from past experience is a guide to the future. It is accepted unquestioningly, on instinct rather than on evidence, and because it is universally shared it is hardly even noticed.

The sceptically inclined philosophers do not shake our confidence in the belief that past experience is a guide to the future. What they do is, first, make us conscious of the belief and, secondly, embarrass those of us who advocate rationality; since here is a belief which is not apportioned to the evidence but which gives the collection of evidence its purpose.

6

The doubts of philosophical sceptics can be ignored or dismissed as ridiculous, because what they are questioning is 'common sense'. A more noticeable threat to the rational approach is the area of judgements of value, as suggested in Chapter 2. Whereas people have a strong and coinciding belief about the relevance of past experience in predicting the future, on questions of right and wrong they have strong beliefs which often diverge. Such divergencies can leave us at a loss, just as the philosophical sceptic can leave us at a loss.

Consider the opposing positions on capital punishment. So long as the issue is held to turn on how far capital punishment deters potential murderers, the dispute can in theory be resolved. We would look for culturally similar countries with similar crime rates, one of which consistently applied the death penalty and one of which did not. We would then compare the murder rate in each. However, I suspect that all the talk about deterrence is something of a smoke-screen: both sides talk about it because both sides are convinced that they can win on this ground, and because it is something to talk about. The underlying dispute is about whether those who have committed certain sorts of crime deserve to be done to death. On this level, argument quickly gives way to rhetoric. Those who support capital punishment are accused of favouring cruel and unnatural punishment; those who oppose it are accused of lacking feeling for the victims, as if the only way of showing proper feelings were to demand the death of the criminal. Each side has an implacable conviction of rightness and it is difficult to see where rational argument can take us. Some bad arguments are tried, often begging the question. Even where relevant considerations can be found they seem somewhat oblique.

For example, there is the risk that an innocent person will be convicted and done to death before the discovery of fresh evidence to clear his name. Obviously no judicial system is free from the risk of miscarriage of justice. Reparation can be made, in part at least, if the convicted person is still alive, but a posthumous pardon is hardly recompense. Though, as I have said, this seems to be a relevant consideration—something which counts in some degree against capital punishment—it is hardly central. Defenders of the death penalty would regard this risk of a miscarriage of justice as an inevitable part of dispensing true justice, and it is almost certainly not for this reason that most abolitionists oppose it. Abolitionists are against the death penalty because it seems to them abhorrent in itself, and trying to find some merely circumstantial argument in its favour conveys no hint of the depth of feeling involved.

There may of course be some argument, so far unthought of, which could definitively settle the issue one way or the other. But it does not seem to be that sort of a dispute. It has a peculiar recalcitrance, like the problems raised by philosophical scepticism. For trying to establish the legitimacy or otherwise of capital punishment is similarly trying to establish what seems 'just obvious': only now both sides disagree about what is obvious.

An approach was suggested in Chapter 2 by seeking some general principle which both sides would accept and which would entail the rightness, or wrongness, of capital punishment. Suppose we can find some principle, *P*, which everyone would accept. Suppose that from *P* it follows that capital punishment is acceptable. Then, on pain of inconsistency, abolitionists would have to give up their objections to capital punishment. The trouble is, I doubt if there is any general principle about which abolitionists would feel so confident. If accepting *P* led to condoning the death penalty they would take this as a proof that there was something wrong with general principle *P*. That capital punishment is wrong is a conviction more firmly held than any general principle. (Of course, the same would happen in reverse. If some principle entailed that capital punishment was wrong, many defenders of capital punishment would doubtless say 'So much for the principle'.)

Nor is it only such weighty matters as life and death that throw up these flat and uncompromising disagreements. A good example occurred in a faculty meeting at one university. The question arose whether, at the presentation of degrees, there should be a break with tradition: instead of awarding degrees in order of merit, it was proposed that they should be awarded in alphabetical order. The outstanding students, it was argued, already had reward enough, and the near-failures would not be so pointedly singled out.

What quickly emerged was that although there were strong feelings on both sides nobody could come up with any strong arguments for either position. Some thought the change appropriate, others thought it inappropriate. Someone said that the Divinity faculty would never do it. One person denounced it as a communist plot. Someone else said it was a change in the right direction. Professor X reckoned that the stigma of being branded a near-failure would encourage the lazy students to work. Dr Y felt that if Professor X were to boo and hiss the worst students as they collected their degrees this might be even more effective. Maybe there were real considerations that the august body missed, but I think not. This item, in itself small, impinged on deep basic beliefs about how conspicuous success and failure should be. People's instinctive beliefs on this diverge. It is the presence of instinctive divisions such as this that gives rise to the large number of bad arguments attending proposals for change which were discussed in Chapter 17.

7

So what does rationality mean in this context, and what can logic do?

Where judgements are confused, or not thought through, reason can help. People often want things which are impossible to have together; for example, a market economy, job security, and no inflation. Obviously, then, a want has to be tested against the constraints involved in the fulfilment of other wants. Again, people sometimes express support for a principle which, thought through, commits them to things they would not approve of (see again the discussion of the dope pedlar's defence in Chapter 17). They are prone to indulge in special pleading. Where judgements are partial in this way, rational discussion is of value, though it need not produce agreement. Everyone is inclined at times to argue one-sidedly for a course of action. We are all familiar with the joke about the well-heeled business man who pleads the need for managerial incentives and condemns the avarice of his shop-floor workers. Logic can point out the partiality of the pronouncement—one man's need for incentives is another man's avarice—but is unlikely to resolve the disagreement. It is more likely that new arguments in defence of managerial incentives will be found, less easily attacked. Convergence may eventually come, but may not.

There seem likely to remain situations where one cannot reason a way forward, even with a commitment to reason on both sides.

Worse, however, in some cases reason can appear almost obscene—armchair attempts to demonstrate that something disgusting is not, after all, disgusting. The problem is that people have strong and opposed convictions on whether something is disgusting.

Susan Stebbing wrote a book in the 1930s called *Thinking to Some Purpose* which discusses the relation between thinking and doing:

> On the one hand there is the danger of rushing into action without thinking about what we are doing . . . On the other hand, there is the danger of indulging in academic detachment from life. This is the peculiar temptation of those who are prone to see both sides of a question and are content to enjoy an argument for its own sake. The present writer is at times beset by this temptation. But thinking is primarily for the sake of action. No one can avoid the responsibility of acting in accordance with his mode of thinking. No one can act wisely who has never felt the need to pause and think about how he is going to act and why he decides to act as he does. (Stebbing, p. 23)

I do not see the problem in quite this way. It is not that reason determines the way we should act but tempts us into the byways of an argument. Rather, reason does not always determine—or does not always fully determine—the way we should act. Opting one way or the other on issues such as capital punishment, abortion, approving or disapproving of equality of life-style, these are things which we do, and feel strongly about, but where nevertheless we do not know how to set about proving our decisions to be the right ones. We make decisions which we cannot fully argue for; hold attitudes which we cannot fully defend.

This seems to me the crucial gap which Susan Stebbing slides over. It is a severe limit to the rational approach. In certain decisions the head cannot get us there; the heart has to.

8
There's more to life than logic.

Is this, then, what I am claiming? It strikes me as certainly true but a dangerous claim (like 'To make an omelette you have to break eggs'). On the surface it is a truism; there is more to life than thinking straight. But the suggestion is probably that thinking straight is a responsibility we can shirk: follow our instincts and all will be well. Mostly I object to this because I haven't much faith in other people's instincts. But my own have shown up on occasion, I now think, as distinctly fallible. That is why we need to think hard about moral questions, to make sure that we are consistent, to try to see proposals as they will affect others and not just ourselves, and to try to anticipate any problem that the changes we favour might bring with them. I do not think that reason can fully determine the way we opt in moral issues, but we should be sure so far as we can that our feelings are coherent and impartial. We should drive rationality as far as it will take us.

Appendix 1: 'If . . . then' and '→'

The problem is that so far as statements of the form '$p \rightarrow q$' are concerned, whether the statement as a whole is true or false depends on whether the parts are true or false. For 'If p then q' the position is less clear-cut.

In the case where p is true and q false, statements of the form '$p \rightarrow q$' are false, and as we saw in Chapter 3*, the same is true of 'If p then q'. For example, the claim that if the sun shines then Jane is happy is shown to be false if it is true that the sun is shining and false that Jane is happy.

In every other case the truth table for '$p \rightarrow q$' comes out true, but when '$\rightarrow$' is replaced with 'if . . . then' the results are less obvious. For example, take any two true statements, p and q. Since both are true then it is true that $p \rightarrow q$. However, putting 'p' = 'the Sun is larger than the Moon', and 'q' = 'Edinburgh is in Scotland', reveals a problem. Many people are inclined to reject the statement 'If the Sun is larger than the Moon then Edinburgh is in Scotland', although both component parts are true. Doubts arise because there is no *connection* between the two facts. An 'if . . . then' statement seems to require a connection between p and q, whereas in the case of '$\rightarrow$' there need be no connection: all that is claimed is that we don't have p true and q false.

This need for a connection would explain why statements of the form 'If p then q' are false where p is true and q false. For if it turns out that p is true and q false there *cannot* be a connection between p and q.

However, the issue is a contentious one in the philosophy of logic and many would argue that the account above exaggerates the difference between '$\rightarrow$' and the ordinary 'if . . . then'. Apart from questions of truth or falsity there are other ways our statements can be assessed; as irrelevant or misleading, for example. It is not normally appropriate to assert things of the form 'If p then q' when we know that both parts are true, and it may well be that our confusion over statements like the one above is that they break the normal conventions of assertion rather that they actually say something false. Readers wishing to know more are referred to Stephen Read, pp. 64–95, for a full discussion.

Appendix 2: Modern Logic and Aristotle

I

Aristotle was the first person to develop a logic of arguments with 'all' and 'some'. His systematic treatment survived virtually unchallenged until the latter half of the nineteenth century, when it was superseded by developments stemming from mathematics. However, Aristotle's system seems a very natural one, at first glance more akin to ordinary language than that which superseded it, and it is worth looking closely at the issue over which the two treatments diverge.

Aristotle held the apparently reasonable belief that if every *A* is a *B* then at least one *A* is a *B*: if every cat is a carnivore then at least one cat is a carnivore; and the corresponding belief that if no *A* is a *B* then at least one *A* is not a *B*: if no cat is a carnivore then at least one cat is not a carnivore. In both cases the second statement is apparently weaker than the first and follows from it. By changing our example we can illustrate, rather than simply explain, what is involved. Consider the following line of letters:

R T K S V N H J

It is true to say that every letter in the row is a capital. But it is also true to say that at least one letter in the row is a capital (V, for example). The second claim is weaker than the first, but obviously also true. Now consider another line of letters:

r t k s v n h j

Here it is true to say that no letter is a capital, but also true to say that at least one letter is not a capital (t, for example). Of course, the converse implications do not hold. If at least one letter is a capital it does not follow that all are, and if at least one letter is not a capital it does not follow that none is. One example will suffice to refute both suggestions. Consider this line:

r T K s V n h J

Aristotle's logic of syllogisms, then, appears to fit in well with common-sense views on how the words 'every', 'some', and 'no' inter-relate. But there are features of this treatment which are somewhat disturbing. Consider the following statements:

(1) Every ghost is noisy.   (2) No ghost is noisy.
(3) Some ghost is noisy.   (4) Some ghost is not noisy.

If every ghost is noisy then at least one ghost is noisy; if no ghost is noisy then at least one ghost is not noisy. There is also the possibility that at least one ghost is noisy and at least one ghost is not noisy. But in any event we seem to be committed to the existence of at least one ghost, whether noisy or not. And obviously it is not just ghosts; we are committed to the existence of goblins, unicorns, anti-gravity machines, and whatever else we talk about. This is a weakness of the Aristotelian system. Indeed, unless some way is found of limiting the objects we are permitted to talk about, arguments are sanctioned which are invalid—which go from true premisses to false conclusions.

Suppose I begin with the true statement 'No cat is an animal with three tails'. In Aristotle's system (and that which replaced it) this is equivalent to 'No animal with three tails is a cat'. Now we argue that if no animal with three tails is a cat then at least one animal with three tails is not a cat. So, beginning with the true statement 'No cat is an animal with three tails', we arrive by moves permitted within the system at the unacceptable statement 'At least one animal with three tails is not a cat'. Something is wrong.

2

Modern logic denies the inference from 'Every A is a B' to 'At least one A is a B'; also the inference from 'No A is a B' to 'At least one A is not a B'. Since the argument in the paragraph above involved the second of these moves, it would not go through in modern logic. The modern system involves a different analysis of 'every' and 'no'. Under this interpretation, as we saw, statements beginning with 'every' and 'no' are treated rather as complicated 'if . . . then' statements.

'Every *A* is *B*' is regarded as equivalent to 'If anything is an *A* then it is a *B*'. Under this interpretation, 'Every cat is a carnivore' is taken to mean 'If anything is a cat then it is a carnivore'; it is not to claim or imply that there are cats which are carnivorous, or even that there are cats at all. Hence we cannot move validly from 'Every cat is carnivorous' to 'Some cat is carnivorous', for the latter *does* imply the existence of cats.

Now this interpretation of 'every' is quite a departure from our ordinary beliefs about how the word works. It is not entirely unfamiliar; there are a few examples in science of its use, for example: 'Every body moving with the velocity of light has infinite mass', or 'Every body not acted upon by a force continues in a state of rest or uniform motion in a straight line'. There is no suggestion in these cases that there are any bodies actually moving with the velocity of light, or that there are any force-free bodies. However, such examples as these are comparatively rare, and the main attractions of the new interpretation are its convenience for solving the problems of the old, and the ease with which it can be developed to deal with quite complicated sentences, rather than its consonance with ordinary language. The new interpretation does not commit us to the view that if every ghost is harmful then it must follow that at least one ghost is harmful. For 'Every ghost is harmful' means only 'If anything is a ghost then it is harmful'. We have not implied the existence of ghosts.

In entirely the same way, modern logic takes 'No *A* is a *B*' as equivalent to 'If anything is an *A* then it is not a *B*', or 'Nothing is both an *A* and a *B*'. Neither commits us to the existence of anything which is *A*, so we can remain suitably sceptical about the existence of ghosts, three-tailed animals, and the like.

Answers to Exercises

1 ARGUMENTS

1.1   To make an assessment of modern art is an impossible task.

1.2   Increasingly people turn to astrology.

1.3   Not an argument: no conclusion.

1.4   Stern—and enforced—limits at black-spots would have a far greater effect than an overall curb simply for legislation's sake. (A conclusion, despite the absence of a grammatical signal.)

1.5   Customers are the real winners. But see example on p. 3.

1.6   Conclusion: William won't vote for a communist. Hidden premiss: No churchgoer will vote for a Communist.

1.7   Conclusion: A reduction in the present penalty for drunken driving would have a beneficial effect. Hidden premiss: Whatever makes the jury more ready to convict drunken drivers is beneficial. (Or perhaps two hidden premisses: (1) If the jury is more ready to convict then drivers will be more cautious, and (2) If drivers are more cautious this will be beneficial.)

1.8   Conclusion: many young men in modern industrial society join gangs and turn to lawlessness. Hidden premisses: (1) The young men in modern industrial society must find some way of achieving status, and (2) Lawlessness is a way of achieving status.

1.9   The machine contains a mixture of fabrics.
These different fabrics have a liking for different kinds of dirt.
∴ The dirt . . . becomes evenly spread over other garments.
And
The dirt . . . becomes evenly spread over other garments.
∴ Washing machines fail to wash really clean.

1.10   Conclusion: Capital punishment for terrorists will act as a deterrent.

1.11   It is not really a calamity (that a large part of control has been wrenched out of parents' hands by pop culture).

2 PROOFS

2.1 Irrelevant. The first reason is that it avoids public disorder; the second that gaol is not a deterrent. Neither shows that capital punishment is a deterrent.

2.2 Irrelevant. Argues for the success, not the morality, of the methods.

2.3 Begs the question. The 'reason' offered is a restatement of the conclusion.

2.4 Bracket the middle sentence. Trying to show that the movement of people causes immediate costs without any necessary increase in production. Successful, I think.

2.5 Question-begging description of suicide as murder.

2.6 If the reasons offered are relevant it can only be because it is assumed (in a question-begging way) that the extension of the public sector is wrong.

2.7 Reading between the lines, the argument appears to be: The drug could change someone's attitude to life and work.
∴ It is irresponsible to advocate its use.
The reason offered begs the question by assuming that a change in outlook would be bad. Also, branding the action 'irresponsible' rather begs the question against having a right to do it.

3 VALIDITY: 'IF . . . THEN'

3.1 Put p for 'there is violence on the football field' and q for 'there is violence amongst the fans': If p then q; q; ∴ p. Invalid. Affirming the consequent.

3.2 Put p for 'the money supply is held steady' and q for 'the rate of inflation will fall': If p then q; p; ∴ q. Valid.

3.3 Same abbreviations as above. If q then p; p; ∴ q. Invalid. Affirming the consequent.

3.4 Simplified, the argument is:
If there is a slump in shares then there will be a rise in unemployment.
There is not a slump in shares.
So unemployment will not rise.
Let p = 'there is a slump in shares' and q = 'there will be a rise in unemployment': If p then q; Not p; ∴ Not q. Invalid.

3.5 p = 'the President was physically endangered' and q = 'the alarm expressed was justified': If p then q; Not p; ∴ Not q. Invalid.

3.6 p = 'the advertising of cigarettes is prohibited', q = 'the government will lose revenue . . . sales': If p then q; Not q; ∴ Not p. Valid.

3.7 p = 'each man has a definite . . . his life' and q = 'each man is a machine' (the premiss does not quite say this, but it seems to be what is intended): Like 3.5, invalid.

3.8

p	q	$\sim$	$(p \,\&\, q)$
T	T	**F**	T
T	F	**T**	F
F	T	**T**	F
F	F	**T**	F

The column in bold results from negating the right-hand column, the one for $p \,\&\, q$.

3.9

p	q	$\sim p$	$\&$	q
T	T	F	**F**	T
T	F	F	**F**	F
F	T	T	**T**	T
F	F	T	**F**	F

The two are not the same. The truth table for 3.8 results from negating $p \,\&\, q$, while that for 3.9 results from joining $\sim p$ with q by '&' (the column in bold type above).

3.10   Putting p = Marion called, q = John was happy, we get $\sim p \rightarrow \sim q$, q, ∴ p. The truth table is:

p	q	$\sim p$	$\rightarrow$	$\sim q$,	q,	∴	p
T	T	F	**T**	F	T		T
T	F	F	**T**	T	F		T
F	T	T	**F**	F	T		F
F	F	T	**T**	T	F		F

The argument is valid. The only case where both premises are true is the first row, and the conclusion is also true in that row.

3.11   The truth table for $(p \to q)$ & $(\sim p \to \sim q)$ is as follows:

p	q	$(p \to q)$	&	$(\sim p \to \sim q)$
T T		T	**T**	F *T* F
T F		F	**F**	F *T* T
F T		T	**F**	T *F* F
F F		T	**T**	T *T* T

The column under $p \to q$ is the standard one, that for $\sim p \to \sim q$ is shown in italics, and the result of joining them by '&' is shown in bold. It is the same as the table for '$p \leftrightarrow q$'.

4 VALIDITY: DISJUNCTIONS AND DILEMMAS

4.1 p = 'the witness saw the accused enter the bank', q = 'the witness is a liar': Either p or q; not q; $\therefore$ p. Valid, on either use of 'or'.

4.2 p = 'the statesmen of the period were gullible fools' and q = 'the statesmen were lining their pockets . . . the citizen': Either p or q; p; $\therefore$ Not q. Invalid, if inclusive 'or'. Valid, if exclusive 'or', since the possibility of their being gullible and corrupt is ruled out.

4.3   John is clever = p, John is hardworking = q. The exclusive 'or', as said earlier, is given by $(p \lor q)$ & $\sim(p \& q)$. So the argument is laid out and tested as below:

p	q	$(p \lor q)$	&	$\sim(p \& q),$	p	$\therefore$	$\sim q$
T T		T	**F**	F	T		F
T F		T	**T**	T	T		T
F T		T	**T**	T	F		F
F F		F	**F**	T	F		T

It is valid. Only in the second row are both premises true and in that case the conclusion is also true.

4.4   On the inclusive 'or', with the same substitutions as in 4.3, the argument is:

p	*q*	(*p* ∨ *q*),	~*p*	∴	*q*
T	T	T	F		T
T	F	T	F		F
F	T	T	T		T
F	F	F	T		F

The third row is the crucial one, since only there are both premisses true and the conclusion is also true.

The truth table for the exclusive 'or' has F in the first row where the inclusive 'or' has T. The third row is still the crucial one.

4.5   The truth table for the first premiss, $p \to {\sim}q$, results from joining *p* with ~*q* by '→'. It is shown as a single step. Similarly for $q \to {\sim}r$ and $p \to {\sim}r$.

p,	*q,*	*r*	$p \to {\sim}q,$	$q \to {\sim}r,$	∴	$p \to {\sim}r$
T	T	T	F	F		F
T	T	F	F	T		T
T	F	T	T	T		F
T	F	F	T	T		T
F	T	T	T	F		T
F	T	F	T	T		T
F	F	T	T	T		T
F	F	F	T	T		T

The argument is invalid because in the third row we have true premisses and a false conclusion.

4.6   The truth table is:

p,	*q,*	*r*	(*p* & *q*) → *r,*		∴	*p* → (*q* → *r*)	
T	T	T	T	T T		T T	T
T	T	F	T	F F		T F	F
T	F	T	F	T T		T T	T
T	F	F	F	T F		T T	T
F	T	T	F	T T		F T	T
F	T	F	F	T F		F T	F
F	F	T	F	T T		F T	T
F	F	F	F	T F		F T	T

The resultant columns for premiss and conclusion are both shown in bold. There is no row where the premiss is true and the conclusion false, so the argument is valid.

Answers to Part (i)

4.7   With obvious substitutions: If and only if p then q; q; $\therefore$ p. Valid. (Compare with example 3.3.)

4.8   Dilemma (hence valid). Conclusion: Either jobs will increase or noise nuisance will abate.

4.9   Either air traffic grows or it declines. If it grows then noise nuisance will increase. If it declines then jobs will decrease. So either noise nuisance will increase or jobs will decrease.

4.10   Conclusion comes first. p = 'the dead do not rise', q = 'Christ is not raised', and r = 'your faith is vain': If p then q; if q then r; $\therefore$ if p then r. Valid.

4.11 p = 'the book contains pornographic passages', q = 'the book will be widely read', giving: If not p then not q; p; $\therefore$ q. Invalid. Given p = not not p, it denies the antecedent.

4.12 p = 'an industry is making a loss', q = 'an industry is making a profit', r = 'it should not be propped up with taxpayers' money', and s = 'there is no point in taking it over'. Dilemma. The first horn could be challenged by showing that there are strategic or other reasons for subsidizing an industry rather than letting it die or contract. The second horn could be challenged by showing that an industry could be run more efficiently or more in the public interest by public ownership. Escaping between the horns is possible if an industry is just breaking even. But that case seems insignificant.

4.13   Dilemma. Supply 'Either the government will not reduce . . . or the government will reduce . . .'. Either not p or p; if not (unless) p then q; if p then r; $\therefore$ either q or r.

4.14   If you love someone then you hurt them; so if you hurt them then you love them. Resembles 'If p then q; q; $\therefore$ p'. Differs by saying 'If p then q; $\therefore$ if q then p'. Invalid. Test by finding an example where 'if p then q' is true and 'if q then p' false.

4.15   Conclusion given first. Reformulated, with p = 'there is civilization', q = 'there is leisure', and r = 'there is slavery': If p then q; if not *r* then not *q*; ∴ if not *r* then not *p*. Using the equivalence given, we get: If *p* then *q*; if *q* then *r*; if *p* then *r*. Valid.

4.16 Truncated dilemma: *p* = 'Jones carries more stock', *q* = 'Jones will attract . . .', and *r* = 'Jones will run up debts'. Either not *p* or *p*; if not *p* then not *q*; if *p* then *r*; ∴ either not *q* or *r*.

4.17 *p* = 'motive . . . are present' and *q* = 'the accused . . . charged'. If *q* then *p*; *p*; ∴ *q*. Invalid, affirming the consequent.

4.18 *p* = 'a negotiator is acceptable', *q* = 'a negotiator takes a responsible view of labour relations', and *r* = 'a negotiator is a committed capitalist'. If not *q* then not *p*; if *q* then *r*; ∴ if not *r* then not *p*. Using the equivalence rule of 4.11, it becomes a hypothetical syllogism, as 4.11.

Answers to Part (ii)

4.7(ii) The truth table for '↔' is given in 3.11.

p	*q*	*p* ↔ *q*,	q	∴	*p*
T	T	T	T		T
T	F	F	F		T
F	T	F	T		F
F	F	T	F		F

Valid.

4.10(ii) The truth table is:

p,	*q*,	*r*	*p* → *q*,	*q* → *r*,	∴	*p* → *r*
T	T	T	T	T		T
T	T	F	T	F		F
T	F	T	F	T		T
T	F	F	F	T		F
F	T	T	T	T		T
F	T	F	T	F		T
F	F	T	T	T		T
F	F	F	T	T		T

Valid.

4.11(ii) The truth table is:

p	q	~p → ~q,	p,	∴	q
T	T	F **T** F	**T**		T
T	F	F **T** T	**T**		F
F	T	T **F** F	**F**		T
F	F	T **T** T	**F**		F

Invalid, from the second row.

4.14(ii) The truth table is:

p	q	p → q,	∴	q → p
T	T	T		T
T	F	F		T
F	T	T		F
F	F	T		T

Invalid, from the third row.

4.15(ii) Essentially the same truth table as 4.10. The main columns of the second premiss and conclusion are in bold.

p,	q,	r	p → q,	~r → ~q,	∴	~r → ~p
T	T	T	T	F **T** F		F **T** F
T	T	F	T	T **F** F		T **F** F
T	F	T	F	F **T** T		F **T** F

etc.
Valid.

4.17(ii) Truth table:

p	q	q → p,	p,	∴	q
T	T	T	T		T
T	F	T	T		F
F	T	F	F		T
F	F	T	F		F

Invalid, from second row.

4.18(ii) The truth table is the same as 4.10 and 4.15. Valid.

5 GETTING THE PREMISSES RIGHT

5.1   Man's ideals, hopes, etc. must be realized.

5.2   The appetites for food and sex should manifest themselves in parallel ways. And man's appetite for food, rather than for sex, should provide the model.

5.3   Takes for granted what it tries to show, that all events must have a cause.

5.4   If most people prefer corporal punishment to a long punishment, hard to see how it can be a better deterrent for most people.

5.5   Begs question.

5.6   Forbids anything but work. If any activity became so general that people spent all their time at it then again no work would be done.

5.7   A prima facie inconsistency between supposing that few schools outside the state system are good, and that they attract a disproportionate number of good teachers.

5.8   Doesn't counter the charge of neglect, but excuses the neglect. Doesn't show the criticism to be 'unfair' in the sense of 'false'.

6 STICKING TO THE POINT

6.1   Begins with the claim that all intelligent people will express themselves in philosophical thinking. Later weakened to suggest that some intelligent people are unfitted by inclination or training for philosophy.

6.2   Begins by asserting that advertising has nothing to do with alcohol abuse. Qualified by asserting that other influences are more important. Later seems to imply that government persuasion could counter alcohol abuse, so why cannot advertising promote it?

6.3   Justifications rather weak. Why seek adventure in that way? Final claim is that money would not otherwise be better spent, not that it *could* not be better spent.

6.4   Shapes as if to challenge the truth of the belief about schizophrenia, but goes on to talk about the effects of the belief.

6.5 Begins by implying that to be swayed by irrelevances is bad or silly (excessively contemptuous view of people to suppose they are). Ends by saying (rhetorical question) that it is not bad or silly.

6.6 Seems to be arguing that loss of faith has made the world a worse place. In fact argues that loss of faith has made it no better.

6.7 Begins by claiming that power now goes to the most intelligent. Ends by claiming that it goes to those who most want it.

6.8 The evidence does not show that low-level radiation is normally beneficial; only that it is beneficial as a prelude to a high dosage.

7 MEANING AND DEFINITION

7.1 Government expenditure is not spent on the government but on public goods. So it is hard to see what the government is sacrificing.

7.2 Restoring to Parliament an air of honesty (for tactical reasons). A backhanded compliment?

7.3 Uses 'sacrifice' so widely that a very rich person, who saves only what he cannot find a way to spend, nevertheless makes a sacrifice in not spending it.

7.4 Another shift in the meaning of 'God'.

7.5 What is attacked is 'uncritical' and 'unreflective' patriotism. Is patriotism in itself uncritical, or just some brands of it?

7.6 'Truly joined together': tightens up normal meaning of 'going through a religious wedding ceremony in good faith', so that the divorce of the 'truly' joined together is ruled out by definition.

7.7 'Censorship' has bad overtones; 'ensuring greater responsibility' less so. In practice they seem to come to the same.

7.8 'Freedom' has favourable connotations but different descriptive meanings. An attempt to narrow the descriptive meaning. *Laissez-faire* is freedom from bureaucratic controls; but equally, security is freedom from fear, and prosperity freedom from want.

7.9 I find the first part less convincing, partly because 'extremist', like 'terrorist', has negative connotations and partly because the end may not justify the means.

7.10   Better: 'Sport ought to be above (unconnected with) politics.'
        Whether right or wrong, it is not inconsistent to campaign for
        their separation.

8 DIVISIONS AND DISTINCTIONS

8.1   To me, 'unwise' suggests 'foolish', rather than 'not wise'. The
        suggested classifications (a) wise/unwise, (b) wise/average sens-
        ible/unwise are both possible. But it is easier to deny that 'William
        is unwise' is the contradictory of 'William is wise' under (b) than
        (a). Neither classification is clear-cut, since there are borderline
        cases.

8.2   Shows perhaps that we should talk of necessities relative to a given
        society, biological necessities, and so on. Not that no distinction
        can be drawn at all.

8.3   Disagreement doesn't show that *no* real distinction exists. (See
        Section 6.)

8.4   'Third alternative' is bad grammar; third possibilities can occur,
        however.

8.5   The objection takes 'extrovert' as never wanting to be alone,
        'introvert' as never wanting company. But even on less extreme
        definitions the classification might be unsatisfactory (if most
        people are somewhere in the middle).

8.6   I think claiming that a foetus is really or essentially a human
        being.

8.7   Apparently questioning the distinction between human and non-
        human cells on the ground that there are borderline cases.

9 'ALL' AND 'SOME'

9.1   (1)   (2)   (3)

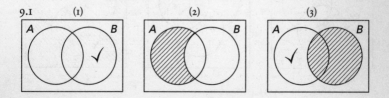

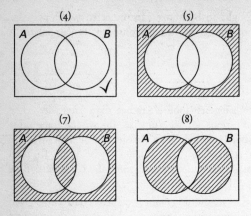

9.2 Things which are: (4) *A*s and *C*s but not *B*s; (5) *A*s, *B*s, and *C*s; (6) *B*s and *C*s but not *A*s; (7) *C*s but not *A*s and not *B*s; (8) not *A*s, not *B*s, and not *C*s.

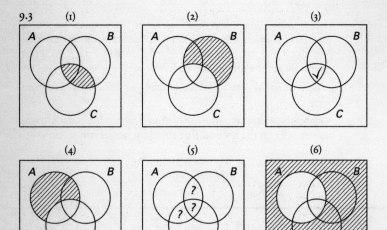

9.4

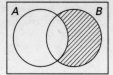

(A = 'the brave';
B = 'those who deserve
the fair' (Equivalent to
'Only As are Bs', or 'All
Bs are As').

9.5

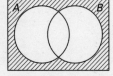

9.6

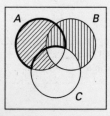 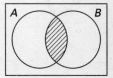

(1) Everything not A is
B (Nothing is not A
and not B)

(2) No A is B

10 ARGUMENTS WITH 'ALL' AND 'SOME'

10.1

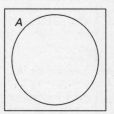

A = 'successful people', B = 'thoughtful people',
and C = 'patient people'. All As are Bs; all Bs
are Cs; all As are Cs. Valid. (Remember the rule
for 'only'.)

10.2

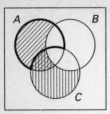

A = 'vitamins', B = 'cheap things', and C = 'nutritious things'. All As are Bs; all Cs are Bs; all As are Cs. Invalid. (Area A, B, not C may not be empty.)

10.3

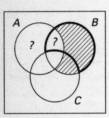

A = 'selfish people', B = 'good parents', and C = 'intelligent people'. No As are Bs; some Cs are As; some Cs are not Bs. Valid.

10.4

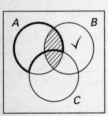

A = 'feedback mechanisms', B = 'purposive mechanisms' and C = 'complicated mechanisms'. All Bs are As; some As are not Cs; some Bs are not Cs. Invalid. (Tick may be in A, not B, not C.)

10.5

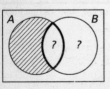

A = 'tenant', B = 'one entitled to vote', and C = 'ratepayer'. No A is B; some Bs are not Cs; some As are not Cs. Invalid. (No tick in A.)

10.6

A = 'weak people', B = 'people tempted to lie', and * = 'Bill'. All As are B's; * is B; * is A. Invalid. (No definite * in A.)

10.7 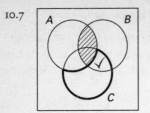 A = 'child offered . . . High School'; B = 'child accepting . . . St Joseph's' and C = 'child amongst . . . town'. No A is B; some Bs are Cs; some Cs are not As. Valid.

10.8 Either like 10.2 or like 10.6 (with * = 'the philosophical writings of Kant'). Invalid.

10.9 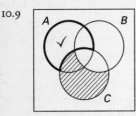 A = 'delegate', B = 'one voting for . . . stoppage', and C = 'one branded as irresponsible'. To be shown: All Cs are Bs; some As are not Bs; $\therefore$ some As are not Cs. Valid.

11 GROUPS AND INDIVIDUALS

11.1 Parts have a life-span. Doesn't follow that the whole does. If new entities constantly arise the Universe may last forever.

11.2 The rest taken together buy less; it doesn't follow that each of them buys less.

11.3 Similar to 11.1.

11.4 Each strives to safeguard his share. Doesn't follow that any is concerned to safeguard the country (though interests may coincide).

11.5 Not everyone can work harder than everyone else, only one person can.

11.6 Toss a coin; take turns as decision-maker. These are just the most obvious suggestions.

11.7 Collectively the statesmen failed. Individually few could have done anything to prevent war, perhaps.

11.8 It may be that national safety as a whole comes first without its being the case that increasing national safety by a small fraction comes first.

12 PROBABILITY, EVIDENCE, AND CAUSES

12.1   No. Let, e.g. A = 'whales', B = 'mammals', and C = 'land animals'.

12.2   The most obvious suggestions: burglar could have acquired a key; burglar could have found a door or window open, which someone subsequently relocked.

12.3   (1) Most Irishmen wear a shamrock on St Patrick's Day.
        (2) Most who wear a shamrock on St Patrick's Day are Irish.

12.4   This could mean that people have operated few reactors for many years; or many reactors for few years.

12.5   Comparative risks differ, and the degree of risk is what counts.

12.6   Presumably the claim is akin to the one about smoking. If so the response doesn't meet the point.

12.7   A standing condition. One then has to explain why wars are relatively unusual, and why man's aggressive nature channels itself in this direction rather than, e.g., frequent fist-fights.

12.8   Could show that newer immigrant groups come from intellectually less stimulating cultures than older immigrant groups did, or that performance on the tests is influenced by knowledge of or cultural similarity to the American way of life, etc.

12.9   Too quick. We need to know whether there are more men than women drivers, whether men drive more, whether they are more likely to be convicted if found guilty, etc.

13 PROBABILITY: STATISTICS

13.1   The mentally ill take up more beds because they do not respond so quickly to treatment as other illnesses.

13.2   We need to know what proportion of the whole population has been inoculated. (If it was higher than three-quarters then inoculation on the face of it has been of value.)

13.3   H H H H T T T T
                        H H T T H H T T
                        H T H T H T H T

Each vertical sequence has a one-eighth probability of occurring.

13.4 Two ways of getting 'one of each'—H, T as well as T, H. So the odds are one in four for each, not one in three.

13.5 If the lottery is fair, then only the number of tickets bought, and not their distribution, matters.

13.6 If supersonic transports do nearly as much damage as cows in fields (the whole cow population) then it is not reassuring, unless we know that cows do little damage to the ozone layer.

13.7 A 10 per cent rise followed by a 10 per cent rise *on that* gives a rise of 21 per cent over two years. (Try with actual values.)

13.8 Either a very remote chance came up, or somebody miscalculated the odds against such happenings.

13.9 Only if the shoes are just as likely to be acquired by non-Chinese as by Chinese and everyone wears one pair of shoes throughout the year.

14 ANALOGIES

14.1 Compares emotion to a contained liquid. A common but perhaps suspect comparison: some 'blocked' emotions may just disappear.

14.2 A 'dog in the manger' denies others the use of something which is of no value to himself. Harold's boat may be unseaworthy/uninsured, but Harold may hope to rectify that.

14.3 Fails on its own terms. The Bible message must be genuine, and date and stamp are marks of authenticity.

14.4 No obvious reason to expect such a resemblance between people and nations.

14.5 Compares the expression of rival views to invasion in war. If so, then freedom of speech is not 'vital' but disastrous.

14.6 One person may have thousands more 'votes' than another. Strange democracy!

14.7 Unconvincing, because potential terrorists can read newspapers and storms can't.

14.8 Unhelpful analogy, because one often does throw things away when they aren't working properly.

15 INDIRECT PROOFS

15.1 $p =$ 'people are happy ... benefits' and $q =$ 'few will work ... security:

Not q

∴ Not p.

15.2 Put $p =$ 'the universe is expanding' and $q =$ 'the spectrum ... red':

q

∴ p.

Invalid as a formal argument. We need a way of blocking alternative explanations of the red shift.

15.3 Given, n^2 is odd. Assume also n is even, having the form $2k$. Then $n^2 = 4k^2$, i.e. twice $2k^2$. So the assumption leads to the conclusion that n^2 is even, contrary to what we were given.

15.4 The speaker is not telling the truth: either he is not a Martian, or Martians sometimes tell the truth.

15.5 Doesn't follow. The two 'if ... then' statements are not contradictory. It does follow that Chambers is innocent. Suppose he's guilty; then Brown is innocent; but if Brown is innocent, so is Chambers (given). So Chambers can't be guilty. See section 3.

15.6 Against the claim that if there is unemployment then business men are happy: p and not q, ∴ not (if p then q). Valid.

15.7 No. (This barber could exist.)

15.8 If all behaviour is predetermined then our apparently deliberately chosen policy is also predetermined.

16 AUTHORITY AND REPUTE

16.1 Self-refuting.

16.2 Einstein cited outside his area of expertise. His arguments need to be assessed.

16.3   An attempted diversion. Any proposal for moderate change will attract those who want wider change, and those who want wider change will obviously not be committed to the *status quo*. But no reason to suppose that the less wide-ranging proposals must lead on to the wider (if the wider are not desired), or that they are proposed in bad faith.

16.4   More difficult. People are entitled to change their views, but if they do so too often we may suspect them of just following fashion.

16.5   Weak. Why look for 'evidence' (indirect) of the thinness of the argument when the argument is spread out for inspection?

16.6   Why assume that the opposition have no *case* to put?

17 PRACTICAL REASONING

17.1   That the trend *should* be supported is what needs showing.

17.2   Like 'progress'; the opposition might not agree that the changes were reforms.

17.3   A variation on the 'one-way' move—the *status quo* is so bad anything's better.

17.4   False consolation.

17.5   Slippery slope argument; but why should further demands be met?

17.6   It seems unlikely that anyone can know what people will endure. Also, what they decide about what they *should* endure will probably affect what they *will* endure.

17.7   Assumes that there can be no defensible midway position. But this seems unlikely.

Further Reading

In this book the emphasis has been mainly on sound and unsound reasoning in ordinary contexts. However, deductive reasoning is capable of great formal development, and this is the subject of logic as an academic discipline. Those reading further in the subject need to know how far the books recommended take them into formal, symbolic logic. This accounts for the system of classification below. There are some logic books which are good to teach from but which may not be so easy for a reader working alone. In this category I would put: Allen, Colin and Hand, Michael, *Logic Primer*, MIT, 1992.

The books below have enough by way of explanation for the reader to manage alone, although many require hard work to master them.

Informal

FISHER, ALEC, *The Logic of Real Arguments*, Cambridge University Press, 1988.
Nicely written, with an emphasis on theoretical examples. Examines and discusses quite difficult, theoretical passages.

KIERSKY, JAMES and CASTE, NICHOLAS, *Thinking Critically*, West Publishing Co., 1995.
Covers roughly the same material as my book, but in more detail.

Formal

COPI, I. M., *Introduction to Logic*, Collier MacMillan, 9th edn., 1993.
Something of a classic. Contains material on informal logic and inductive argument, but the main emphasis is on formal logic.

FORBES, GRAHAM, *Modern Logic: A Text in Elementary Symbolic Logic*, Oxford University Press, 1994.
Despite the subtitle, this is a thorough, comprehensive coverage of the logic of propositions and quantifiers, including material on non-standard logic. Clearly written, but demanding.

HEIL, JOHN, *First-order Logic*, Jones and Bartlett, 1994.
Good presentation of the logic of propositions and quantifiers.

HODGES, W. A., *Logic*, Penguin, 1977.
Uses a tableau technique for testing arguments. Rewarding, but demands close study.

LEMMON, E. J., *Beginning Logic*, Nelson University Paperbacks, 1971.
Something of a classic. Covers the logic of propositions and quantifiers. Again, demands close study.

Bibliography

ARDREY, ROBERT, *The Territorial Imperative*, Collins, 1967.

BECK, W. S., *Modern Science and the Nature of Life*, Penguin, 1961.

BENTHAM, JEREMY, *The Book of Fallacies*, John C. H. L. Hunt, 1824.

BORING, LANGFELD, and WELD (eds.), *Foundations of Psychology*, Wiley, 1948.

CALDER, NIGEL, *Violent Universe*, BBC, 1973; Futura, 1975.

CARLYLE, THOMAS, *Lectures on Heroes*, Chapman & Hall, 1894.

CARROLL, J. B., *Language and Thought*, Prentice Hall, 1964.

CHURCHILL, WINSTON, *History of the Second World War*, Cassell, 1959.

CROSLAND, ANTHONY, *The Future of Socialism*, Jonathan Cape (revised edn.), 1964.

DOYLE, SIR A. CONAN, *The Adventures of Sherlock Holmes*, John Murray, 1974.

DRAKE, STILLMAN (tr.), *Discoveries and Opinions of Galileo*, Doubleday, 1957.

EMMET, E. R., *Learning to Think*, Longman, 1965.

EVANS, DAVID S., *Teach Yourself Astronomy*, English Universities Press, 1952.

FLEW, ANTONY, *Thinking About Thinking*, Fontana, 1975.

HADFIELD, J. A., *Psychology and Morals*, Methuen, 1964.

HUME, DAVID, *A Treatise of Human Nature, Book One*, Collins, 1962.

HUYGENS, *Treatise on Light*, 1690.

JEANS, SIR JAMES, *The Mysterious Universe*, Penguin, 1937.

LEWIS, C. S., (1) *Mere Christianity*, Fontana, 1970.

—— (2) *The Problem of Pain*, Fontana, 1957.

MELVILLE, HERMAN, *Moby Dick*, Cresset, 1946.

MILL, J. S., *A System of Logic*, Routledge, 1974.

MORONEY, M. J., *Facts from Figures*, Penguin, 1969.

Muggeridge at the Microphone, BBC, 1967.

NIEBUHR, REINHOLD, *The Nature and Destiny of Man*, Nisbet, 1941.

NIETZSCHE, FRIEDRICH, *Beyond Good and Evil*, tr. Hollingdale, Penguin, 1990.

PAP, ARTHUR, *Semantics and Necessary Truth*, Yale University Press, 1958.

POWELL DAVIES, A., *The Meaning of the Dead Sea Scrolls*, Mentor, 1956.

QUINE, W. V. O., *From a Logical Point of View*, Harper n.d., MIT Press, 1960.

READ, STEPHEN, *Thinking About Logic*, Oxford, 1995.

RICHARDS, I. A., *Principles of Literary Criticism*, Routledge, 1926.

ROOK ARTHUR (ed.), *Origins and Growth of Biology*, Penguin, 1964.

ROWNTREE, DEREK, *Statistics without Tears: A Primer for Non-mathematicians*, Penguin, 1991.

RUSSELL, BERTRAND, *My Philosophical Development*, Allen & Unwin, 1975.

SCHNEIDER, *Scientific American*, July 1966.

STEBBING, SUSAN, *Thinking to Some Purpose*, Penguin, 1952.

TAYLOR, A. J. P., *Origins of the Second World War*, Hamish Hamilton, 1963.

THEOBALD, ROBERT, *The Rich and the Poor*, Mentor, New York, 1961.

THOULESS, R. H., *Experimental Psychical Research*, Penguin, 1963.

—— *Straight and Crooked Thinking*, Pan (revised edn.), 1974.

TOLSTOY, LEO, *War and Peace*, tr. C. Garnett, Pan, 1972.

WELLS, H. G., *Guide to the New World*, Gollancz, 1941.

WOLFF, PETER (tr.), *Breakthroughs in Physics*, Signet, 1965.

Index